TRANSFORMATIVE PEDAGOGIES AND THE ENVIRONMENT

Creative Agency through Contemporary Art and Design

Edited by
Marie Sierra and
Kit Wise

Part of the Curated Series:
Transformative Pedagogies in
the Visual Domain

Series Curators:
Dr. Arianne Rourke and
Dr. Vaughan Rees

TRANSFORMATIVE PEDAGOGIES AND THE ENVIRONMENT

Creative Agency through Contemporary Art and Design

Edited by
Marie Sierra and
Kit Wise

Part of the Curated Series:
Transformative Pedagogies in
the Visual Domain

Series Curators:
Dr. Arianne Rourke and
Dr. Vaughan Rees

COMMON GROUND RESEARCH NETWORKS 2018

First published in 2018
as part of the New Directions in the Humanities Book Imprint
doi: 10.18848/978-1-86335-010-5/CGP (Full Book)

Common Ground Research Networks
2001 South First Street, Suite 202
University of Illinois Research Park
Champaign, IL 61820 USA

Library of Congress Cataloging-in-Publication Data

Names: Sierra, Marie (Marie A.), editor. | Wise, Kit, 1975- editor.
Title: Transformative pedagogies and the environment : creative agency
  through contemporary art and design / edited by Marie Sierra and Kit Wise.
Description: Champaign, IL : Common Ground Research Networks, 2018. | Series:
 Transformative pedagogies in the visual domain | Includes bibliographical
  references and index.
Identifiers: LCCN 2017058832 (print) | LCCN 2018005716 (ebook) | ISBN
  9781863350143 (e-book) | ISBN 9781863350105 (hardback : alk. paper) | ISBN
  9781863350129 (pbk. : alk. paper)
Subjects: LCSH: Transformative learning--Environmental aspects. |
  Interdisciplinary approach in education. | Art in environmental education.
Classification: LCC LC1100 (ebook) | LCC LC1100 .T74 2018 (print) | DDC
  333.7071--dc23
LC record available at https://lccn.loc.gov/2017058832

Cover Photo Credit: Bernadett Butson and Zeeshan Khan

Table of Contents

ENDORSEMENT

Ingeniously, this book combines new pedagogies with new syllabus: it connects the contemporary emphasis on active learning and the pressing challenge of environmental discourse. To a backdrop of many centuries of studio education—always organic, intuitive and critical—art and design furnish a necessary educational paradigm for how we grapple with teaching the unknown. As the editors Marie Sierra and Kit Wise say, "the very practice of art and design, by virtue of its ability . . . to hold opposing views in tension, provides a platform to engage with environmental issues". Their intelligent and reflective book *Transformative Pedagogies and the Environment: Creative Agency through Contemporary Art* demonstrates the important research activity occurring in studio teaching in Australia, the U.K., and New Zealand, showing how critically engaged and thoughtful pedagogical practice involves students in the key issues of environment. It reveals how inspired studio teaching can engage students with broader issues of community, politics, and empowerment, so they enter their professions with real experience of the agency and catalytic potential of art and design.

Associate Professor Robert Nelson
Associate Director Student Learning Experience
Monash University, Office of Learning and Teaching

Transformative Pedagogies and the Environment

ACKNOWLEDGEMENTS

The editors would like to acknowledge their respective universities, UNSW Art & Design, and the University of Tasmania, Tasmanian College of the Arts, for their support of the book. To the Series Curators, Associate Professors Vaughan Rees and Arianne Rourke, of UNSW Art & Design, thank you for the invitation to participate in the project. A special thanks to the authors from Australia, the UK, and New Zealand, for sharing their insightful and innovative work. High commendation and thanks to Dr Robert Rowe for his careful copy editing and proofreading, and knowing how to turn a phrase. And to our respective partners and families, your constant support was felt and invaluable, thank you.

Transformative Pedagogies and the Environment

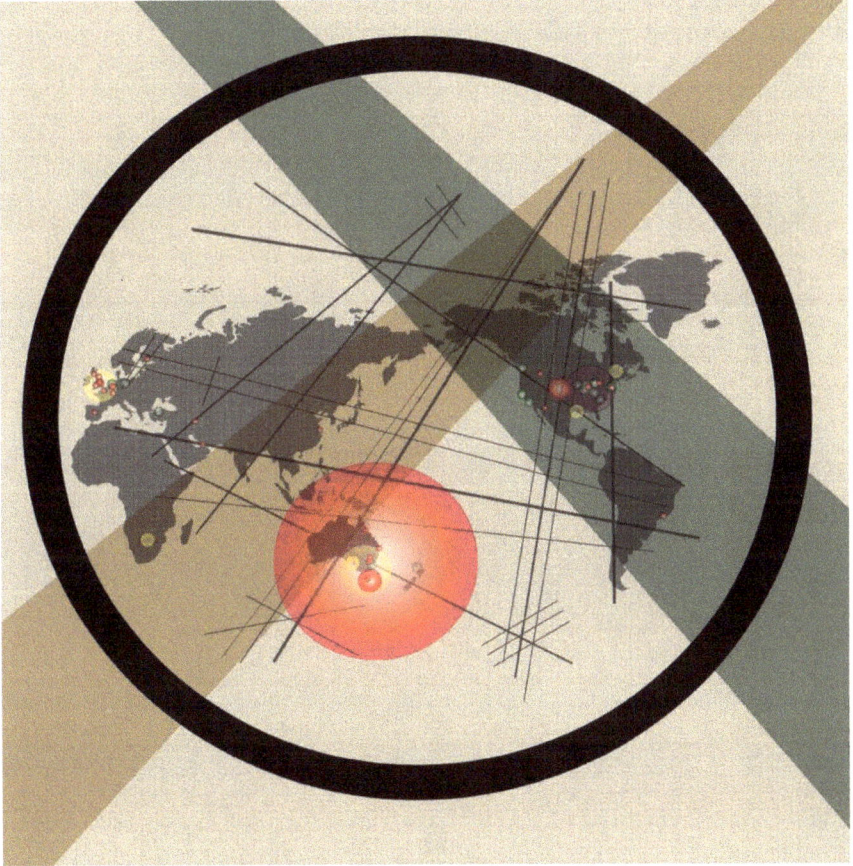

Mapping the Global Reach of Authorship for
Transformative Pedagogies in the Visual Domain

Transformative Pedagogies and the Environment

Curators' Essay

Dr. Arianne Rourke and Dr. Vaughan Rees

The Editors of *Transformative Pedagogies and the Environment: Creative Agency through Contemporary Art*, Professors Marie Sierra and Kit Wise explore, in the first book of eight in the Curated Series: *Transformative Pedagogy in the Visual Domain*, interdisciplinarity through various relationships in higher education between art and design and, science and engineering.

Through a lens of global issues, thoughtfully selected pedagogical exemplars of studio practice and case studies, the sixteen authors make explicit the methodologies and personal approaches to a common concern, the environment. During a time of global political disruption and ecological concern the need seems even more acute to equip university students to be active agents in dealing with environmental imperatives. Through these ten chapters the reader will engage with a broad range of strategies, some of which may be perceived as quite radical and emotional. However, in this collection of text and images is an overall argument that art and design is well placed as a domain (or interconnecting with other disciplines) in which tertiary students can actively engage through creative practice with fundamental global concerns.

The genesis for this series *Transformative Pedagogies in the Visual Domain* emerged from The Curators' observing and experiencing how a fertile field of higher educators were strategically creating visual material to ignite both a knowledge transfer and indeed knowledge exchange, between the educator and the student. One of the advantages of working in higher education is the opportunity to observe throughout the various disciplines and modes of delivery, the extraordinary variety of pedagogical practices where visual material is an important primary ingredient for promoting an engaging rich educational environment. For the last few years both Curators have identified examples of best practice within their professional network and created a place to publish where a practitioner can reflect on practice and share examples of best practice to a wider, critical and appreciative international audience. This opportunity creates an ongoing practice of discipline specific practitioners not only exhibiting, researching and creating outcomes within their main focus but also to contribute to the scholarship of pedagogy about how practice and higher level thought is communicated and shaped within a creative learning environment.

During this time the network formed into a Community of Practice that crossed professional disciplinary boundaries, geographical locations, cultural constructs, contemporary and traditional methods, varied research methodologies and theories. This community is corralled within a framework of overlapping territories of higher education, pedagogy and the visual. Taking on the premise of a Community of Practice as Wenger, McDermott, and Snyder (2002) argued, where: "Groups of people…share a concern, a set of problems, or a passion about a topic, and…deepen their knowledge and expertise in this area by interacting on an ongoing basis" (p.4). As our network expanded we were able to see naturally forming clusters of knowledge and sufficient depth within the Community of Practice to create this series with eight separate books with each focussing on the visual, higher education and pedagogy within: the environment, Asia region, contemplation, community engagement, innovation and entrepreneurship, innovative learning, work integrated learning and, the embodied.

The legacy of Donald Schön's (1983, 1987) pivotal work on the modelling reflective practice and educating the reflective practitioner created scholarly guidelines, that seem to naturally fit with many visual educators as his notion of a purposeful reflective mode resonates with those in the creative industry education sector. Sellars (2012) when commenting on Schön's (1983, 1987) reflective practice model, argued the importance of educators beginning this process by reflecting on their "own individual experiences and perspectives," believing there is a need to "consider these in their contextual variations and draw upon the theoretical, professional strategies that they have encountered or plan to explore" (p.466). This approach permeates throughout the book series where many point of views and theories as well as practices are shared and united under the visionary core idea of recognising the important role visuals play in both the communication, engagement as well as "meaning" of learning. Through case study examples, theories and personal reflections, authors have provided a visual lens for observing and studying the thought processes and actions of their students, audiences and participators whose lives have been enriched through their unique visions, creative approaches and experiences. With technology bombarding our tertiary learning spaces with its avalanche of visual imagery, there has risen an imperative need to develop multi-modal literacy (Kress & van Leeuwen, 2001) skills to understand the complex ever-evolving interconnected visual world, this series envisages to contribute further knowledge and understanding to this field.

The series of eight books would not have been possible without the dedicated work of sixteen book Editors, who reviewed and then selected 163 authors from all over the globe to contribute their reflections and transformative pedagogical approaches to assist in understanding the visual world. Authors from twenty-one countries and ninety-eight different educational institutions and businesses have contributed to the series their expertise from fields as varied as lyrical prose writing to sports psychology, with educators from health sciences to cultural anthropology and business entrepreneurship.

The global contribution of so many authors and editors, their geographical location and associated institutions offered the opportunity to present visually the numerical and locality data generated by the authorship of this book series. Graphic designers Bernadett Butson and Zeeshan Khan working with the Series' Curators, visually mapped the global reach and the critical mass of the authorship. A graphic language of colour saturation and intensity, organic and mechanical shapes, structuring and focusing lines and the relationship between these elements (influenced by Russian artist Wassily Kandinsky 1866–1944, and his 1923 highly graphical painting, *Circles in a Circle*) present the visual overview (Mapping the Global Reach of Authorship for *Transformative Pedagogies in the Visual Domain*) seen on a previous page and acts as a basis for the various coloured and cropped versions that are printed on the covers of the eight books.

This inclusive series brings together practitioners from all stages of academia from Early Career Researchers to Emeritus Professors, from beginning teachers to retired educators with many years' experience who have come together to contribute their inspirational insights for the *Transformative Pedagogy in the Visual Domain* book series.

REFERENCES

Kress, G. & Van Leeuwen, T. (2001). *Multimodal discourse*. London: Routledge.

Schön, D. A. (1983). *The Reflective Practitioner*. San Francisco: Jossey-Bass.

Schön, D. A. (1987). *Educating the Reflective Practitioner*. San Francisco: Jossey-Bass.

Sellars, M. (2012). Teachers and change: The role of reflective practice. *Procedia - Social and Behavioral Sciences*, 55, 461–469.

Wenger, E., McDermott, R. & Snyder, W. M. (2002). *Cultivating communities of practice*. Boston, Massachusetts: Harvard Business School Press.

Transformative Pedagogies and the Environment

CHAPTER 1

The Interdisciplinary Witness: Interdisciplinary Pedagogy and Speaking the New

Marie Sierra, Kit Wise, and Ross Brewin

ABSTRACT

Interdisciplinarity has become an increasingly important goal for both industries and universities around the world, championed as a necessity if the "wicked problems" of our times are to be addressed. Creative practices such as art and architecture have long histories of interdisciplinarity and therefore play an important role in preparing students for careers that will necessarily be situated in an environmentally challenged future. This chapter cites several art projects that collaborated across art, architecture, science and engineering, and which in turn engaged transformative pedagogical approaches to connect audiences and students with ecological imperatives. The case studies demonstrate different interdisciplinary perspectives and methodologies being effectively combined in the making of contemporary art and design. As institutions, universities have always been characterised by the evolution, splitting, and reforming of disciplines such that "routine interdisciplinarity" driven by emerging challenges is a defining feature (Davies & Devlin, 2010). Boyer acknowledged this imperative in his seminal 1990 report for the Carnegie Foundation for the Advancement of Teaching, where he introduced the notion of a scholarship of integration: "the work of the scholar also means stepping back from one's investigation, looking for connections, building bridges between theory and practice" (Boyer, 1990).

This model of research through "integration" and of engaging theory with practice is a feature of the inquiry-based learning processes that characterise the pedagogic objectives of projects undertaken at several Australian art and design schools. For this chapter, examples include Monash Art Design Architecture (MADA) at Monash University, Tasmanian College of the Arts at the University of Tasmania, UNSW Art & Design, and the Victorian College of the Arts at the University of Melbourne. In all of these institutions, far-reaching collaborative approaches engage with real-world problems and issues.

INTRODUCTION

Discussion of theoretical models for interdisciplinarity extend over at least forty years, from Apostel, Berger, Briggs, and Michaud's *Interdisciplinarity: Problems of Teaching and Research in Universities* (1972) to Barrett's "Is Interdisciplinarity Old News? A Disciplined Consideration of Interdisciplinarity" (2012), and include considerable debate around the precise terms used and their meaning. Interdisciplinarity, often highly desired by academics and students alike, is debated in Australian university contexts. However, Australian funding models create a financial "envelope" in the shape of Schools or their parent Faculties, so there is little incentive, indeed often disincentives to sharing students across these boundaries. Double degrees are a more common structure for creating interdisciplinary experiences in the Australian context, as clearly demarcated lines can be established between these "envelopes" and tracking of where the funding attached to a student can be established, often with after-the-fact transfer of funds between bodies. Nonetheless, there is a fair degree of pedagogical permeability between the disciplines of art, design, and architecture which allows for fertile interdisciplinary activities and learning. For example, these areas share similar practice-based or practice-led research approaches, often delivered through project-based and concrete learning experiences. They also have overlapping histories, and such past allegiances bode well for cross fertilisation in a shared future full of environmental challenges. This in itself can create a platform for transformative pedagogical approaches.

THE LANGUAGE OF INTERDISCIPLINARITY

One of the most significant challenges for interdisciplinarity is language, and before addressing the case studies of transformative pedagogies formed around environmental learning, some clarity of terms is of benefit. Additionally, defining shared terms and values across disciplines is a complex and iterative process, so it is particularly valuable to give some consideration to the terms used in this project, as well as the conditions in which those terms are used.

For the sake of expediency, this chapter uses the general term *interdisciplinarity* (ID) in preference to multi-disciplinarity, cross-disciplinarity, transdisciplinarity, or similar. However, it is important to note that each of the many terms used points to different combinations, processes, and outcomes. Familiarity with these terms allows the various approaches used in the case studies to be identified and some of the discoveries of the projects to be better understood.

Martin Davies and Marcia Devlin's book chapter "Interdisciplinary Higher Education" (2010) provides a useful summary of the varied and often contested terms used to describe ID over the last twenty years. Franks et al. (2007) also provide an excellent overview of the field in "Interdisciplinary Foundations: Reflecting on Interdisciplinarity and Three Decades of Teaching and Research at Griffith University, Australia." These effectively represent a "universe" of interdisciplinarities. See Table 1 for an overview of interdisciplinarities listed in the order of their disciplinary specificity. The following definitions are drawn from

Davies and Devlin's text (2010, pp. 10–14). For further discussion relating to this table, and associated definitions of disciplinary combinations, see "Hyperdisciplinarity and Beyond: The Beginning or the End? Enabling interdisciplinarity in the creative arts" (Wise, 2013).

Table 1.1: Terms Commonly Used to Describe Interdisciplinarity (ID)

Term Used	Description[a]
Disciplinarity	The understanding of disciplines is that they are "thought domains – quasi-stable, partially integrated, semi-autonomous, intellectual conveniences – consisting of problems, theories and methods of investigation"; i.e., consist of specific histories, methods, communities, and language.
Multidisciplinarity	Disciplines contributing from their own perspective—co-existence: "everyone does his or her own thing with little or no necessity for any one participant to be aware of the other participant's work"; e.g., the development of a public artwork.
Cross-disciplinarity	The investigation of a topic normally outside a field, without engaging with expertise relevant to that topic; essentially the sampling of another discipline. This model rarely involves the transfer of methodologies and only the topic is "new"; e.g., the physics of music: physics students may not learn much about music, nor are musicians able to undertake research into physics.
Interdisciplinarity	"The emergence of insight and understanding of a problem domain through the integration or derivation of different concepts, methods and epistemologies from different disciplines in a novel way." Key terms that arise in this definition are "integration" and "novel." These qualities lead to an "axis" of ID, depending upon their degree.
Relational ID	"Two or more disciplines . . . contributing their particular disciplinary knowledge on a common subject"; i.e., looking at a problem through two perspectives. Unlike multidisciplinarity, there is explicit acknowledgement of the other's perspective. However, the two perspectives are not integrated in a meaningful sense, but are simply listed.
Exchange ID	"Critique and critical exchange of views between disciplines, while maintaining robust disciplinary specificity"; i.e., a contested argument: strong engagement, but little willingness to integrate views or to generate anything "novel."
Pluridisciplinarity	This model "requires two or more areas to combine their expertise to jointly address an area of common concern." Pluridisciplinarity demonstrates one of the two defining features of ID: the integration of approaches. It is cooperative and collaborative; e.g., in pursuing solutions to real-world problems such as AIDS, climate change, or the developments in cognitive science requiring input from a diverse range of fields. While there is integration through collaboration, the outcomes may not be "novel": the outlines of the contributing disciplines do not change. However this model does perhaps best describe institutional-level goals; for example, those of the ARC.

Modification ID	Disciplines are integrated as in pluridisciplinarity, but are coordinated by a higher directive such that the disciplinary sub-contributions are modified to some degree, and the individual contributions require synthesis to generate their own outcomes. For example, medical research that coordinates the collaboration of biology, physics, and psychology. The higher directive evaluates and combines the lower-level integrations to develop them beyond their discipline boundaries.
Transdisciplinarity	"The collapse of academic borders and the emergence of new disciplines." This assumes that the "parent" disciplines are re-formed and ultimately dissolved and presumably represents paradigm shifts in disciplines themselves. Transdisciplinarity may represent a purely theoretical possibility in institutional terms, although art history would suggest that the creative practices employed in art production may approach this model; e.g., the history of the avant-garde or the emergence of Dadaism.

[a] Definitions of interdisciplinarities are drawn from Davies and Devlin (2010, pp. 10–14).

ALIGNMENT AND INFLUENCE

Given the above array of terms, interdisciplinarity (ID) can be expected to have a diverse range of meanings for different stakeholders. Similarly, the processes, outcomes, and perceived benefits of ID are diverse and even divergent. In the most of the case studies presented in this chapter, multiple approaches were undertaken, often simultaneously. However, two points of emphasis can be identified: *alignment* and *influence*, which together describe a sliding scale that can be considered indicative of the degree of integration of the disciplines.

1. **Alignment** (Multidisciplinary): Outcome or problem-focused interdisciplinarity.
   In the inquiry-based learning processes, multiple skill sets are brought together to achieve a specific outcome. Disciplines align with each other in order to apply their knowledge to specific parts of a problem.

2. **Influence** (Pluridisciplinary): Experiential or process-focused interdisciplinarity.
   Experiential or open-ended ID learning experiences do not revolve around a specific problem or brief, but allow participants to absorb alternative methodologies, perspectives, and knowledge through processes with which other disciplines engage. This could be described as disciplines influencing each other through porous engagement that generates ruptures in practice, analogous to moments of innovation. The movement from one knowledge system to another can be described as pluridisciplinary, as it is characterised by significant integration of disciplines as well as the novelty of the outcomes generated.

Interdisciplinarity, with its dual vehicles of alignment and influence, allows us to see problems in new ways. Combining perspectives, looking through the eyes of others, we can find unexpected relationships, meanings, and even solutions. The relationship between alignment and influence can be demonstrated using university art and design school projects as case studies; three Australian examples are given below. A further consideration is how these insights are visualised for others: how do we communicate the new ideas found through interdisciplinary collaboration? and how do we share what we have seen?

By way of illustration, Jean Cocteau suggested that art makes science visible. This could be described as a multidisciplinary relationship—art's ability to visualise is aligned with science's ability to generate exciting data representing new discoveries. In such an analysis art simply functions as illustration, translating esoteric scientific discourse into a public form. However, if we consider the semiotic conditions of this translation it is possible that a more complex interdisciplinary relationship is at work.

If we consider a disciplinary exchange as a form of discourse—disciplines speaking to each other—we are able to question what happens to the condition of each discipline in the act of "speaking." The twentieth century linguist Emile Benveniste considered the "'shifters' or indicators of enunciation," pronouns, which allow the speaking subject to "appropriate language in order to use it" (as cited in Agamben, 1999, p. 114). Beneveniste notes that these "shifters" have the sole purpose of indicating, within the act of speech, who is speaking relative to the other(s) addressed by the speech act. They do not refer to any external reality, but only to "a 'reality of discourse,' and this is a very strange thing. *I* cannot be defined except in terms of 'locution,' not in terms of objects as a nominal sign is" (as cited in Agamben, 1999, p. 116). In the instance of scientific communication, the scientist that "speaks" of the discipline—what is seen, the data collected, methodologies used, or discoveries witnessed—is relative to the act of speaking itself. In the act of speaking, the subject "disappears."

Giorgio Agamben argues that the consequence of this is profound; the "I" that speaks is necessarily other than the "I" that experiences, resulting in the incapacity of the self (in the Heavy Metal example, the scientist) to ever truly speak. There is a dislocation between the actual speaker (scientist) and the figure that speaks (scientist as narrator). "The subject of enunciation is composed of discourse and exists in discourse alone. But, for this very reason, once the subject is in discourse, he can say nothing; he cannot speak." (Agamben, 1999, p. 117). At the same time, this "I"-other that does speak has "nothing to say," as it is solely a construct of enunciation, an "other" to the "I" that experiences (Agamben, 1999, p. 117). According to Agamben, the seeing scientist is not the speaking scientist, because the scientist who speaks of what is seen is constructed by language, rather than being empirically established. Logically, Agamben is therefore drawn to ask "who is the subject of testimony?" (Agamben, 1999, p. 120). Alternatively, in the context of this illustrative example, how is science communicated authoritatively?

Agamben goes on to suggest that the authentic subject who can speak of that which has been witnessed can never be defined; its manifestation is at best "indistinct." Any witness (here, the seeing scientist) is unable to speak as, from a linguistic perspective, the "I" that occurs in enunciation is not the "I" that witnessed:

"Testimony takes place [in] a zone of indistinction in which it is impossible to establish the position of the subject, to identify the 'imagined substance' of the 'I' and, along with it, the true witness" (Agamben, 1999, p. 120). The scientist is unable to truly speak—or rather, to speak truly.

The consequence of Agamben's (1999) argument is that there is no authoritative "I" that speaks; authorship itself is ambiguous. Given the communicative status of the witness is unstable (in this illustration, the scientist), Agamben goes on to argue that the role of the artist (or novelist, designer, etc.) means that communication becomes both collaboratively possible, and valuable. The artist, skilled in visual languages, brings expertise to the communication of what was seen—establishing an ambiguous, compound self of witness–speaker in the space opened up by the dislocation of author from witness. For Agamben, this compound author can be understood as a model of collaboration between disciplines in order to share new knowledge.

From the perspective of modes of interdisciplinarity, this may represent *transdisciplinary* collaboration, where the voices of the contributing disciplines become reformed, and "indistinct," shifting their boundaries to generate a new modality. Agamben provides a theoretical model of how disciplines are able to come together to speak the world anew, forming innovative identities that enable (indeed require) them to move beyond their epistemological boundaries.

Such transdisciplinary levels of maturity in the interdisciplinary relationship are uncommon and require clear guidelines for participants, a continual monitoring of respectfulness, agreement that boundaries are permeable, and the development of trust over time. Alignment and influence are foundation stones of this maturity, and the case studies that follow demonstrate instances where these two traits were established, often reaching a state of transdisciplinarity and its "collapse of academic borders." The higher state of transdisciplinarity's "emergence of new disciplines" may also arise organically from these interactions, particularly in the practicing lives of the generations of students who experience these projects in their formative years. Having experienced the application of transformative pedagogy to the "wicked problem" of the environmental imperatives of their future, they are best placed to form new disciplines by harnessing the creative agency of art and design. Whether university structures can become equally malleable and responsive remains a question.

CASE STUDY: MONASH UNIVERSITY'S MADA AND THE RIVER DERWENT HEAVY METAL PROJECT, MONA

In July of 2013, Kirsha Kaechele of The Museum of Old and New Art (MONA) in Hobart, Tasmania, invited a group of scientists, artists, architects, and students to a symposium to discuss the potential for creative interdisciplinary projects to tackle a heavy metal pollution problem in the River Derwent. Like many rivers the Derwent has an industrial history, but one with specific heavy metal contamination issues. During the week-long symposium, the group of scientists outlined the extent of the pollution problem and challenged those from the creative disciplines to dream up responses that could actively engage the public with ongoing research and remediation strategies for the river.

Staff and students from Monash Art Design & Architecture (MADA), Monash University, Melbourne, participated in this symposium. They then returned to Melbourne to embark on a three-month exploratory design process that eventually led to the proposal of a series of interrelated projects to be located at MONA. The projects operated at the nexus of science, art, and architecture aiming to publicly communicate the pollution problem, symbolically contribute to pollution remediation, and provide a set of social hubs at which to gather.

The first projects, *Heavy Metal Retaining Wall* and *Oyster Hatchery*, were realised over an intense five-week period leading up to the launch of MONA's River Derwent Heavy Metal Project at the beginning of the summer for MONA's Festival of Music and Art (Mofo). The construction actively involved MADA staff and students, project staff at MONA, and a number of local tradespersons.

Scientists at the initial symposium discussed the potential of employing biological systems to contribute to the remediation of pollution. Particular attention was paid to oysters, a known efficient natural bio-filter. Such harnessing of natural processes to remediate industrial contamination has previously been a point of collaboration between artists and scientists. One well known art example that also addressed heavy metal contamination was artist Mel Chin's 1991 work *Revival Field*, wherein he worked with scientist Dr Rufus Chaney to develop a work that used hyperaccumulator plants to draw heavy metals from soil (Chin, 1991).

In order to explore these ideas further for the River Derwent Heavy Metal Project, MADA engaged closely with the Tasmanian oyster industry, which was extraordinarily supportive of the project. As well as donating materials and equipment, they provided live oysters and expertise in maintaining the *Oyster Hatchery* installation. James Calvert was a key member of the local industry that contributed to the project. Appropriately, it was James's father who was the first person to set up a commercial oyster farm on the River Derwent. Interestingly, this venture ended poorly when a number of local dignitaries were rendered physically ill from consuming oysters that were likely contaminated with heavy metals; the capacity of oysters to concentrate heavy metal pollutants was little understood at the time. However, successive generations of his family have helped establish the world-renowned quality Tasmanian oysters are known for today.

The development and execution of the projects involved a group of twelve final-semester Bachelor of Architecture students and a number of postgraduate students from Fine Art. MADA staff leading the project were architects Ross Brewin and Alysia Bennett, and artist Kit Wise. A design studio was held where students were invited to formulate individual responses to the brief before combining into small groups to develop common ideas. These ideas were then discussed with a review panel consisting of curator Kirsha Keachele and Steve Devereaux from MONA, engineer Peter Felicetti, and practice professors Callum Morton and Nigel Bertram from MADA. A number of key ideas emerged from this panel discussion, which were then developed by the whole group.

At the end of the semester, MADA art and architecture staff and students travelled to Hobart and presented the collaborative proposals to representatives of MONA, including Kirsha Kaechele and owner David Walsh (Figure 1.1). Scientists and members of the local art community were also consulted. The projects were accepted for development, commencing an intense period of project design development.

Aspects of the project commenced construction in Hobart in December 2013, with some art components produced simultaneously in Melbourne. The artists worked alongside the architects, responding to subtle changes in the plans as well as further sharing their respective ways of working. The *Oyster Hatchery* project was complimented by a live video feed from oyster baskets established in the Derwent on site at MONA, a late addition to the project that became possible through the support of the University of Tasmania's Institute for Marine and Antarctic Studies (IMAS), the oyster industry, and MONA.

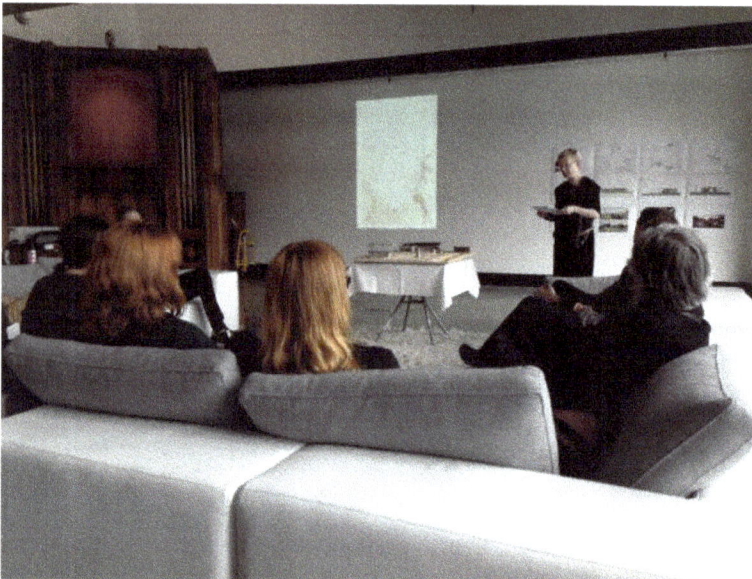

Figure 1.1: Student Biatta Kelly Presenting Ideas for Heavy Metal to David Walsh, Kirsha Kaechele, MONA and MADA Team, 2013.

In MADA's participation in MONA's River Derwent Heavy Metal Project, the process of *alignment* between artistic practices and scientific knowledge was taken as the primary response to the brief. The ability of oysters to filter heavy metals manifested from scientific knowledge, and led the Architecture students to develop structures that would allow this to be undertaken as part of the artwork. Engineers advised on the feasibility of the elements designed; further feedback was sought from scientists on the functionality required. Lighting technicians and software programmers developed data presentation formats for the installations.

The process of *influence* can be found in MADA's Heavy Metal Project in the dialogue between the artists and the architects concerning the designs for structures, wherein different perspectives were brought to the formal decision making. There was also a two-way discussion as both artists and architects generated ideas in response to the conceptual themes that arose, such as how to present trace metals and minerals in a visible form. Discussion with scientists about their languages for representing the metals—such as the periodic table of elements—also led to design considerations based on translating these representations into structural components, and they became apertures punctuating the wall element (Figure 1.2). Finally, observation of the different working processes of scientists, artists, and architects generated new ways of making, extending the usual methodologies of each, such as the use of real time scientific data feeds of river health becoming a time-based light installation. Influence was evident here as practitioners were allowed to absorb alternative methodologies and perspectives, as well as knowledge, through studio processes which were derived from other disciplines. New paradigm-shifting relationships were identified between ideas and approaches through such "blue-sky" experimentation.

Figure 1.2: MADA Heavy Metal Project on Site at MONA, Hobart, 2014

CASE STUDY: UNIVERSITY OF MELBOURNE'S VCA AND THE VICTORIA HARBOUR YOUNG ARTISTS INITIATIVE

The School of Art, Victorian College of the Arts (VCA), University of Melbourne, is home to a studio area called Sculpture & Spatial Practice. In 2008, the property development corporation Lend Lease, which had significantly progressed new apartment housing developments in a docklands area adjacent to the central business district of Melbourne, contacted Sculpture & Spatial Practice to see if student artists would be interested in an outdoor exhibition of their work to showcase the Victoria Harbour site. While interested in the offer, staff were keen for the students to be treated as emergent professionals, and for the project to succeed both pedagogically and publicly. Fortunately, Lend Lease was willing to negotiate on their initial approach agreeing to an idea that was put to them, which was to provide funding towards organising the exhibition in the same way a public art commission would be run. Students would voluntarily enter preliminary ideas for artworks to a panel of Sculpture & Spatial Practice staff and representatives from Lend Lease, with a few of these ideas selected by the panel to go forward into development for a short-run outdoor exhibition of public art in the Victoria Harbour area. The project also gained support from the City of Melbourne as the docklands area was a major project with strong government interest; the City of Melbourne has a strong history in supporting public artworks, including those of a temporary nature.

This project had several benefits for the students and for Lend Lease as the client. The students were exposed to the process of public art commissioning, but in a relatively safe environment where understanding of the needs and desires of the client were mediated through staff. Staff were consistently available to provide advice to students, with some staff having extensive experience in developing or commissioning permanent public art works. This gave Lend Lease, as client, exposure to a new cohort of emerging artists with their innovative and sometimes irreverent ideation, allowing them to step away from the fine detail of the project while in development to focus on the celebration of the work and the venue for its opening launch and the duration of the exhibition. This befitted their overall aim to draw attention to the amenity of the Docklands area as a new place to live, recreate, and do business.

The *Victoria Harbour Young Artists Initiative* project ran for seven years after its inception in 2008. Marie Sierra, then head of Sculpture & Spatial Practice, inaugurated the project and ran it for two years; having previously Chaired the City of Melbourne Public Art Committee, she was able to support the students' understanding of the commissioning process from the client side. Lecturer Mark Stoner had successfully completed many public art projects and was also critical to the success of the project, as was lecturer Kate McMahon who provided urban planning scholarship. From 2010, Sculpture & Spatial Practice came under Simone Slee's leadership, with project curation and coordination by lecturer Laura Woodward; during this period the project changed name to *Rising*. Over time the project became further refined and, in 2012, *Rising* was awarded the Australia Business Arts Foundation's Australia Council Young & Emerging Artists Award. The Australia Business Arts Foundation, which has now changed name to Creative Partnerships Australia, notes the relationship between the students and clients on their website:

> Between five and eight second and third year students are awarded a commission for a four-week temporary public art exhibition at Victoria Harbour. Students work directly with Lend Lease and City of Melbourne representatives to ensure their artworks comply with technical and safety standards.

> Both partners share a vision for the role of temporary and ephemeral art in a public context and specifically the contribution of art to Victoria Harbour's sense of community. Lend Lease has a policy of supporting emerging artists considering a career in public art, while the S&SP stream is committed to

offering ambitious practical experience for students to develop their art practice.

The project has made a significant contribution to the students' academic and professional artistic success. As well as receiving top marks and prizes, many students have continued to exhibit in artist run or public galleries.

This project is a model example of the VCA's goal to create dynamic links with industry partners. For Lend Lease, the project has generated excellent feedback from residents and visitors to Docklands.

"It introduced me to the possibility of using alternate platforms – outside of the gallery space – to exhibit work. This project revealed that working collaboratively greatly enriches the creative process and enhances the outcome."

Ben Taranto, student (Creative Partnerships Australia, n.d.).

The *Victoria Harbour Young Artist Initiative / Rising* concluded in 2014. During its lifespan, the project drove alignment and influence between the disciplines of urban planning, engineering, architecture, and landscape architecture. Also, even though technical advice at the VCA was always to hand and very thorough, students had to seek specific technique and material advice from suppliers, as the works had to endure not only an outdoor, seaside environment, but one that had a robust night life posing many challenges for public health and safety. For the first run in 2009, timber boardwalk areas of the Docklands precinct were still being laid when the students made their first site visit; this meant they had to read and interpret building plans in order to understand very basic elements of the site, such as the extent and reach of the pedestrian areas and the points of interface with the water below. Hard hats and hi-visibility vests had to be worn and the site manager guided our visit.

Two student projects that are indicative of alignment and influence of cognate but distinct fields are from the 2008 and 2009 exhibitions respectively. Aerin Langworthy and Rachael Bauman completed a work called *AS4602* in the first exhibition, which, while appearing simple, was a challenge to clear through risk management as its installation and de-installation had to be done from a dinghy out on the water. Aerin and Rachael wrapped fluorescent safety vests around a number of timber pilings that were several meters out into water from the edge of the decking, the wooden piles therefore mimicking the bodies of construction workers who had until only very recently been all over the area (Figure 1.3).

Figure 1.3: Aerin Langworthy and Rachael Bauman, AS4602,
Victoria Harbour Young Artists Initiative, 2008

The work focused the sense that this post-industrial landscape was, yet again, in a process of rapid transition through human intervention after a period of abandonment. The area was once the site of habitation and a source of food supply for Indigenous people; then a colonial port, eventually deserted for deeper water elsewhere; and now after a lengthy phase of neglect while the city busied itself with development downtown, it was suddenly again the focus of an anthropocentric urge to "reclaim" the waterfront. The work echoed Raymond Williams's observation that:

> The idea of nature contains an extraordinary amount of human history. What is often being argued, it seems to me, in the idea of nature is the idea of man; and this not only generally, or in ultimate ways, but the idea of man in society, indeed the ideas of kinds of societies. (Williams, 1972, p. 150)

Because the work was in the water, the students had to deal with more than one government body with jurisdiction over the area. In this case, the state Port Authority had to have knowledge of the project, a layer of bureaucracy most other students didn't have to negotiate. Lecturer Mark Stoner assisted with the boating end of the art installation as he had the most experience on the water, but the students had to work with safety officers and the site manager to ensure all appropriate checks and clearances were in place. Simply finding out who had to give clearance, and in what order, was a learning curve in itself, alerting students to the politics of public space, private ownership, crown land, use value, and entitlement.

The following year when the exhibition ran, Ben Taranto and Aaron Cooper used part of the docklands infrastructure, an orange steel sheet that functioned as a balustrade for a sloping walkway, to mount silicone casts of mussels in exactly the same shade of orange (Figure 1.4). Technical issues needed to be solved: how to connect the silicone mussels to the steel sheet without damaging it, but in such a way that the public could not easily remove them. An engineer and a safety officer had to clear the work, and Ben and Aaron spent a lot of time with the suppliers of the silicone to resolve issues of materiality and adhesion.

Ben and Aaron's final work, called *Biologically Foul*, pointed to how humans refer to structures, including the hulls of boats as "fouled" when occupied by organisms, such as mussels. More importantly, they were questioning how these species might experience humans claiming of the waterfront for their own needs.

Figure 1.4: Ben Taranto and Aaron Cooper, *Biologically Foul*,
Victoria Harbour, Melbourne, Young Artists Initiative, 2009

The politics of the underwater world was of particular interest to Ben, who had previously made a living as a diving instructor; this married well with Aaron's interest in ecological and ethical issues. Working together brought these concerns into alliance and the resulting work highlighted the idea that:

> The whole idea of nature as something separate from human experience is a lie. Humans and nature construct one another. Ignoring that fact obscures the one way out of the current environmental crisis – a living within and alongside of nature without dominating it. (Wilson, 1992, p. 13)

The Docklands precinct of Melbourne is indicative of a maturing city, which is readdressing its waterfront and industrial heritage rather than turning away from it. As a site that blends history with the contemporary world, all the students involved in the exhibition series learned how to work cooperatively with other discipline areas. For example, *alignment* between disciplines was borne out in language. While working within an art school, part of what a student is taught is the vocabulary of art; outside of the discipline, these terms may have little or even confused meanings. Students needed not only to learn new terminologies, but also to explain themselves clearly, often using lay terms to describe what they were doing, to the clients and other professionals with whom they came into contact. In terms of *influence*, the real-world environment of the project drove first-hand experience of alternative methodologies and perspectives, because the university structure and its lecturers were no longer the only authority with which the students needed to concern themselves. The processes of negotiating their projects with people who did not know them or their work to achieve affordable on-time outcomes, required them to reframe the assumptions they held about the reading and purpose of their work in a way the studio classroom can rarely achieve. At a formative stage in their careers as professional artists, these aspects of alignment and influence were a leap forward in understanding the broader context of art, and how it's perceived in the public realm.

CASE STUDY: UNSW ART & DESIGN AND PROJECT X

Another important Australian case study that demonstrates alignment and influence was Project X, hosted by the University of New South Wales (UNSW) in 2007–09. Initially Project X was formed as a cross-Faculty project to bring together students from different disciplines. The students worked in groups, responding to a real-world brief with a client, with one response selected by a jury to culminate in an actual built form. Project X was then selected to be a case study for the Studio Teaching Project (STP), a multi-university project supported by a grant from the now-disestablished Australian Learning and Teaching Council Ltd., an initiative of the Australian Government Department of Education, Employment and Workplace Relations. The aim of the STP was to examine the drivers, value, curriculum structures, and empirical nature of the studio learning environment to identify and celebrate its value and contribution in the tertiary education context.

Project X structured interdisciplinary interaction between students from three UNSW Faculties: the College of Fine Art (now UNSW Art & Design), Faculty of Built Environment, and Faculty of Engineering. Students from fine art, design, architecture, interior architecture, construction management, and engineering, among other cognate disciplines, were brought together over a two-week intensive period to work together towards a collaborative outcome. The focus of this multidisciplinary design workshop was for the students to resolve a given design problem, doing so by working with fellow students from other disciplines. Due to the sheer size of UNSW, in the majority of cases the students from these different faculties and disciplines had never met each other, nor indeed had many of the staff. The academics involved cited this interdisciplinary project as "an exciting and viable way of achieving educational goals in both professional and non-professional degrees" (Longbottom et al., 2009). Design, as a discipline, is extraordinarily positioned for interdisciplinary activity. As Victor Margolin defined it:

Design, as various scholars have suggested, is a contingent practice whose techniques, goals, and objectives are continually changing. What is fixed about design is that it is an art of conception and planning whose end result is product, whether that product is a material object or an immaterial service or system. Design is also an integrative activity that, in its broadest sense, draws together knowledge from multiple fields and disciplines to achieve particular results. It has both a semantic dimension and a technical or operative one. (Margolin, 2000, p. 1)

Figure 1.5: UNSW Project X Work for the Organising Committee,
ConnectED International Conference on Design Education in Development, 2007

Project X had three iterations. The first, in 2007, was a Design Studio, which led to a Design Development & Construction Workshop (Figure 1.5) resulting in a large temporary artwork in the centre of the UNSW main campus. The client was the Organising Committee for the ConnectED 2007 International Conference on Design Education. The finished work formed a physical centrepiece to the event (Figure 1.6).

Figure 1.6: UNSW Project X Finished Work for the Organising Committee,
ConnectED International Conference on Design Education, 2007

The second and third iterations of Project X worked with the College of Fine Art in the role of the client. There was a project for the construction of a teaching conference space, the client being College of Fine Art's Imaging the Land International Research Initiative (2008). For this, a prototype, temporary building was erected at the main UNSW campus. The third iteration was the construction of an artist's studio at Fowlers Gap in remote outback NSW where UNSW has an Arid Zone Research Station, and the College of Fine Arts holds intensive courses. This project had a permanent outcome: the artist's studio is still in place on site, and is used by science students as well as art and design students when they visit. Both the second and third projects went through stages of concept and design development, then academic assessment, and finally industry assessment with the client involved. From there, they progressed to construction, often with materials donated from industry.

The UNSW Project X series demonstrates a high level of alignment and influence between disciplines. This arises from how they structured interdisciplinary interaction around the common goal of responding to a client brief with a built outcome. They also had a high level of integration *between* alignment and influence, as the discipline areas had to continually respond and adapt to the expectations, knowledge, language, processes, and overall approach of each discipline generating a constantly negotiated space against the backdrop of a looming deadline.

As students are adapting to aligning their disciplines with other disciplines, and to the acceptance of influence on their working processes, they also become more familiar and comfortable with the flexibly required in the professional context. This skill is particularly important in fields where one works directly with clients, usually through the mechanism of a client brief and in fast-changing work environments. In this instance, Agamben's idea of the compound witness can be understood as a way to introduce this flexibility into who is the "author" of the envisioned work: both the client and the architect contribute to what is produced or "spoken" in response to the brief.

Further, working on briefs for sites such as UNSW's Fowlers Gap Arid Zone Research Station raises many issues of sustainability, appropriate technology, materials resourcing, and design sensitivity to the environment—all issues of escalating importance in the world of the graduating cohort. What kind of role design students will hold as ecological citizens when they become fully fledged professionals is foregrounded by real-world projects, as they rub against not only "wicked problems," but one another—in multi-cultural and internationalised student cohorts, varied world views and value sets are ensured. Their contribution to nature as social construct may also emerge, framed by the contingent relationships of design and its notions of style, as noted by Baudrillard:

> The very "rediscovery" of the body is a recycling of the body, just as the "rediscovery" of Nature — in the form of a countryside trimmed down to sample specimens framed against an immense urban sprawl, partitioned and "domesticated" as green belts, nature reserves, or as a backdrop for weekend cottages — is actually a recycling of Nature. In other words, Nature is no longer at all a primeval and original presence symbolically opposed to culture, but a *simulation model,* a "consommé" of the recirculated signs of nature; in short, it is nature *recycled.* If this is not yet the situation everywhere, it is nonetheless the current tendency. And whether it is called the management or preservation of nature reserves and the environment, it always involves the recycling of a nature condemned by its very existence. Nature as event, and as knowledge, is governed in this system by the *principle of the latest trend.* Functionally, it has to change like fashion. It has the value of *ambience,* and therefore is subject to a cycle of renewal. (Baudrillard, 1990, p. 65)

UNSW also explored the value of interdisciplinary real-world studio projects through a Faculty of Built Environment project that addressed another complex issue worthy of the title "wicked problem". They employed Boyer's principles of application and integration (1990) to engage Architecture, Interior Architecture, Landscape Architecture, and Planning and Urban Development students to develop a community facility for people with schizophrenia: "The qualitative feedback revealed a significant potential for interdisciplinary design studios to provide integrative and personally transformative learning experiences for students and community members" (Corkery, Roche, Watson, & Zehner, 2007). Mental health is becoming a contemporary public issue of critical importance. Increasingly, designers will be called upon to develop intelligent solutions that foster wellbeing.

As Penny Sparke noted, "design inevitably perpetuates the ideology of the system it serves" (Sparke, 1986, p. 205). It is both a social and ecological imperative that new generations of designers learn to operate within these moral and ethical responsibilities.

CONCLUSION

The case studies presented in this chapter indicate divergent interdisciplinary perspectives and methodologies being combined effectively not only in, but through, the making of contemporary art and design. The imperatives of client briefs, public exhibitions, and built forms are elements that students will experience in their professional lives. They have the effect of driving different disciplines to a common goal, providing a reason for both students and staff to resist boundaries and set definitions. The "routine interdisciplinarity" noted by Davies and Devlin (2010) is given impetus by such projects, animating awareness and responsibility through an alignment and influence between disciplines.

Similarly, by encountering the "other" of the client, students who may have previously been siloed in their discipline specificity must embrace processes and ideation that could otherwise have easily been overlooked or avoided. They need not only to look for connections, but also, as Boyer recognised, build bridges between the common aspects of theory and practice in their cognate realms.

Finally, recognising that collaboration between disciplines, as well as between artist/designer and client, is founded on a compound identity where the solution or vision is realised through a shared "speaking" of that idea, suggests a deeper form of bridge building. These case studies point towards the ways in which disciplines can align, influence, and even interweave to enable the more profound innovations associated with the transdisciplinary, and transformative pedagogy.

REFERENCES

Agamben, G. (1999). *Remnants of Auschwitz: The witness and the archive*. New York, NY: Zone Books.

Apostel, L., Berger, G., Briggs, A., & Michaud, G. (Eds.) (1972). *Interdisciplinarity: problems of teaching and research in universities*. Paris, France: Organisation for Economic Cooperation and Development. Retrieved from https://www.researchgate.net/publication/234737333_Interdisciplinarity _Problems_of_Teaching_and_Research_in_Universities

Baudrillard, J. (1990). *Revenge of the crystal: Selected writings on the modern object and its destiny, 1968-1983* (P. Foss & J. Pefanis, Trans.). Leichhardt, NSW: Pluto Press Australia Ltd in association with Power Institute of Fine Arts, University of Sydney.

Barrett, B. D. (2012). Is interdisciplinarity old news? A disciplined consideration of interdisciplinarity. *British Journal of Sociology of Education, 33*, 97–114. http://dx.doi.org/10.1080/01425692.2012.632868

Boyer, E. (1990). *Scholarship reconsidered: Priorities of the professoriate.* The Carnegie Foundation for the Advancement of Teaching.

Chin, M. (1991). *Revival Field.* Retrieved from http://melchin.org/oeuvre/revival-field

Corkery, L., Roche, B., Watson, K., & Zehner, B. (2007). Transforming design studio learning and teaching through real world, interdisciplinary projects. *ConnectED 2007 International Conference on Design Education.* Sydney, Australia: University of New South Wales. Retrieved from https://www.researchgate.net/publication/266471685_Transforming_Design _Studio_Learning_and_Teaching_through_Real_World_Interdisciplinary _Projects

Creative Partnerships Australia. (n.d.). Retrieved from https://www.creativepartnershipsaustralia.org.au/resources/case-studies /sculpture-and-spatial-practice-school-of-art-vca-the-university-of -melbourne-and-lend-lease

Davies, M., & Devlin, M. (2010). Interdisciplinary higher education. In M. Davies, M. Devlin, M. Tight (Eds.), *Interdisciplinary higher education: perspective and practicalities* (pp. 3–28). Bingley, England: Emerald Group Publishing. http://dx.doi.org/10.1108/S1479-3628(2010)0000005004

Franks, D., Dale, P., Hindmarsh, R., Fellows, C., Buckridge, M., & Cybinski, P. (2007). Interdisciplinary foundations: reflecting on interdisciplinarity and three decades of teaching and research at Griffith University, Australia. *Studies in Higher Education, 32,* 167–185. http://dx.doi.org/10.1080/03075070701267228

Longbottom, D., Bell, G., Vrcelj, Z., Attard, M., Hough, R., & Carrick, J. (2009). Project X: the experience of student-led multidisciplinary design courses across 3 faculties at UNSW. *Curriculum development in studio teaching,* v4, STP case studies of effective practice. In S. Wilson & K. Watson (Eds.). Retrieved from http://online.cofa.unsw.edu.au/studioteaching/pdfs/Case StudyCarolLongbottomX_SWedit.pdf

Margolin, V. (2000). Building a design research community. Retrieved from http://victor.people.uic.edu/articles/designcommunity.pdf [originally published as: Margolin, V. (2000). Building a design research community. In

S. Pizzocaro, A. Arruda, & D. De Moraes (Eds.), *Design plus research: Proceedings of the Politecnico de Milano Conference* (pp. 17–19). Milano, Italy: Politecnico di Milano.]

Sparke, Penny. (1986). *An introduction to design and culture in the twentieth century.* New York, NY: Harper & Row.

Williams, R. (1972). "Ideas of Nature." In J. Benthall (Ed.), *Ecology, the shaping enquiry: a course given at the Institute of Contemporary Arts* (pp. 146–164). London, England: Longman.

Wilson, A. (1992). *The culture of Nature: North American landscape from Disney to the Exxon Valdez.* Cambridge, MA: Blackwell.

Wise, Kit. (2013). Hyperdisciplinarity and beyond: The beginning or the end? Enabling interdisciplinarity in the creative arts. In J. Holmes (Ed.), *The CALTN papers: The refereed proceedings of the Creative Arts Learning and Teaching Network Symposium* (pp. 192–213). Hobart, Australia: Creative Arts Learning and Teaching Network. Retrieved from https://itunes.apple.com/au/book/the-caltn-papers/id694491942?mt=11JonathanHolmes

CHAPTER 2

A Placement for Everyone

David Cross

ABSTRACT

This chapter outlines a collaboration between staff and students towards transformation in our university/art school. A primary influence has been the Artist Placement Group (APG), which from 1966 to 1979 negotiated for artists to be placed in business, industry and governmental organisations. In 2012, I designated my job at University of the Arts London (UAL) as an artist's placement, with a remit to promote engagement with the ecological and social-economic crisis.

In 2013, our Vice Chancellor signed the People & Planet "Green Education Pledge" committing UAL to engagement with sustainability. As an artist on a placement, I wrote to thank him, and provided summaries of research connecting climate change to the financial system. I warned of the financial risks of fossil fuels as "stranded assets," and the reputational risks of an uncritical relationship with Royal Bank of Scotland, with its aggressive investments in fossil fuels. I identified opportunities to advance sustainability by working with our university's providers of energy, insurance, and banking.

I gave lectures connecting art, climate change, and finance, proposing that UAL should divest from fossil fuels, and reinvest in democratically controlled renewable energy. With students I formed a campaign group, *Divest UAL*. In November 2015 UAL announced that it would divest its endowments of £3.9 million from fossil fuels, and sign the UN Principles for Responsible Investment. That month, the UK Government launched a consultation paper pushing for fundamental changes to Higher Education: allowing universities to change governance structures, drop their obligation of public service, and transfer their assets.

Although these proposals seem designed to destroy education as a public good, we could *détourne* them to reclaim and transform our university/art school. Our task now is to develop a viable model of UAL as a cooperative, not-for-profit social enterprise, working creatively to become truly sustainable.

INTRODUCTION

In this essay, I will outline how connections between my art practice and my work as an academic have reinforced my commitment to art education as a public and common good. These links and affinities have motivated me to overcome the separation between living as an artist and earning a living as an academic, by unilaterally designating my academic job as an artist's placement. Informing my teaching, practice and research is an engagement with the relationship between visual culture and "sustainability" as a conjunction of environment, development and social justice.

The approach taken here is led by my practice as an artist and as such is both theoretical *and* empirical: it draws on conceptual ideas and operates through context-based actions/interventions, at the juncture of institutional critique, artistic practice and (participatory) action research. Through seven sections—*The Kettle is a Crucible*, *The Limits to Growth*, *"Context is Half the Work," Engagement and Procurement*, *Master of the Universe, Seen to be Done*, and *Athenian Democracy?*—whose themes have emerged from a sequence of actions/interventions (comprising debates, encounters, events, performances, and presentations) over the past few years, the essay describes my work with a self-selecting group of students to persuade our university to divest from fossil fuels. These interventions have made visible some of the institution's structures, practices and assumptions, and seem to have brought about a small change in their articulation. Our work on the single issue of divestment has led to an open-ended collaboration, in which we have begun to collectively define our common aim of envisioning and modelling our university as a co-operatively owned and controlled social enterprise. Through collaborating with students in this way I have sensed the possibility of becoming not only a subject, but also an agent, of institutional change. I can only speak for myself, but this sense of possibility has transformed my image of the institution, and of my place within it.

From 1991 until 2014, I worked in artistic collaboration with Matthew Cornford, as Cornford & Cross, making art projects that critically engaged with particular contexts and situations. Most Cornford & Cross projects were realised as commissions, with public money for artists' fees and a production budget connected to aims, objectives, terms, and conditions that were more or less explicitly described by the commissioner. Drawing from the various instances of institutional critique practiced by artists including Michael Asher, Hans Haacke, and Mierle Laderman Ukeles, we often engaged with the assumptions we felt to be implicit within a commission as a crucial aspect of the overall context.[1]

Many of our projects were structured around the realisation of sculptural installations, which by addressing the viewing subject in spatial terms, aimed to avoid being reducible to a spectacle. Other projects invited people to critically engage with the conditions of spectatorship or with their relationship to the artwork as a commodity form. Producing temporary articulations of materials, which we borrowed or hired and dispersed afterwards, was one of several ways as artists we amplified the power of the budget, and as an environmentalist I pushed my commitment to

---

[1] See http://www.cornfordandcross.com (accessed April 1, 2016).

sustainability. In all our works, the aim was to form an aesthetic paradox, or crisis of incompatible elements and forces, to resist the closure of meaning and the creation of a false consensus. I was particularly interested in identifying latent conflicts in situations, provoking the formation of contestatory "publics," and mobilising uncertainty in order to offer moments in which heightened self-awareness might activate social agency.

Matthew and I had never expected to earn a living, much less make money from producing critical art works. To sustain our practice, we aimed for basic economic security, plenty of cultural stimulation, and a great deal of intellectual freedom. After graduating from the Royal College of Art in 1991, we each took up teaching posts in art schools. Contributing to the book, *Curating and the Educational Turn*, we set out the influences, interests, and concerns linking our collaborative art practice to pedagogy, which we related to a sequence of changes in government policy for higher education in Britain (Cornford & Cross, 2010).

Following the Global Financial Crisis of 2007–08, and the political program of austerity imposed in its wake, public funding in the UK for the kind of art projects we offered was withdrawn. As Matthew turned his attention to a study of the historic demise of art schools across Britain (Beck & Cornford, 2014), I began to review the problems inherent in my dual position as an artist and academic. Previously I had tried to give sculptural form to critical and resistant impulses, while opportunistically negotiating the transformations of the university. Recognising such contradictions, how could I develop a coherent relationship to the possible futures of the university/art school?

THE KETTLE IS A CRUCIBLE

Figure 2.1: Parliament Square, London, December 9, 2010
Source: Photograph by David Cross

University of the Arts London (UAL) is the result of an ongoing process of transformation, parts of which I have experienced first-hand, as a student at Saint Martin's School of Art from 1986–89, and then as an academic since taking up a post at the London Institute in 2002. In 1986, the Greater London Council was abolished by the Conservative government under Prime Minister Margaret Thatcher, and seven independent London art schools and colleges—Camberwell School of Arts and Crafts, Central School of Art and Design, Chelsea School of Art, the College for Distributive Trades, London College of Printing, London College of Fashion, and Saint Martins School of Art—were merged to form the London Institute, incorporated as a higher education body in 1991, awarded university status by the Privy Council in 2003, and re-named University of the Arts London in 2004. In 2003, Byam Shaw School of Art was taken over by Central Saint Martins College of Art and Design and Wimbledon School of Art was renamed Wimbledon College of Art, becoming part of UAL in 2006.[2]

But as well as these mergers and acquisitions, perhaps the most significant transformation of UAL came about as part of a broader historic reversal of the status of higher education in Britain. In November 2009, the former Chief Executive Officer of British Petroleum, John Browne, The Lord Browne of Madingley, was appointed by the UK coalition government to lead an enquiry into student fees. Published in October 2010, "The Browne Report," as it is known, recommended that undergraduate student fees could be increased to £9,000 a year, to be funded by government-backed loans rather than grants. This permitted the state to withdraw funding for higher education, maintaining a residual support for science, technology, engineering, and mathematics, but resulting in the total withdrawal of funds for the teaching of other subjects at undergraduate level, including arts and design (Browne et al. 2010).

The higher education sector's response focused on defending art and design in terms of its economic value. On 1 December 2010, Universities UK published *Creating Prosperity: the role of higher education in driving the UK's creative economy* (Universities UK, 2010). This report, which was launched at UAL, deploys the terminology of competitiveness, employability, and entrepreneurship to push for art and design education to be transformed to serve a business agenda. Endorsing the report, Nigel Carrington, Vice Chancellor of UAL wrote, "The contribution of creative graduates to an innovative knowledge economy must be recognised and celebrated if the UK is to maintain and enhance its standing on the world stage" (Higher Education News, Leeds University 2010, para 9). The report, and Carrington's public statement, apparently opposed the government funding cuts, but by "framing" the value of art and design education in economic terms, his argument followed the BBC's coverage of the austerity agenda, which as media theorists Jilly Boyce Kay and Lee Salter have shown, "discursively normalises neoliberal economics" (2014, p. 754).

Cultural critic Terry Eagleton once referred to "the conservative's privilege of not having to name himself" (1992, p. 34). In my view, whereas traditional conservatism

---

[2] For a brief history see, for example, https://en.wikipedia.org/wiki/University_of_the_Arts_London (accessed April 2, 2016).

used privilege to avoid scrutiny, neoliberalism doesn't evoke privilege as such, but it does promote exclusivity, claim exemption, and masks its values with a "neutral" logic of technical efficiency (such as when a financial rationale is given for privatisation of a public good). Opposing not only the cuts to education, but also the whole political program of austerity, the students took a principled position, and articulated their views. Rejecting the premise that they would protect their individual interests, the students acted collectively, demonstrating in public by occupying organisations and institutions, demanding tax justice, and defending education not as a private transaction, but as a public good, which is valuable in its own right.[3] As I wrote at the time:

> On 9 December 2010, the day that the British parliament voted on Browne's proposal to cut education funding and triple university fees, Matthew Cornford joined me in the procession to Parliament Square in London.
>
> We were surrounded by thousands of young people, many of whom were about to experience the breaking of an election pledge by Liberal Democrat leader Nick Clegg, who had won the student vote on a promise not to increase tuition fees. Shocked by this betrayal, their first contact with the police was an ordeal of treachery and provocation. At the moment in their lives when they prepared to take their place in society, young people were confronted with the flagrant and systematic betrayal of their rights by those in power.
>
> The "kettle" or secure cordon is a police tactic of surrounding large numbers of people before closing in, forcing the people into close confinement in a way that seems calculated to humiliate and provoke. As well as affronting our human dignity (in front of the Houses of Parliament, thousands of citizens were confined in the open for hours without food, drinking water or toilets), the authorities infringed our civil liberties: having been held without warning, without explanation and without charge, we were only allowed to leave the secure cordon one at a time, down an intimidating corridor of riot police, who made us stop in front of a bright light and a digital camera to be recorded close-up by a professional police photographer.
>
> Beyond the ranks of police in riot gear, on horseback and in reinforced vehicles, some people may have drifted back to the shops and cafés. But it seemed to me that many more were jolted out of the desolate individualism of consumerism into a galvanized, collective condition of citizenship. (Cross, 2011)

---

[3] See for example the statements issued by some of the student occupiers:
https://ucloccupation.wordpress.com/demands/ *and* http://lseoccupation2010.blogspot.co.uk/p/public -statement-and-demands.html. For a full list of all the student occupations see http://anticuts.com/2010/11/27/list-of-university-occupations/ (accessed April 2, 2016).

I don't know whether that day produced a lasting change for anyone else. But for me, the kettle was more than a lesson in the school of hard knocks—it was an experience that changed my understanding of my place in the world. Shortly afterwards, at a meeting of senior academics at UAL, I proposed that we hold an open debate on the purpose of higher education. A senior professor rejected my proposal, dismissing the fees increase as "just a switch of income stream." Another, still more senior, professor told me that it was too late for discussion about the marketisation of education, claiming with a shrug, "it's already happened." While the first professor used a bureaucratic abstraction to disavow the injustice of the change in which they were participating, the second imposed a narrative closure on the progress of events in a bid to forestall connections between education and democracy. Refusing to accept the confinement that such a closing down of the argument would produce, my colleague and friend Hayley Newman and I held an open debate, *Education as a Public Good* (Cross & Newman, n.d.).

THE LIMIT TO GROWTH

Figure 2.2: The British Petroleum Deepwater Horizon Oil Rig, April 2010
Source: Photograph Provided to The New York Times *by a
Worker Who Asked Not to Be Identified*

In that debate, I argued that education should be valued as a public good because the benefits of education accrue not only to individuals, but also to society. As John Holmwood has argued, "The public university matters to everyone, we contend, because it is a condition of citizenship and full participation in economic, cultural and political life" (2011, p. 11).

Yet in a widely cited definition of the public good, micro-economists Andreu Mas-Colell, Michael Whinston, and Jerry Green, write:

> A public good is a commodity for which use of a unit of the good by one agent does not preclude its use by other agents. Put somewhat differently, public goods possess the feature that they are *non-depletable*. Consumption by one individual does not affect the supply available for other individuals. Knowledge provides a good illustration. The use of a piece of knowledge for one purpose does not preclude its use for others. (1995, p. 359)

One problem with this conventional definition is that it presumes that public qualities are inherent to goods, rather than socially constructed. Moreover, social constructions can advance the interests of specific social groups over those of the wider society, as the imposition of debt as a condition for access to higher education shows. If we could set aside questions around the project of intellectual property, we might agree that the "consumption" of knowledge by individuals may not affect the supply available for others. But with education, changes to the supply certainly affect consumption. Though personal debt may not *preclude* the use of knowledge for the public or common good, it greatly increases the pressures and incentives for knowledge to serve private interests instead.

How might a conception of art education as a public good relate to the aim of promoting a critical engagement with the contested ideal of "sustainability"? [4] Following the Brundtland Report (United Nations World Commission on Environment and Development, 1987), I have engaged as an artist with the discourse of sustainable development, which aspires to "development that meets the needs of the present without compromising the ability of future generations to meet their own needs" (1987, para 27, Chapter 2, Section IV). Yet corporations and governments have used the term *sustainability* to distract from, or produce consent for, profit-seeking activities that have contributed to resource depletion, climate change, and ecological collapse. In so doing they have not only damaged the global commons, but also undermined the possibility of trust between individuals and organisations. This is part of our predicament under capitalism, in which contemporary visual culture is increasingly aligned with the ideologies of consumerism and competitive individualism. While public space is flooded with imagery serving private interests, visual literacy is instrumentalised as a set of marketable skills, and correspondingly marginalised as a faculty of citizenship.

Security, health, and justice are prime examples of public goods, and all are threatened by ecological damage, resource depletion, socio-economic inequality, and instability. Yet editorial coverage in the private media variously misrecognises or downplays the threats, and propagates doubt as to their causes, while advertising and mainstream entertainment recuperate our critical understanding of the crisis and our relationship to it. So it is no accident that many people still don't know, or don't care,

---

[4] I argue for "sustainability" as a conjunction of environment, development and social justice as opposed to the corporate recuperation of the term sustainability to conceal and distract attention from ecological destruction.

how far ecological destruction has gone, how quickly it is accelerating, and how great are the dangers.

Art education, as a public good, could enable people to understand that these problems are neither "natural" nor inevitable, and that our perception of them is ideologically conditioned. As artist and theorist Victor Burgin describes it: "The message is ideological not simply because it is wrong in what it says—simply to be mistaken is not necessarily to be in a state of false-consciousness—it is ideological because it misrepresents the actual material condition of the world *in the service of specific vested interests*" (1999, p. 43). Straying wilfully beyond the boundary of art into the utopian terrain of activism, I think that art education as a public good can, and should, complement the criticism of what is, with an imagining of what could, and should, be.

The British Petroleum oil rig *Deepwater Horizon* exploded and sank in April 2010, killing 11 crew and devastating the environment. The disaster exemplifies a tendency identified in 1972 in *The Limits to Growth*: as more easily accessible or higher quality deposits of non-renewable resources are depleted, the fraction of capital machinery needed to extract whatever resources are left increases, proportionate to their value (Meadows, Meadows, Randers, & Behrens, 1972). As expenses rise and revenues fall, corporations try to sustain their profit margin by cutting costs.

Addressing the student Occupation at University College London in January 2011, I pointed out that when the disaster happened, Lord John Browne was no longer Chief Executive Officer of British Petroleum. Yet it had been under his leadership that BP had been rebranded as "Beyond Petroleum," and cut operating costs so ruthlessly that the oil company fatally compromised its safety standards leading up to this disaster. Why then had Browne been appointed to lead an enquiry into financing Higher Education, if not for his skill at extracting value by "externalising" risks, costs, and losses onto the public and commons? I said the official title of the Browne report, *Securing a Sustainable Future for Higher Education*, should be recognised as a cynical bid to recuperate the progressive ideal of sustainability.

The students of the UCL Occupation warmly received my talk, and after an intense discussion of the need for limits to the expansionist logic of privatisation, they quickly returned to work, collectively resisting the neoliberal assault on the public university. I was impressed by the productive energy of their "communities of practice" (Wenger, 1998) and how, in drawing on the practices of art, activism, and disobedience, the students were exploring possibilities for transformative education as part of a broad social movement against government austerity programs. After a while, I didn't mind that I couldn't tell whether their methods were a means to an end, or an end in themselves.

"CONTEXT IS HALF THE WORK"

Figure 2.3: *Education: Not Knowing* for *The Individual and the Organization: Artist Placement Group 1966–79*, Raven Row Gallery, London, 2012
Source: Photograph by Neil Cummings

The Individual and the Organization: Artist Placement Group 1966–79 was an exhibition at Raven Row Gallery, London, from September to December 2012, curated by Antony Hudek and Alex Sainsbury, in consultation with Barbara Steveni. As part of the exhibition program, Neil Cummings, my colleague at Chelsea College of Art, UAL, invited me to facilitate one of five themed discussions. "Education: Not Knowing" was a public discussion based on the discursive approach of the Artist Placement Group (APG). In it I shared the ambition to reintroduce the progressive ethos and critical methods of APG in the present.

In my collaborative practice with Cornford & Cross, I had been influenced by how APG went "out of the studios and into the institutions of society, from object-based work towards information, to site-specific work and to social relationships" and by their key axiom: "context is half the work" (*Context is Half the Work*, 2015, p. 2). With my interest in the relationship between cultural and economic value systems, and my experience of administration in educational institutions, I was intrigued by the APG conceptual ideal of the "open brief" as a binding but indeterminate agreement between artists and their host organisations. Linking the APG themes of "placement" and "education," ("Education: Not Knowing," 2012) and following Hayley Newman's self-appointment in 2011 as artist in residence in the City of London, I proposed that the artists' placement could be developed and applied today, by artists interpreting their employment in a university/art school as a placement in an organisation. I didn't know whether this could relocate the site of institutional critique from the museum and gallery to the university, or bypass the dichotomy between art and activism. But I decided to try it myself: there and then, I designated my academic post at University of the Arts London as an artist's placement. This unauthorised and open-ended experiment positioning UAL as the context for my work has caused me headaches, but it has also helped me make new connections between my roles of academic and artist, and shifted the relationship of research to my practice.

BUSINESS ENGAGEMENT AND PROCUREMENT

Figure 2.4: UAL Vice-Chancellor Nigel Carrington Signs the
"People and Planet Green Education Pledge," March 2013
Source: Photograph Copyright 2013 by UAL

Nigel Carrington became Vice-Chancellor of University of the Arts London in 2008, following a career in law and business. In March 2013, Carrington signed the People & Planet "Green Education Declaration" committing UAL to, "decisive and strategic action within our institutions and collectively to bring about a world-leading, sustainable higher education sector" (Green Education Declaration signatories, n.d.). In my new role as an artist on a placement, I wrote to him to say that this was a bold and admirable move. But ambition quite rightly raises expectations, and I said we would need to act fast, if we were to keep up with students. I sent him and his executive team summaries of the latest research connecting climate change to instability in the financial system. Alerting them to the financial risks of fossil fuels as "stranded assets" (Ansar, Caldecott, & Tilbury, 2013) and the reputational risks of our relationship with UAL's bank, the Royal Bank of Scotland (RBS), I suggested that UAL faced a significant opportunity to be the first university in Britain to divest from fossil fuels.

In April 2013 the then Director of Strategic Development and the Director of Finance invited me to discuss my proposals. I bought a smart shirt (firm collar, horizontal blue stripes), put together a presentation and went up to the executive suite to give it my best shot. Hoping to persuade these Directors to switch our university's finances away from RBS, I showed them that in 2000 RBS acquired NatWest Bank in what was described as the "largest hostile takeover battle in UK corporate history"

(Reputation Institute, 2010), leading to over 18,000 job losses (CNNMoney, 2000).[5] By 2008 RBS had made so many reckless loans that, being "too big to fail," the UK taxpayer bailed it out. A Cabinet Office spokesperson said, "the failure of RBS played an important role in the financial crisis of 2008–09 which, together with other macroeconomic factors, triggered the worst recession in the UK since the Second World War" (BBC News, 2012). I noted that RBS was heavily invested in fossil fuels—especially coal and "unconventional" or extreme fuels from tar sands and fracking (Evans et al., 2010),[6] and that since our Vice Chancellor had publicly pledged to make UAL a sustainable university, an uncritical business relationship with The Royal Bank of Scotland contradicted our values and posed a risk to our reputation. But I hit a cool, smooth wall of denial and resistance from the Directors. To end the meeting, one of them asked, "If we started to ask ethical questions, where would it lead?"

I came away not knowing whether I should feel alarmed at their complacency or embarrassed at my naivety. But soon after, I was appointed to a working group on sustainability, and tasked to draw up a university strategy for Business Engagement and Procurement. The strategy I proposed combined engagement with procurement through intellectual and creative interaction with the university's business providers of energy, insurance, and finance.

First, I noted that the UK government was expanding nuclear power, mingling tar sands fuel with conventional fuel, promoting fracking (despite intense public opposition), and cutting funding for wind and solar power. Yet renewable energy was falling in price, while the end of fossil fuels was in sight. So I proposed that, in partnership with our energy supplier, staff and students at UAL engage with themes of "Power and Transformation."

Second, I noted many independent advisors had warned that the UK government should be taking urgent action to prepare for the disasters and emergencies of climate change (Committee on Climate Change, 2014; Grantham Research Institute, 2016). Edward Snowden's leaked information had revealed that in the USA and Britain, invasive surveillance and defence planning were increasingly concerned by the risk of civil unrest triggered by climate change catastrophes, energy shocks, and socio-economic crises (Ahmed, 2013). So I proposed that with our insurers, we develop cultural responses to "Hazard and Risk."

Third, I noted that unlike RBS, some banks were delivering the kind of change needed to avoid systemic collapse. I gave the example of Triodos Bank (n.d.), which only finances organisations that benefit the environment and society, and publishes details of every loan that it makes. I highlighted that unlike RBS, Triodos was exceptionally well capitalised, and so avoided exposure to the "Big Three" credit ratings agencies Fitch, Moody's, and Standard & Poor's, which were implicated in the subprime mortgage scandal that led to the global financial crisis. So I proposed that with our bank, we should embark on practice-led research into themes of "Value and Exchange."

---

[5] This was reported widely in the media at the time.
[6] See also, http://platformlondon.org/2010/02/27/new-platform-report-reveals-rbs-is-uk-bank-most -involved-in-financing-loans-to-tar-sands-companies.

Prior to this, I had proposed at a one-day UAL research and enterprise event that with an ethical bank like Triodos, UAL could establish a dedicated fund of around £5 million to lend at super-low interest rates to its graduates to start up social enterprises. The decisions to lend would be made by a panel including staff and students of the university. Certainly, some of these loans would fail, but by sharing risk with its own alumni, I thought UAL could improve its reputation with students. I called Triodos Bank, who said that this was an exciting new idea with great potential and that they could help to make it happen. However, before going any further, I decided to discuss the idea with students. Although I was disappointed by their cool response, I felt I could not argue when the students explained they already had more than enough debt to last a lifetime.

MASTER OF THE UNIVERSE

Figure 2.5: David Cross, *Master of the Universe*, 2015,
Academic Robe, Theatrical Makeup
Source: Photograph by Karel Doing

Throughout 2013 and 2014, I gave lectures across UAL and beyond connecting climate change and finance to our art institution, see; for example, *Mapping Art Practices* (Standpoint Gallery, 2014). Inspired by the global fossil fuel divestment campaign started by Bill McKibben (2012), 350.org and People & Planet,[7] I proposed that UAL should divest from fossil fuels, and reinvest in energy that is not only renewable, but also decentralised, diversified, and democratically controlled. In response, BA sculpture student Georgia Brown and several other students came

---

[7] See http://350.org and https://peopleandplanet.org (accessed April 2, 2016). The divestment movement, represented most strongly by these two organisations was, in my view, catalysed by Bill McKibben's (2012) *Rolling Stone* article "Global Warming's Terrifying New Math."

forward; together we formed a campaign group, *Divest UAL*. Our regular but informal discussions explored how our different positions and skills might combine to result in action: the students set up an online petition and Facebook group, I painted canvas banners for marches, the students held campaign stalls at UAL events, I provided research material on climate change and finance, Georgia Brown submitted Freedom of Information requests, and we all went on demonstrations.

This process of collaboration between staff and students could be described in terms of "horizontality," drawing on the observations Olivier Desvoignes (of the artistic collaborative *microsillons*) has made of his own collaborative artistic practice. Discussing how Michel Foucault's model of power can be understood as exercised within the social body rather than from above, Desvoignes writes: "For us, working at the micro-level of the pedagogical exchange is a way to imagine a kind of transformation that could be, to use Foucault's term, capillary, from the bottom toward the top." Bypassing the bottom-up/top-down opposition of "verticality," Desvoignes draws on anarchist, feminist, and libertarian pedagogies to develop the concept of horizontality in power relations between students and tutors (2015).[8] According to this principle, he argues, horizontality might be extended to other power relations, such as between academics and the university's administrative, managerial, governing, and executive functions.

Although the research I have done with students is artistic and practice-led rather than social science-based, our process does resemble the social science method of (participatory) action research. Argued to evolve out of the work of the radical educationalist Paolo Freire (1970), in this kind of research, iterative cycles of learning by a group in a situation gradually produce social agency through a transformation of awareness. Most pertinently our research aligns with the purpose of (participatory) action research in terms of practicality, usefulness, and sustainability:

> A primary purpose of action research is to produce practical knowledge that is useful to people in the everyday conduct of their lives. A wider purpose of action research is to contribute through this practical knowledge to the increased well-being—economic, political, psychological, spiritual—of human persons and communities, and to a more equitable and sustainable relationship with the wider ecology of the planet of which we are an intrinsic part. (Reason & Bradbury, 2008, p. 4)

However, an important distinction between more traditional modes of (participatory) action research and the work described here, concerns the relations of power that exist between researcher and researched. When focusing (participatory) action research on the university itself, institutional power relations fall under scrutiny.

At an annual staff appraisal, I was told that I was working very hard, but that nothing I was doing was having any effect—I was just a lone researcher, and unless I showed that I really cared, my institutional relationships could wither and die. The chance to redeem myself came one Saturday in July 2015 near the end of term, when I

---

[8] I supervised Olivier Desvoignes's PhD from 2010–15.

took part in *TransActing – A Market of Values* at Chelsea College of Arts in London, curated by Critical Practice (2015).[9] I wanted to signal a transition from my previous way of making sculptural installations, towards a more embodied engagement with the situation unfolding around me. So I hired my graduation robes for Master of Arts at the Royal College of Art, and paid a makeup artist to give my head and hands the appearance of putrefaction in homage to the Occupy movement's use of the zombie as the figure of contemporary capitalism.

I made a revolting spectacle of myself as the living dead: a professional academic, warning of ecological catastrophe, and the destruction of value through the pursuit of money, yet implicated in the commodification of my own cognitive and affective labour. In a one-person pageant of academic heritage, I "acted out" as a lone researcher, a spectator rather than a participant in the positive exchanges going on around me. I stumbled around *TransActing – A Market of Values*, recalling the tradition of the robed mystic in the marketplace, dispensing predictions, knowledge, or wisdom in return for payment, but I barely spoke and asked for nothing. *Master of the Universe* refers both to the financiers who caused the global financial crisis, and to the Masters of the University struggling to negotiate the resulting paradoxes and conflicts.

A new example of such a conflict was soon to emerge. After term had ended, I was tasked to organise a scheme in which Readers and Professors would teach into the undergraduate and postgraduate courses. I asked about the key issues the scheme aimed to address, and was told that despite a high score in the national Research Exercise Framework (REF), our university faced a major reduction in research funding. I responded as an artist on a placement, and in September 2015 I submitted a discussion document, *From Practice-Led Research to Research-Led Teaching,* in which I argued for a dynamic relationship between teaching, practice, and research; and a methodology based on participatory action research in which issues would be defined and decisions would be taken collectively. I wrote:

> Severe cuts look set to continue for the foreseeable future. The UK Government Spending Review, *A Country that Lives within its Means …* [HM Treasury (2015)], aims to eliminate the fiscal deficit by focusing on security while protecting core public services. The Government does not class either Higher Education or the Arts and Humanities as core public services. Following cuts of £12 billion to welfare services, the Government is requiring its Departments to identify where a further £20 billion of cuts can be made by 2019–20.

> The funding cuts appear threatening not only because they are swift and deep, but also because they are a manifestation of hostile and unjust policies. Moreover, the funding cuts pose a "wicked problem" because we who must respond have different or conflicting interests, and the consequences of our decisions could include irreversible harm to the system that we share with

---

[9] See also http://www.criticalpracticechelsea.org/wiki/index.php?title=Market_of_Values (accessed April 2, 2016).

others. For example, the interests of research staff with relatively secure employment contracts could conflict with those of teaching staff, especially Visiting and Associate Lecturers whose security could be eroded by reductions and restructuring of teaching budgets.

Besides their material impact, funding cuts have a pernicious effect of presenting as rational and inevitable a regime of compliance based on inequality of access to information and resources. For UAL this poses a particular danger, because so much of our value is "cultural capital" based on a reputation for creativity and risk-taking in a supportive environment of respect, trust and goodwill. Treating the funding cuts as a technical problem of restructuring to balance income and expenditure might seem like a positive approach. But we would do better to recognize that this is also a test of our organizational culture and values.

Articulating an ethos for connecting research with teaching, Holmwood has invoked the Robbins Report of 1963, which argued that: "education should take place in an environment in which research (or scholarship) and teaching occur alongside each other…universities should meet the aspirations of those who work in them to apply themselves to scholarship, research and the development of knowledge." (Holmwood, 2011, p. 7).

Following Holmwood, my proposal was not an expression of nostalgia, but an active attempt to connect practice-led research and research-led teaching in order to inform a pedagogic transformation with the progressive values of another era.

SEEN TO BE DONE

Figure 2.6: Fossil Free "Die-in," Divest UAL,
Central Saint Martins, London, 29 October 2015
Source: Photograph by Georgia Brown

45

Representation is a key concept in the political sphere, as it is in visual culture. The axiom, "justice should not only be done, but should manifestly and undoubtedly be seen to be done,"[10] connects the political to the visible. Similarly, campaigning for social justice calls not only for patient work behind the scenes, but also the highly visible display of solidarity as a symbolic public act.

In March 2015, a large group of students went into Occupation at Central Saint Martins, to protest against UAL's closure of Foundation Courses in Art and Design, and to make demands including democratisation of the university, and financial transparency (UAL students, 2015). The Occupation lasted four weeks, until the UAL Vice Chancellor instigated legal proceedings against its leaders, who were summoned to appear before a judge of the Royal Courts of Justice, and served with an injunction permanently banning them from taking part in any occupational protest of UAL premises (Slawson, 2015).

In June 2015, the Vice Chancellor (Carrington, 2015) gave a speech to the UK Policy Forum, in which he referred to artists as "super consumers of culture and fashion" (para 26) and said, "creativity is not just about challenging convention. It is also a highly marketable skill and has an economic impact" (para 17). Although the Vice Chancellor has questioned the replacement of publicly funded student grants with loans for greatly increased tuition fees, he appears to share the UK Government's aim of transforming the relationship between universities and students to one structured around consumption and the market. In sharp contrast, the Council for the Defence of British Universities (CDBU) robustly denounces the marketisation of education, in which "universities are equated with businesses, value is defined purely in economic terms, and students and staff are set up in opposition as consumer and vendor respectively, working to serve conflicting interests (to pay as little as possible for the product purchased and to charge as much as the "customer" will take)" (CDBU, 2016, para 2).

Yet although students could gain tactical advantage by exercising their rights as customers under legislation such as the Consumer Rights Act (2015), so far they have chosen not to. Students of the Occupation and the Fossil Free campaign have not claimed the role of consumers of educational services, choosing instead to act as *participants* in their education and *members* of their university. Moreover, through their creative and critical labour, and by developing their social and professional networks, students are producers of what Pierre Bourdieu has termed "cultural and social capital," without which the university/art school could not exist as such (Bourdieu, 1986).

The same day that Carrington gave his speech, I was speaking at an event organised by students from Camberwell College of Arts in an independent space nearby (Cross, 2015). I suggested a thought experiment: imagine the university/art school without students. This would pose an economic challenge to the university, which would lose three quarters of its income. But perhaps, with some tough choices

---

[10] This legal maxim and ruling derived from the principle of natural justice was expressed by Lord Chief Justice Hewart in 1924 in the leading English case R v Sussex Justices, Ex parte McCarthy ([1924] 1 KB 256, [1923] All ER Rep 233) famous for establishing the principle that the mere appearance of bias is sufficient to overturn a judicial decision.

made by the Human Resources department, new business partnerships and a financial restructuring to leverage out value from its assets (Toporowski, 2013), a rebranded university could offer a range of professional services to the culture industries, and so continue to compete in the global marketplace. For a while, life might seem to continue as normal, as it does at the end of term. But if the students stayed away when the new term began, what would academics and technicians and librarians do? With paperwork sorted, teaching projects completed, books returned to the library, workshops and studios tidied, it would soon become clear that without students, then academics and technicians, and also administrators, managers, directors, and governors would all be surplus to requirements. In theory, having withdrawn from the neoliberal university/art school, students could set up or join up with an independent art school, whether as a radical exercise in autonomy or a more affordable alternative to art education as a debt trap. But in practice, withdrawal would mean surrendering the buildings and their contents: canteen, library, studios, letterpress, printing, darkrooms, and workshops. We might then ask, who owns the university/art school?

On 29 October 2015, *Divest UAL* students staged a "die-in" at Central Saint Martins, near the site of the Occupation of six months earlier. In the busy concourse of the art school, housed in a corporate building rented from private property developer Argent, whose security staff patrols the premises, the students spread out their banner, then lay down and "died."

Ambiguously poised between defiance and capitulation, their action complemented carefully gathered evidence and reasoned argument for divestment with a sudden, psychological affect. I have seen public die-ins involving many more participants, but I was moved by the *Divest UAL* campaigners' solidarity and courage. Carried out in a place where they are well known, the students' gesture as a minority was to put themselves in a position of symbolic vulnerability, highly visible on the unstable border between art and activism.

In November 2015 UAL announced that it would divest its endowments of £3.9 million from fossil fuels, and sign the United Nations Principles for Responsible Investment. But in the official announcement the work of *Divest UAL* was not visible. So, having been invited to present an update on sustainability to the November 2015 meeting of the UAL Professors and Readers Committee, I said that congratulations were due—to the *Divest UAL* group for their inspiring work, and to UAL for responding to them.

ATHENIAN DEMOCRACY?

Figure 2.7: Architect's Vision for Stratford Waterfront, Part of the Exciting New
Education and Cultural District, "Olympicopolis," at Queen Elizabeth Olympic Park
*Source: Image Copyright 2015 by Forbes Massie/
London Legacy Development Corporation*

At the February 2016 meeting of the UAL Professors and Readers Committee, I was again invited to give an update on sustainability. This time, referring to the UK Government's consultation paper *Fulfilling Our Potential: Teaching Excellence, Student Choice and Social Mobility* (Department for Business, Innovation & Skills, 2015), I said:

> Understandably, discussion of the paper has mostly focused on the burdens and risks of a bureaucratic evaluation of "teaching excellence." But the paper contains far more radical proposals for fundamental changes to Higher Education, which include freeing up universities to change their own governance structures, ending universities' obligation to operate in the public interest, and allowing universities to transfer their assets (presumably into private ownership).

> The Government's stated aim is to create a competitive market amongst "education providers." If we at UAL try to compete with deregulated private commercial rivals, we risk becoming like them: ruthless, unstable, and unsustainable.

> However, I believe we could use the Government's proposals differently to:

- reform UAL's governance structure to make it more democratic,
- enshrine in our constitution a commitment to sustainable social benefit, and
- transfer the university's assets into a trust dedicated to delivering that aim.

> As a not-for-profit cooperative social enterprise, UAL would be uniquely placed to develop collaborations with public sector, private sector, and voluntary sector organisations to envision and realise the transition to a more sustainable society. Our university could move beyond teaching creativity, to become a creative organisation, with an institutional culture centred on transformative pedagogy and research that engages with societal challenges.

I invited my colleagues to join students in collectively developing a viable model of UAL as we believe it should be: an experiment in creativity and learning as co-determination, which recognises different forms of value.

In March 2016, our Vice Chancellor gave an All Staff Briefing, in which he presented "Delivering transformative education" as the first of UAL's four strategic areas until 2022 (UAL, 2015, July, p. 12), and showed a selection of successful creative projects in partnership with external stakeholders that have contributed positive social benefit. For UAL's strategic area of "An Inspirational Environment," he showed a digital visualisation of the major new building project on the site of the 2012 Olympic games in East London. Introducing the 2015 Report and financial statements, the Vice Chancellor noted, "over the next five years UAL will invest more than a quarter of a billion pounds in regenerating areas of London" (p. 10).

Assuming the bulk of this sum is borrowed on our behalf, we might hope that the Vice Chancellor's gamble pays off. But even if the scheme succeeds financially, then staff and students face the task of reconciling the university's ambition of being a world leader in sustainability with the actuality of a vast growth based on a precarious mix of leveraged finance and student debt. In his Policy Forum speech, the Vice Chancellor wrote, "taken as a whole, what the cultural and educational institution will be doing at Olympicopolis is to create a machine to change culture, not simply exhibit it" (Carrington, 2015, para 8).

When he invited questions, I thanked him for featuring socially engaged projects showing that the value produced at UAL is more than monetary. I said that his response to the government's consultation paper, like many others, had focused on Teaching Excellence, but passed over the radical proposals that would permit universities to change their structures of governance, and transfer their assets. Referring to the risks of competing with unregulated commercial "educational providers', I asked him whether UAL could redefine itself as a co-operative social enterprise.[11] His reply was immediate and unequivocal: "No. We are a monstrously complex organisation now, so trying to run with a new organisational model would be a risk too far. Having said that, we do listen—we have a fortnightly meeting with the

---

[11] For a compelling account of co-operative education, see Joss Winn (2015, pp. 39–55).

Students Union. But you can't have a thousands-strong Athenian democracy" (Carrington, 2016).

CONCLUSION

Through the seven sections of this essay I describe a series of actions/interventions that respond to major changes in UK higher education in ways that relate to the emancipatory ideal of transformative pedagogy. In the *The Kettle is a Crucible* I suggest that the shared experience of adversity—in this case through arbitrary confinement as a form of collective punishment for those demanding social justice—could produce a new collective identity or social subjectivity, quite unlike the individualism that serves the status quo; following that, using the figure of Lord Brown who spans the extractive fossil fuel industry and the higher education system, *The Limits to Growth* aligns a critical engagement with the contested ideal of "sustainability" to that of promoting a conception of art education as a public good. *Context is Half the Work* signals the potential that the APG approach offers for overcoming the separations produced by institutional categories, and hence for redirecting critical attention and creative energy in a more open process of learning. *Business Engagement and Procurement* develops that possibility by proposing that the business operations of the university/art school which are usually held apart from the curriculum offer concrete examples for staff and students to engage with these issues through "live projects." *Master of the Universe* takes a more cathartic turn—in a performance which collapses the distinction between artist and academic, I address the psycho-social aspects of education both as a professional, and a personal process of transformation. This double effect of transformation is also articulated in *Seen to be Done*, but from the student perspective. I present student occupations and "die-ins" as strategies to engage with representation as a concept central to the political and cultural spheres, produce interaction between tangible and intangible forms of value, and highlight the complementary relationship between cognitive and affective labour. Finally, *Athenian Democracy?* recounts a more agonistic mode of exchange that reveals a potential conflict between the aim of "delivering transformative education" and the institutional context of a hierarchy.

Described as "actions" in terms of activism and action research, or as "interventions" in fine art practice, the work has taken forms of debate, encounter, event, performance, and presentation. Each one draws on APG's potential to focus critical and creative attention, and directs it onto the university/art school to inform the intersection of transformative pedagogy and ecological thinking. Two APG ideas have been of particular relevance: the view that "context is half the work," and the "open brief."

In terms of the context, and as noted in the introduction to the APG exhibition at Raven Row, "in the face of general indifference and frequent antagonism, APG dared to imagine the (inevitably asymmetrical) intersection of opposing value systems" (Hudek & Sainsbury, 2012, para 4). Today, the university/art school is a context of intersection between the opposing value systems of culture and neoliberal economics. The university structures the relationship between them by separating its academic life as a place of learning from its executive functions as an engine of capital accumulation. This disconnection limits the potential for art practice, teaching, or research to inform the key decisions that shape the learning environment, and correspondingly extends the potential for the executive to do so. The organisations and institutions in which the original APG projects took place were different from those of art education, yet when the institution hosting an artist's placement is a university/art school, such differences and the assumptions underpinning them no longer hold. The result is impossible to predict, but a breaching of critical thresholds between cultural and economic value systems could be productive, as art's criticality is turned on the institutional and pedagogic processes that give rise to it. The APG concept of the open brief offered a radical premise "that artists would be paid a wage by the host organisation, regardless of the material output of their placement" (Hudek & Sainsbury, 2012, para 3). Imagining such a transaction in the university highlights a key difference between staff and students in the pedagogic exchange: academics are paid by the university; students pay to the university. Complementing the economic transactions is the assessment process, in which academics award credits to students in recognition of their labour and/or production.

The university/art school regulates the encounter between the transgressive impulse of the "creative," and the controlling impulse of "industry." The stated aim of UAL is to deliver transformative education, while enhancing graduates' employability in the creative industries. Conversely, applying the APG method of the open brief in the university/art school can advance an emancipatory transformative pedagogy through an indeterminate exploration of the structures and practices of the university, and of the broader social value of art and design education. Discussion of how the "creative industries" relate to consumerism could extend to considering how far the ideology of infinite economic growth on a finite planet is compatible with a respect for human rights, and an understanding of ecological systems as the basis of life on earth.

But divergent impulses can exist within people, as well as between them: artists may challenge the gallery, while seeking recognition from the social system the gallery is part of; students and staff may question the institution, while claiming the status and authority that it confers. Similarly, the university/art school fosters the creativity and tolerates the criticality of its staff and students, while limiting their freedoms and controlling the economic value that they produce and provide. Because such tensions rarely result in explicit dissent, the problems they can cause are more intractable for being difficult to identify. Research carried out by members of the psychology department at UCL, the London Business School, and Queen Mary University has shown that perceived inconsistencies between an institution's environmental policies and its actions, such as investing in fossil fuels, reduces staff and students' intentions to engage in pro-environmental behaviour (Skipper et al., n.d.). Citing this research, and connecting the discourses of environmental education and social justice, Jane Holder has argued for a pedagogical approach to fossil fuel divestment, based on recognition of the "intangible and multifarious ways by which an institution instills values and learning in its students" (2015, p. 235).

Just as "transformative education" is open to different or even opposing interpretations, "sustainability" is a deeply contested concept. Seeking to reconcile environment, development, and social justice issues, Kate Raworth has described a framework for sustainable development with a "foundation" of human rights and a "ceiling" of ecological limits, creating a safe and just space for humanity (2012, p.4). I propose that through exploring social practices, value systems, and material exchanges, transformative pedagogy in art and design could inhabit such a space as a field of cultural interactions. That calls for pedagogies that are transformative in the emancipatory sense. Such transformation could be framed at the personal, organisational, or societal level, but I am more interested in the relationship between continuity and change *across* those levels because, like the students who inspire me, I am looking to connect how I live with how I learn.

Practical Suggestions for Transformative Pedagogy around "Sustainability"

- Enable interaction in which staff and students show and discuss their interests, ambitions, and concerns, and say how they relate to the environment.
- Help the group to set up or change their learning situation, and/or try somewhere else. Discuss what is better, and who should decide?
- Engage with real issues and work on "live" projects, for which there is no set approach and the outcomes cannot be known in advance.
- Discuss meta-issues, such as the relationship between difference and commonality, or between opinions and values.
- Acknowledge different subject positions, and say how they are relevant to the environmental issue in hand.
- Share or hand over control, such as for choosing reading material, facilitating a discussion, or arranging an event. Discuss who should take the credit if it goes well, and who should take responsibility if it goes wrong.
- Invite everyone in the group to work in pairs. Each person should listen carefully to their counterpart, who will describe a transformative experience which relates to the environment. One by one, listeners relate the account they have heard back to the group.

REFERENCES

Ahmed, N., (2013, June 14). Pentagon bracing for public dissent over climate and energy shocks [Blog]. *The Guardian*. Retrieved from https://www.theguardian.com/environment/earth-insight/2013/jun/14/climate-change-energy-shocks-nsa-prism

Ansar, A., Caldecott, B., & Tilbury, J. (2013). Stranded assets and the fossil fuel divestment campaign: what does divestment mean for the valuation of fossil fuel assets? *Stranded Assets Programme*, Smith School of Enterprise and Environment, University of Oxford.

BBC News. (2012, January 31). *Former RBS boss Fred Goodwin stripped of knighthood*. Retrieved from www.bbc.co.uk/news/uk-politics-16821650

Beck, J., & Cornford, M. (2014). *The Art School and the Culture Shed*. Kingston upon Thames, England: Centre for Useless Splendour, Kingston University. Retrieved from http://instituteformodern.co.uk/2014/the-art-school-and-the -culture-shed-book

Bourdieu, P. (1986). The forms of capital. In J. Richardson (Ed.), *Handbook of theory and research for the sociology of education* (pp. 241–258). New York, NY: Greenwood Press.

Browne, J., Barber, M., Coyle, D., Eastwood, D., King, J., Naik, R., & Sands, P. (2010). *Securing a sustainable future for higher education: an independent review of higher education finance*. Retrieved from https://www.gov.uk/government/publications/the-browne-report-higher -education-funding-and-student-finance

Burgin, V. (1999). Art, common sense and photography. In J. Evans & S. Hall (Eds.), *Visual culture: The reader* (pp. 41–50). London, England: Sage.

Carrington, N. (2015, June 17). *Policy Forum London speech: The role of higher education in supporting the creative economy*. Retrieved April 2, 2016 from blogs.arts.ac.uk/vice-chancellor/2015/06/17/policy-forum-london-speech -the-role-of-higher-education-in-supporting-the-creative-economy

Carrington, N. (2016, March). Response to author's question at all staff briefing [Transcribed by D. Cross]. London, England: Chelsea College of Arts.

CDBU. (2016, January 14). *Response to the green paper* [CDBU Update]. Retrieved March 28, 2016 from http://cdbu.org.uk/cdbu-response-to-green-paper

CNNMoney. (2000, February 15). *Royal Bank wins battle*. Retrieved from http://money.cnn.com/2000/02/15/europe/natwest

Committee on Climate Change. (2014). *Managing climate risks to well-being and the economy: ASC progress report 2014*. Retrieved from https://www.theccc.org.uk/publication/managing-climate-risks-to-well-being -and-the-economy-asc-progress-report-2014

Context is Half the Work. A partial history of the Artist Placement Group. (2015). Berlin: Kunstraum Kreuzberg.

Cornford, M., & Cross, D. (2010). A Dialogue on Art School. In P. O'Neill & M. Wilson (Eds.), *Curating and the educational turn* (pp. 262–270). London, UK/Amsterdam, Netherlands: Open Editions/De Appel.

Critical Practice [Curators]. (2015, July 11). #TransActing: A Market of Values. Retrieved April 2, 2016 from http://www.criticalpracticechelsea.org/wiki /index.php?title=TransActing:_A_Market_of_Values

Cross, D. (2011, March 26). *The kettle is a crucible* [Text for student fanzine distributed at TUC "March for the Alternative"].

Cross, D. (2015, June 17). The University Beyond Neoliberalism. In J. Clarke & L. Wright (Organisers), *Conversas 3* [public discussion]. London, England: Peckham Pelican.

Cross, D., & Newman, H. (n.d.). *Education as a public good* [Video file, 2 parts]. Retrieved from https://vimeo.com/19390335 & https://vimeo.com/19473799

Department for Business, Innovation & Skills. (2015, November) *Fulfilling our potential: Teaching excellence, student choice and social mobility*. Retrieved from https://www.gov.uk/government/consultations/higher-education -teaching-excellence-social-mobility-and-student-choice

Desvoignes, O. (2015). *Blackboards were turned into tables… Questioning 'horizontality' in collaborative pedagogical art projects* (PhD thesis). University of the Arts London. Retrieved from http://ualresearchonline.arts.ac.uk/8730

Eagleton, T. (1992). The crisis of contemporary culture. *New Left Review, 196*. Retrieved from https://newleftreview.org/I/196/terry-eagleton-the-crisis-of -contemporary-culture

Education: Not Knowing [Public discussion]. (2012, November 13). *The individual and the organization: Artist Placement Group 1966–79*. Retrieved February 6, 2017 from http://www.ravenrow.org/events/education_not_knowing

Evans, M., Howarth, C., Kellay, A., Laboucan, B. J., Mercredi, M., Minio-Paluello, M., Schling, H., Smith, K., Thomas-Muller, C., & Wood, A. (2010). *Cashing in on tar sands: RBS, UK banks and Canada's "blood oil."* London, England: Platform. Retrieved from http://platformlondon.org/carbonweb /documents/ciots.pdf

Freire, P. (1970). *Pedagogy of the Oppressed*. New York, NY: Herder and Herder.

Grantham Research Institute on Climate Change and the Environment. (2016, March 24). *UK Government should not have been surprised by this winter's flooding* [Press release]. Retrieved from http://www.lse.ac.uk /GranthamInstitute/news/uk-government-should-not-have-been-surprised-by -this-winters-flooding

Green Education Declaration signatories. (n.d.). Retrieved February 6, 2017 from https://old.peopleandplanet.org/green-education-declaration/signatories

Higher Education News, Leeds University. (2010, December 10). Universities have vital role to play in the creative economy. *Higher Education News*. Leeds, England: Leeds University. Retrieved from http://www.leeds.ac.uk/forstaff /news/article/1362/universities_have_vital_role_to_play_in_the_creative _economy

HM Treasury. (2015). *A Country that Lives within its Means: Spending Review 2015*. Retrieved October 2, 2016 from http://www.gov.uk/government/publications /spending-review-2015-a-country-that-lives-within-its-means

Holder, J. (2015). Fossil free: linking divestment campaigns in universities with legal education. *Environmental Law Review, 17,* 233–236. http://dx.doi.org/10.1177/1461452915609823

Holmwood, J. (2011). Introduction. In J. Holmwood (Ed.), *A Manifesto for the Public University* (pp. 1–11). London, England: Bloomsbury Academic.

Hudek, A., & Sainsbury, A. (2012). Introduction. *The individual and the organization: Artist Placement Group 1966–79* [Online exhibition catalogue]. London, England: Raven Row Gallery. Retrieved February 6, 2017 from http://www.ravenrow.org/texts/40

Kay, J. B., & Salter, L. (2014). Framing the cuts: An analysis of the BBC's discursive framing of the ConDem cuts agenda, *Journalism, 15,* 754–772. http://dx.doi.org/10.1177/1464884913501835

Mas-Colell, A., Whinston, M. D., & Green, J. R. (1995). *Microeconomic Theory*. Oxford, England: Oxford University Press.

McKibben, B. (2012, July 19). Global Warming's Terrifying New Math. *Rolling Stone*. Retrieved from http://www.rollingstone.com/politics/news/global -warmings-terrifying-new-math-20120719

Meadows, D. H., Meadows, D. L., Randers, J., & Behrens, W. W., III. (1972). *The limits to growth: A report for the club of Rome's project on the predicament of mankind.*

R v Sussex Justices, ex p McCarthy. (n.d.). In *Wikipedia*. Retrieved April 3, 2016, from https://en.wikipedia.org/wiki/R_v_Sussex_Justices,_ex_p_McCarthy

Raworth, K. (2012). A safe and just space for humanity: Can we live within the doughnut? *Oxfam Discussion Papers*. Retrieved from https://www.oxfam.org/sites/www.oxfam.org/files/dp-a-safe-and-just-space-for-humanity-130212-en.pdf

Reason, P., & Bradbury, H. (2008). Introduction. In P. Reason & H. Bradbury (Eds.), *The Sage handbook of action research participative inquiry and practice* (pp. 1–11). London, England: Sage Publications.

Reputation Institute. (2010). *Royal Bank of Scotland: A case of reputational risk*. Retrieved from http://www.corporateexcellence.org/index.php/content/download/2627/27460/file/Royal%20Bank%20of%20Scotland%20-%20A%20Case%20of%20Reputational%20Risk.pdf

Skipper, J., Davis, A., Parkin, B., Schenk, P., Tse, H. L., & Jampol, L. E. (n.d.). *Time to divest? Perceived inconsistencies between UCL's environmental policy and actions reduces staff and students' intentions to engage in pro-environmental behaviours* [Working paper, subject to change]. Retrieved February 6, 2017 from https://sites.google.com/a/lab-lab.org/lab-lab/research/green-ucl

Slawson, N. (2015, April 15). University of the Arts London wins injunction against students over protest. *The Guardian*. Retrieved April 2, 2016 from https://www.theguardian.com/education/2015/apr/14/university-of-the-arts-london-wins-injunction-against-students-over-protest

Standpoint Gallery [Organisers]. (2014, June 24). *Mapping Art Practices* [conference]. London, England: Hoxton Town Hall. Retrieved March 26, 2015 from https://www.a-n.co.uk/news/sympoisum-set-to-map-uk-wide-art-practice

Toporowski, J. (2013). *The University as a hedge fund* [Podcast/unpublished paper]. Retrieved from http://www.ucl.ac.uk/urbanlab/news/Futureunivercities/#jantoporowski

Triodos Bank. (n.d.). *About Triodos Bank*. Retrieved April 2, 2016 from https://www.triodos.co.uk/en/about-triodos

UAL. (2015, July). *Report and financial statements: For the year ended 31 July 2015*. Retrieved from http://www.arts.ac.uk/media/arts/about-ual/financial

-statements-public/financial-statements/ual/Financial-report-2015_Amend_1
.pdf

UAL. (2015). *Learning, teaching and enhancement strategy 2015–2022*. Retrieved
from www.arts.ac.uk/media/arts/about-ual/strategy-and-governance
/documents/university-strategy/UAL_LTE_Strategy_2015_Web3.pdf

UAL students: Why We're Occupying Our Art School. (2015, March 21). Retrieved
April 2, 2016 from http://anticuts.com/2015/03/21/ual-students-why-were
-occupying-our-art-school

United Nations World Commission on Environment and Development. (2016). *Our
common future*. Retrieved from http://www.un-documents.net/our-common
-future.pdf

Universities UK. (2010). *Creating Prosperity: the role of higher education in driving
the UK's creative economy*. Retrieved from http://www.universitiesuk.ac.uk
/policy-and-analysis/reports/Pages/creating-prosperity-role-of-he-in-driving
-the-uk-creative-economy%20.aspx

Wenger, E. (1998). *Communities of practice: Learning, meaning, and identity*.
Cambridge, England: Cambridge University Press.

Winn, J. (2015). The co-operative university: Labour, property and pedagogy. *Power
and Education, 7,* 39–55. http://dx.doi.org/10.1177/1757743814567386

Transformative Pedagogies and the Environment

CHAPTER 3

Private Properties: Heuristic Inquiry, Land and the Artistic Researcher

Welby Ings

ABSTRACT

This chapter is concerned with heuristic inquiry. It considers the subjective engagement between the artistic researcher and the physical environment. Drawing on three case studies of practice-led, environmentally focused theses, it examines how subjective forms of engagement with the physical environment can enable artistic researchers to exhume and interpret issues and conditions of land.

By adopting heuristic approaches to their theses the three candidates were able to design research strategies that affirmed imagination, reflection, and flexible approaches to problem solving. In each instance the researcher also explored a unique understanding of the physical environment as a living essence. In the first study this grew out of activist understandings (Burton, 2015), in the second it was framed within an indigenous epistemology (Pouwhare, 2016), and in the third it was related to notions of embodied experience (Steagall, 2016). In each of these instances the researcher operated as an "insider" because being subjective, the context of the research was partly his own. This potentially intimate position stands in a dichotomous relationship to the tenets of positivism that have been fundamental to many other forms of ecological inquiry.

The chapter discusses the advantages and challenges of the heuristic approaches they adopted, using the case studies to unpack the manner in which transformative pedagogical approaches became manifest in the inquiries. It concludes with a summary of strategies that may be employed when supporting and extending such researchers, when they seek to draw into positive connection intimate lived experience with the environments that they study.

INTRODUCTION

Art and the Land

In 2003 the artist Andy Goldsworthy discussed his relationship with land. In a documentary on his work, he stated:

> Art for me is a form of nourishment. I need the land, I need it. I want to understand that state, the energy that I have in me that I also feel in the plants and in the landscape. The energy in life that is flowing through the landscape. It's that intangible thing that is here, then gone – growth, time, change, and the idea of flow in nature. (Donop, Davies, Hill, & Riedelsheimer, 2003)

The inquiring relationship between artists and land has very deep traditions that run well back into history. Although "landscape" as a term to describe specific works of art only entered modern English at the beginning of the 17th century (as an anglicisation of the Dutch word *landschap*), artistic studies of land may be traced back to the frescos of Minoan Greece (circa 1500 BCE) and the fifth century Chinese ink painting tradition of Shan Shui.

Recently, the contributions of artistic practice to understandings of land have permeated disciplines beyond the arts. Significantly, in areas like geographic research, embodied experiences of the landscape and "processes of world-making" (Banfield, 2015, p. 3) have been become manifest in studies where art is deployed as an empirical object. Building upon Rosalind Krauss' influential exploration of art's "expanded field" (1979), researchers have increasingly rethought art as an analytic object and this has resulted in a diversification of investigations beyond those that traditionally employed art as a mode of place-making. Banfield (2015) and Hawkins (2011) have both noted the growth of geographer–artist collaborative projects and the role of personal, practice-based artistic activity in carrying out research that engages creative techniques. Banfield (2015, p. 2) argues that this engagement "is symptomatic of methodological developments across the social sciences more broadly" and forms part of an increasing tendency to integrate qualitative, practice-based methods in traditionally nonartistic disciplinary research.

The Artist as a Subjective Researcher

Brydon-Miller, Berthoin Antal, Friedman, and Gayá Wicks (2011, p. 5) argue that, "art can allow us to see the unseen, to reveal aspects of a landscape in new and sometimes uncomfortable ways." Stevenson proposes that artist-researchers involved in this process "are often engaged in very fluid and often subterranean processes within very complex and interconnected systems" (2013, p. 6). Navigating these systems, she argues, involves significant "periods of incubation and submersion in the creative process" (Stevenson, 2013, p. 3).

Such distinctive approaches to interpreting land pose significant challenges to traditionally objective research because artistic inquiry is often predicated on an integrated relationship between the subjective researcher and what is researched.

Such understandings of research are underpinned by a significant history of thought. In 1958, Polanyi argued that it was impossible to remove the subjective passion and commitment of the observer from an inquiry and contended that these qualities were in fact essential to experiencing and investigating the world. In 1994, Schwandt, building upon Eisner's (1991) notion of the researcher as a connoisseur and "instrument", argued that personality and past experiences provide the sensibilities that make investigation possible. Thus, when artists engage with interpretations of land, or responses to it, the self becomes inescapable because the self is creating, responding to, and evaluating expressions of what is studied. Klein (2010) suggests that in such instances it is not the art work *itself* that constitutes research but rather the evolution of inquiry underpinning its development.

Given this, we might usefully consider *how* certain artistic researchers approach the land when their inquiries are predicated on heuristic methods and embodied levels of engagement with both physicality and meaning.

HEURISTIC INQUIRY

The word heuristic comes from the Greek *heuriskein* meaning "to discover". It relates to a form of inquiry that uses immersion and intelligent, informal questioning to sense one's way forward. Douglass and Moustakas (1985, p. 42) suggest that heuristic inquiries offer "an attitude with which to approach research," rather than a prescribed methodology. They suggest that in its purest form, "heuristics is a passionate and discerning personal involvement in problem solving, an effort to know the essence of some aspect of life through the internal pathways of the self" (Douglass & Moustakas, 1985, p. 63). As such, heuristic inquiry functions without a preformulated hypothesis (Kenny, 2012).

Moustakas (1990) argues that heuristic inquiries must begin with the identification of a question that is deeply felt and has significant emotional ressonance for the researcher. Like Gadamer (1975), he argues that the question must be lived and embodied, and such questions hold considerable potential for a transformative effect on both researchers and the data they process.

Guba and Lincoln (1989) and Moustakas (1990) suggest that to effectively engage with the potentials of such inquiries, researchers must be receptive to information that is collected through the senses. They must be able to respond to nonverbal clues and be capable of "feeling" a question by staying fully with the experience of the phenomenon, irrespective of the shifting forms it may take. Thus, the study of land becomes not a site visit but a condition of being, an incursion into relationships between a location and the self where nuance, imagination and impression may be valued alongside what is explicit and recordable.

In each of the case studies discussed in this chapter, the heuristic inquiry began with a state where the researcher was immersed in a theme or problem. By being embodied in the self and the land, the internal questions this raised meant each candidate made a protean journey. The relationship between the researcher and the studied environment was not fixed, and resonances, meaningful syntheses and pattern recognitions had to be constantly identified, tested, and refined (Pinchbeck, 2006; Kenny, 2012). In this process Douglass and Moustakas suggest:

> The challenge is to examine all the collected data in creative combinations and recombinations, sifting and sorting, moving rhythmically in and out of appearance, looking, listening carefully for the meanings within meanings,

attempting to identify the overarching qualities that adhere in the data. This is a quest for synthesis through realisation of what lies most undeniably at the heart of all that has been discovered. (1985, p. 52)

Kleining and Witt (2000) suggest that the effectiveness of this approach becomes measurable by the richness of the result, its cohesive patterns and inter-subject validity.

Advantages of Heuristic Inquiry

Many artistic thesis candidates intending to work with land based research are drawn to the apparent advantages of heuristic inquiry because its principles seem to correlate with their past experience. They are often familiar with the role of intuition, nonlinearity, and reflexive thinking. They have also utilised embodied connections to the subjects they study. Here the physical and the emotional flow in and through each other, and tacit knowing, operate alongside more explicit processes. For such researchers, heuristic inquiry appears to offer a number of distinct advantages.

First, it is flexible. This quality can be employed to sustain high levels of creative responsiveness because the artist is able to embrace disruption, serendipity, and contradiction as part of a productive process of "coming to know".

Second, heuristic inquiries acknowledge the role and significance of tacit or intuitive knowing, as a fundamental to inquiry (Polanyi, 1958). Because artistic researchers often intuitively connect fragments and identify relationships, they are able to plumb unusual depths of understanding and meaning in a realm of productive unknowing, where they can think and act "between the not yet formed and the formed" (Rosenberg, 2008, p. 114).

Finally, because heuristic inquiries presuppose knowledge as personal, the central position of the self means that it is sometimes possible to draw into close proximity relationships between the phenomenon of study and the nature of the person. With artistic researchers new to the complexities of thesis study, the challenges of longer term inquiry can sometimes be mitigated against when there is a close personal connection to the environment under investigation. A resonant, subjective relationship with the subject can afford higher levels of tenacity because researchers are concurrently drawing on both their emotional connection and their analytical approach.

Challenges of Heuristic Inquiry

Although the inherent flexibility of heuristic approaches may appear attractive, in practice this same flexibility can also prove problematic. In my experience, challenges for early researchers can arise in three particular areas:

First, because artistic research must creatively navigate unknown territory, candidates sometimes seek to minimalise the potential for disruption in their projects. Perhaps such a tendency is not unexpected. Many established conventions in university research emphasise the need to moderate potentials for disturbance.

(Indicative of this is the requirement of applications for thesis study to delineate a single, clearly defined question at the outset of the inquiry.) However, Kleining and Witt note that when working heuristically the "topic of research is preliminary and may change during the research process. It is only fully known after being successfully explored. The topic may be overlapped by another one or turn out as part of a different problem or just disappear" (2000, p. 2).

This protean nature of heuristic questioning can be a challenge. Researchers often operate within professional and academic formulas that have brought them to existing levels of competence. These formulas constitute patterns of security that the mercurial nature of heuristic inquiry can disrupt. In addition to thinking and organisational processes, budgets and time schedules can also suddenly slope sideways when rich new veins of possibility require investigation. Although Sela-Smith (2002, p. 66) suggests that the heuristic researcher must be prepared to surrender to their inquiry, rather than control and manipulate the process so that it moves in the "right" direction, this can be very difficult. Students adopting this approach often encounter high levels of anxiety because heuristic inquiry does not guarantee predictable, unproblematised processes.

Second, because heuristic inquiries embrace diverse potentials, often the inquiry broadens before it narrows. This means that unless researchers are attentive to their research question, they can quickly find themselves swamped with data, struggling in a quagmire of possibilities without sight of firm land. As experiments are generated and give birth to new investigations, increasing bodies of information are generated within the study. Without an astute ability to overview the territory of an inquiry, candidates can begin to teeter under the escalating weight of lost direction. Very specific skills are required to manage the complexity of such research environments. Candidates must be able to temporarily "park" bodies of thinking as they focus on the potential of others. However, they must be able to concurrently articulate the question being addressed in relation to other questions within the research. This is a complex skill that is not highly developed in all thinkers and without it a heuristic inquiry can quickly lose its way in a congestion of movement and irresolution.

Third, as in all subjective inquiries, the heuristic researcher needs to adopt approaches that enable them to balance rigour against the sensitive edge of subjective inquiry. In addressing this issue supervisors must walk a careful line between trust, support, and reinforcing for students the need to separate criticism of the research from criticism of the self. If a student becomes too self-referential, emerging solutions can end up being evaluated against limitations they do not know they possess. This said, an artist employing external feedback in a heuristic inquiry needs to be vigilant. Sela-Smith notes that a "confusion of … different perspectives and different meanings, can fully disorient the researcher doing self-inquiry" (2002, p. 71). Thus, in developing pedagogical approaches for this form of inquiry, care needs to be taken to ensure that subjective insight is preserved while simultaneously ensuring that the student's frames of reference are challenged and extended.

Finally, tied to the significance of the self in heuristic inquiries are issues related to the implications of declaration. The thesis student's research journey will normally go deeper than simply reflecting on actions. Such inquiries can cause them to delve into fundamental concepts of meaning, knowledge, and identity. They will sometimes draw on these in passionate and demanding ways. Accordingly, the subjective self that appears in the thesis can become an exposed personal story that will be read and interpreted by others. The implications and risks of this require careful deliberation.

CASE STUDIES

Because a discussion of the advantages and disadvantages of heuristics can feel a little abstract, the following case studies may provide insights into how the pedagogical implications of supervising such theses have played out inside the lived experience of research. The three theses under discussion were practice-led and undertaken by mature male students with distinctive connections to both the physicality and conceptual meaning of land. The first was concerned with printmaking, the second with interactive film, and the third with photography.

Rene

Figure 3.1: Scorched Print of Kingston Cliffs
Source: R. Burton, 2014

Project and Background

Rene Burton's research project was an artistic response to the "Black Tuesday" bush fires that swept through the small Tasmanian community of Kingborough on February 7th in 1967. His inquiry was framed as a social and ecological palimpsest, concerned with the manner in which fire writes on land, the subsequent environment, and the lived experiences of local residents. He saw the environment he studied as having "been erased and reused, and rewritten on, with each layer of use leaving a readable residue or imprint on the landscape" (Burton, 2015, p. 7).

The inquiry involved long periods of physical immersion in historically fire-damaged sites that he identified from archive material in the local community archives. Using these as references he sought out specific locations wherein he dwelt, recorded, and reflected on time and ecological inscriptions on the land. In addition, he recorded interviews with local residents who had a lived relationship with the area. Data from these were used in film panels that he created as audio-visual palimpsests. He also used written transcriptions from the participants' narrations in a series of prints that he developed for the project (see Figure 3.1). These combined works formed an exhibition *Fire on Parchment* that constituted the final artistic component of his master's thesis.

Prior to embarking on his study, Rene had an extensive history of environmental artistic activism that included, in 2012, an artistic inquiry into New Zealand's most environmentally damaging maritime disaster: the oil spill from the wrecked container vessel the MV Rena. Rene had worked as a volunteer in the clean up of the aftermath of the accident. In a subsequent exhibition called *Beads*, he constructed a work that forced the viewer to engage with filmed images through pollutants from the 350 tonnes of leaked fuel, and the contents of 137 wrecked containers that had damaged the local coastline.

Methodology

In developing the research project for his thesis, Rene adopted a heuristic approach he described as a "self-situated inquiry". Here he fused a "consciousness of the self with a consciousness of the environment" (Burton, 2015, p. 49). Within this dynamic he suggested that the "artist immerses himself in both the physical site of the research and inside the practice that interprets it. In so doing he is engaged in a form of indwelling (where) he senses his way forward in a heuristic manner, drawing on both the tacit and explicit, in a process of interpreting and generating new artistic data" (Burton, 2015, p. 25).

The embodiment, he argued, provided a relationship between himself, the environment, its history and his history. On visits to locations in his research he described walking or sitting for hours, absorbing the smells, sounds, sights, textures, and unspoken stories. He said:

> I allowed the environment to "talk" to me, using my senses to pick up on the physical / explicit. My tacit knowing drew out the missing or underlying tensions and history. I dwelt within the land, conceiving it as an ancient manuscript, layered with evidence and unknowing. From this position I sensed my way towards its layered stories. (Burton, 2015, p. 51)

Such embodied approaches to environmental study are understandable when we encounter artistic researchers who conceive themselves as connected to the land on levels beyond the physical and cognitive. In his thesis positioning statement Rene stated:

I have a deep spiritual attachment to the landscape; I feel it in my bones. This connection is part of a single being; both landscape and person are connected, inherently. One cannot exist without influencing the other. People seek to control the landscape; to divide it, shape it, scrape it back, write on it, and leave our marks on it. Yet we are part of the ecology. Not separate, but a single whole." (Burton, 2015, p. 29)

Pedagogical Discussion

Vilkinas and Cartan (2001) suggest that a supervisory relationship must concurrently embrace paradoxical states where one is both a caring developer and a demander of quality outcomes. For Rene two significant issues illustrate this.

The first concerned the need to balance his political passion and its accompanying rhetoric with the necessity of finding an authentic and considered academic voice. In such instances I tend to encourage politicised students, when embarking on a thesis, to write an initial short chapter that positions themselves as the researcher and places their thesis inquiry in the context of their prior work. This helps them to orient themselves for later discussions related to research paradigms. It also enables the construction of a considered voice that is unencumbered by reference to outside scholarship. It can also move them beyond the rhetoric of ideologically persuasive language that has sometimes become a substitute for considered analysis. The chapter Rene wrote was passionate and self-exposing. He talked about how, as a child, incursions into the bush operated as a salve for anxieties related to his relationship with his father, whose bouts of paranoia were an ongoing source of tension. Rene saw the land as a balance, a respite from complexity and instability. This understanding had accompanied him into adult life.

As he developed his thesis we talked about the implications of such high levels of personal exposure, given that both his family and strangers would be likely to read what he wrote. I explained that his exegesis would be unalterable and publicly available for the rest of his life—and beyond. It would become the mark of both his integrity and scholarship, and it would be available at the click of a mouse. I have found that, when working with inquiries where the self is exposed through the research, such discussions are very important because the implications of self-declaration can be as profound as they are unexpected (Tolich, 2010; Ings, 2014). In this regard I am reminded of Thomas King's observation that "once a story is told … it is loose in the world" (2003, p. 10).

The second pedagogical issue raised by the thesis was unexpected. After making numerous incursions into the district to gather and reflect on data, Rene had begun developing an early set of prints. In these works he layered images on top of each other and experimented with scraping back areas and adding new material over the distressed surface. As the experiments progressed he began painting gel medium over parts of the print. This gel he coated with gunpowder, which he then ignited. By controlling the "burn off", he was able to disturb certain areas of the print using the same erasing element (fire) that had destroyed details of the original site. The ignited prints were filmed and became imagery later used in his audio visual palimpsests. The remaining ash became part of the texture of the print (see Figure 3.2).

Figure: 3.2: Ignited Serigraph with Gunpowder Infused Gel
Source: R. Burton, 2015

However, one night, while this work was drying on the racks in the print room, Rene rode home on his scooter and was struck by a car. The accident was horrific. He suffered a debilitating brain injury and multiple fractures to his legs that resulted in him being confined to a wheelchair for four months. Although I arranged for him to take leave from the thesis to recover, he wanted to continue with the project. While still unable to walk, he began to re-engage with the material that he had been developing. I remember our first supervision session after the accident was held at his home because he could not travel in to the university. He hobbled around the kitchen making dinner and afterwards we cleared the table to critique the four paragraphs of writing that had taken him 12 days to write.

While there is considerable discussion around the role of personal experience in effective supervision (Carter, 1992; Morganett, 1995; Wilson, Wood, & Gaff, 1974), such things take unusual forms. For Rene the self and the research had become linked. This was not a study; it was an immersion in an idea that was inextricably tied to the self. The recovery of the self and the recovery of the thesis became intertwined. There is no road map for such supervision because the researcher and the supervisor are working heuristically. Both parties are required to sense a way intuitively forward through unpredictable variables.

Rene's head injury meant that he was initially unable to work on computers so he was forced to focus solely on analogue techniques. I recall graphically one evening walking up to the print studios above my office because I had heard that he had secured a ride into the university. He didn't know I was there. I watched him as he pulled himself around the room on crutches tenaciously making screenprints of his work. Only one light was burning in the room, defiant against the night. It seemed like a metaphor. In such instances I have come to realise that research can become something deeper than a cognitive investigation; it can be transformative.

Rene's recovery was slow. In the process we talked about treatments to his injuries and treatments to his project. He made small steps forward and around him I adjusted university provisions to accommodate. The metal pins in his legs and his inability to process thinking in ways he had used when he began the thesis impacted significantly on what was discovered and how it was expressed. However, because his research inquiry was not templated, he was able to adjust and fold disruption into new approaches to his work. In his exegesis he said:

> I have continued with the project because it offered something concrete and creative in a trajectory of injury and instability. As a consequence, my practice had to evolve alongside unexpected variables. Being unable to process ideas in the same manner that I did before the accident, I reviewed all of my raw data and experiments. … Due to the extent of my injuries, my adjustments had to be very pragmatic because I had to acknowledge distinct physical and mental limitations. (Burton, 2015, p. 57)

Rene's engagement was not simply an embodiment in a geographical site; it was an immersion in an inquiry. Data and processing became part of a reciprocating dynamic that brought an extraordinary body of research into being, and inside this there was a transformation. In concluding his thesis he wrote:

> The experiences I had in Kingborough have left a lasting mark. I have experienced huge landscapes that became momentary infernos, and then continued to sustain and grow life. Change happens, whether it be a bush fire or a motorcycle accident on an open road. Things that are familiar are destroyed and you salvage meaning from what remains … then you move forward … learning to walk, learning to write coherently, learning to print when you cannot stand. You write new experiences into the fabric of your life. Part of my mental recuperation from the accident was to reconnect with the landscape. As soon as I was able to walk again, I started to journey back into worlds that were physically familiar, but this time at a different pace. Fifteen-minute walks would take up to an hour. These physical restrictions also changed the pace of my practice, slowing it down, allowing me to interact with deeper layers that may previously have been overlooked or gone unnoticed. My thinking burned like a slow, curious flame. (Burton, 2015, p. 78)

Robert

Figure: 3.3. The Quest for Immortality, Film Still from the
Thesis *He iti te manu he nui te korero*
Source: R. Pouwhare, 2016

Project and Background

Robert Pouwhare is a prominent indigenous language activist. He is a direct descendant of Tama-ki-Hikurangi after whom his family's ancestral meetinghouse is named. Prior to undertaking his master's thesis Robert had spent over 40 years dedicated to cultural revitalisation. In the 1980s he became part of the movement that laid a claim for the Māori language both in law and within New Zealand broadcasting. This initiative culminated in the cases being heard at the Privy Council in London. Contemporaneously he became the lead claimant for his tribe in negotiations for land that has been confiscated from his people. These early experiences contributed to a worldview that profoundly shaped how he conceived land and its relationship to meaning. His thesis project, that employed the iconography of land to retell an ancient story of the failure of humans to claim immortality, was predicated within an indigenous paradigm that sought to capture the essence of Te Ao Māori (the Māori world) and Mātauranga Māori (Māori knowledge).

In Māori there is a fundamental understanding that one is "born out of the land and there is a relationship between people and land" (Harmsworth, 1997, p. 7). "Everything in the Māori world has a life force, (mauri), and contamination or degradation of natural resources is seen to damage and diminish the life force and affect the well-being of people" (Harmsworth, 1997, p. 3).

Robert's association with land was deep. He had grown up in a small community in Te Urewera, a remote, rugged forest in the North Island of New Zealand. In the positioning chapter of his thesis he recalled,

> there were barely roads, no electricity and just a flicker of radio. At night our grandparents would sing ancient waiata. Some of this sung poetry retold ancient histories and for them, the contemporary battles against the white man, the evil colonisers who came to steal our land. As youngsters we had no understanding of what the chants meant. All we wanted to do was sleep. But through the power of repetition the old people would drill this

69

information into our brains even when we were in deep sleep. It was not until I grew up that I understood that the oriori (lullaby) was designed to inculcate tribal history, to enduringly educate us about tribal trajectories, ancient hostilities and enmities. (Pouwhare, 2016, pp. 13–14)

Robert brought to his thesis a distinctive epistemology of land. This was based on a Māori view of the world that may be broadly defined as a series of states or dimensions:

- Taha tinana (the material or physical state that we can directly observe and describe),
- Taha hinengaro (the mental or intellectual state that requires us to understand the whole system, with all of its processes),
- Taha wairua (the spiritual state), and
- Taha whanaunga (the related/associative state that is understood over a long period of coexistence and association with the environment (Harmsworth, 1997).

Thus, in Robert's thesis, land was not considered as a geographical construct, it was understood as an expression of living forces (see Figure 3.3). The gods who populated the interactive film he created were all manifestations of the land. Only humans were rendered figuratively. His work was also shaped by a distinctly Māori understanding that there is an implicit connection between *whakapapa* (genealogy) and *whenua* (land) (Rangihau, 1992).

Thus, for Robert, artistically researching land involved a comprehension of the physical, genealogical and metaphysical. In discussing his distinctive treatment of this idea he noted:

It [land (whenua)] exemplifies a multifaceted, different reality; a world that is conceived as an integrated genealogical whole through the mythology. In this work whenua is treated as deeply dramatic. Its covering skies are unstable and time moves across and through it in ways that are unfamiliar. We understand whenua as inherent power, rather than a landscape in which things occur (Pouwhare, 2016, p. 32).

Methodology

The question then existed, "How as an indigenous artist might he research land within such a distinctive epistemological framework?" In such instances traditional Western methodologies generally fall short because paradigmatically they do not emanate from an indigenous perspective. If researching and interpreting the land and one's relationship with it is seen as simply physical, there is no room for understanding and creatively interpreting notions of cosmogony, kinship, genealogy, or the metaphors and frameworks that arise from them.

Accordingly, epistemologically and ontologically his research design operated within a distinctively Māori way of conceiving and progressing creative problem solving. In approaching the project Robert developed Nepia's (2013) indigenous research strategy of "Aratika". In Māori, aratika means to find the "appropriate pathway" (Nepia, 2013, p. 114). Nepia suggests that in using this methodology one may be guided by a sense of immersive discovery that maps on to the principles of tika (truth) and wairuatanga (the spiritual dimension). Inside this, the indigenous researcher may know his or her way forward both cognitively and spiritually.

Pedagogical Discussion

Connell (1985), Ferman (2002), Grant (1999), Pearson and Kayrooz (2004), and Taylor (2006) all argue that supervision is more complex and relationship-oriented than research training. This becomes obvious when we supervise theses about land that emanate from, and draw upon, ways of knowing that are distinctively non-Western. The land in Robert's thesis was pregnant with power. It transcended the physical and was inextricably linked to genealogy, and through that to the identity of the researcher.

In such instances the supervision relationship depends heavily on trust. In developing this, Robert brought to the process the principle of *kōrero* (discussion, conversation, discourse). I spent a great deal of time listening to him and reflecting back what I thought I was hearing. In this process Robert talked about growing up in the forest and his people's grief at the loss of their land. In the depths of these conversations I encountered ideas and words I had never heard. If I did not understand something, he corrected me and explained his thinking. In this process he began to articulate the complex relationships that permeated his work. Following each meeting Robert would add to a draft of his thinking, send it to me, and I would respond within a few days. This process of rapid response meant that as a flow of thinking surfaced it could be maintained and extended. We met regularly, to talk and listen. I have found in such instances that it is better to meet in person than to try to manage things remotely. This is because if a misunderstanding arises it can quickly be addressed in person, and collaboratively you can build much higher levels of trust and insight.

Supporting this process Robert established a network of cultural and technical experts that he described as a raranga (weaving together) of knowledge. He used this input to critique iterations of his film and to challenge or clarify thinking he was unfolding in his exegesis.

Significantly Robert's thesis illustrated the value of drawing into the academy subjective and indigenously oriented understandings. Such voices, when connected to generational occupation of land are able to draw upon what is often rendered physically invisible. Memories of use and subjective narratives of connection may be brought into consideration in a manner that would not be available to an "outside" observer. More significantly this marginalised knowing can also bring with it the epistemological frameworks that shape that knowledge. The place of such paradigms becomes especially significant when dealing with indigenous understandings of the environment, its use and management (Harmsworth, 1997), because such perspectives posit conceptualisations of land from a variety of points of view including the gendered, cosmological, spiritual, and in Robert's case, as a living embodiment of grievance.

Marcos

Figure: 3.4. Vale de la Luna, Atacama Desert, Chile
Source: M. Steagall, 2015

Project and Background

Marcos Steagall is a Brazilian photographer. His professional background has taken him to distant locations in the pursuit of the subjective and the sublime. In recording land he suggests "the photographer engages in a dialogical relationship where the self exists as a dual imprint within the photographic image, because the image carries indexical traces of both the self and the land" (Steagall, 2015, p. 1). Although Marcos already held a PhD when he enrolled in the practice-led doctorate, he wanted to extend his academic study because he was seeking a critical/creative environment in which he might interrogate and expand the parameters of his photography and the theoretical and methodological frameworks surrounding it.

Marcos's work is specifically concerned with an understanding of land that reaches beyond the physical (Whitt, Roberts, Norman, & Grieves, 2001). His photographs depict richly saturated landscapes, devoid of people yet pregnant with possibility and undercurrent. Presence is intense but not tangible because he argues that what we are experiencing in his work is the incorporeal existence of the photographer (see Figure 3.4).

Methodology

Marcos describes his approach to research as both heuristic and embodied. He says, "When I photograph the land, I experience a form of concurrent indwelling and self-search where my physical boundaries and those of the land become fused" (Steagall, 2015, p. 11). Significantly he explores potential photographic locations through a process of walking. This, he suggests, enables him to not only physically experience the contours and details of land but also to "listen" to it from a variation of perspectives. These journeys may take many hours and they occur in silence. His "embodied walking" as a method, is reminiscent of Ingold's (2004) concept of "circumambulatory knowing" (p. 331), and reminds us of Tilley's (1994) assertion that the traversing of a landscape may weave knowledge into the walker's life, and vice versa.

Having found a location, Marcos will sit for hours in one place with his camera, recording the same image over and over as light, time, and atmosphere move incrementally across the site. Within this process he describes

> a harmonious forward motion where the land and my equipment are absorbed into a single creative momentum. Here my sense of rightness (Haseman, 2006) exists beyond explicit description. My practice is oriented by a sensation of pain and pleasure absorbed into a feeling of knowing exactly what to do. The energy radiating from this keeps me exploring, sensing, discovering and formulating and I lose any precise notion of time. (Steagall, 2015, p.12)

Within this his body becomes a tool. He says:

> I explore with my body. I frame possible arrangements with my hands; I physically touch and understand patterns, proportions, relationships and distances. Here textures and colours intoxicate me and suggest meaning. ... The hand-framed image is not fixed but breathing, it moves in relation to my body and I understand what I see as an extension of myself. By expansion the camera becomes an extension of my arm; an orthesis connected to the land. My photographs depict an intermediation of me looking at the land and the land looking at me. Here I am "flesh of its flesh." (Steagall, 2015, p. 12)

Pedagogical Discussion

It would be fair to say that Marcos is a passionate man. He "feels" relationships and his research embraces this. He constructs heuristic approaches that afford high levels of flexibility but are predicated on subjective, physical, and temporal engagement with the land he studies. As a consequence of this, he expects transformation to occur both in his work and in himself.

For such candidates research is rarely stable, so building a culture of reflection is very important. I have found that it is useful to remember that such inquiries are an orchestration of questions. If feedback is framed as questions, rather than advice, and a response is not asked for in an instant reply there is a higher chance that reflection may be taken back into, and reprocessed inside the researcher.

Because the research questions in heuristic inquiries are constantly in a state of change, I have also found it useful to devote time to listening to researchers talk about their work and beliefs. This enables them to articulate thinking of the moment and draw it into explicit expression. When (as in Marcos's case) a thesis must be written in a second language, such an emphasis on talking through thinking can be helpful because it not only encourages language articulation but, more importantly, it reinforces a consciousness of the self.

Because Marcos's engagement with land is both heuristic and self-situated, he adopts strategies to mitigate against the potential limitations of self-referentiality. Accordingly, he has built up a complex network of other professional landscape photographers with whom he shares and discusses iterations of his work. Their discourses also extend to critiques of methodology and thinking that occur when he is in the field. As with Robert, these critical networks operate as a resource and an affirmation of emphases that do not always sit centrally in the academy. In Marcos's case they embrace emerging software and hardware technologies, and approaches to the rigour of photographing in inaccessible or dangerous locations.

This brings us to one final point that may warrant consideration. Holden in 1987 discussed "absorption" as a feature of creative behaviour. Although this state can afford very intense levels of concentration, in this state it can also on occasions render a researcher incapable of recognising imminent danger. This is particularly an issue where the artistic inquiry takes a candidate into physically or socially unsafe environments. As a guide in such situations, I encourage researchers who work with land based inquiries to always take another person with them. If they decide against this, they are expected to inform another trusted person where they are going and indicate what time they expect to be back. In addition, I ask that they check the weather, dress accordingly, discuss what supplies they will have, and clarify their transport details. In remote locations where there is no cell phone reception, these recommendations constitute the fundamental environmental safety guidelines proposed for anyone entering unknown outdoor environments.

PRACTICAL APPLICATION TO TEACHING

In the past 18 years I have supervised over 20 environmentally situated PhD and master's theses. While it would be audacious of me to posit a definitive list of practical recommendations for supporting the heuristic inquiries underpinning such research projects, the following points may be useful considerations because they have all surfaced in one form or another in the case studies discussed in this chapter.

1. Because of the high levels of subjectivity in heuristic approaches to research, at the outset it is useful to discuss with students the implications of self-referentiality in their thesis. As part of this, we need to talk through the necessity when receiving feedback, for them to separate critique of their research from a perceived critique of the self.
2. Disruption and discovery lie at the core of heuristic inquiries, so we must be prepared as supervisors to design systems that normalise the unanticipated, because in practice it can be more disturbing to students than they expect.
3. Because heuristic inquiries can become very personal, it is important to discuss with students the potential impacts of personal declaration, given that their thesis will be an unalterable, publicly available document that will shape the way people will perceive them both artistically and professionally.

4. When working with candidates who operate from epistemological frameworks outside of our own, we must be prepared to listen and reflect back what we are hearing so they are able to clarify their thinking and make explicit the paradigm that supports their research. If we are prepared to decentre ourselves from the role of authoritative advisor we can encourage students to concurrently draw into their research, the expertise of other parties whose epistemologies will transcend our own. As an extension, we need to appreciate that the candidate's thesis will likely be required to stand authentically in at least two (sometimes contrasting) scholarly fields: the academy and the indigenous knowledge environment from which the research emanates (Edwards, 2013).

5. Because heuristic inquiries can result in periods of anxiety, it is useful to assure candidates from the outset that we are prepared to meet with them in person on a regular basis, as they work through disruptions. This will not only ensure that logistical problems can be resolved in a more timely manner, but also that trust, critique, and insight are elevated to higher levels of activation within the research journey.

6. Intelligent questioning lies at the base of effective heuristic inquiry, so it is often a successful strategy to adopt the same approach when supervising. If we can consciously avoid giving advice, we can question from diverse perspectives and thus demonstrate how questioning can be used as an agent for discovery in their research. We might also avoid insisting on immediate replies to questions. By encouraging time to dwell on what is asked (sometimes over the duration of a number of weeks), there is a higher chance that reflection will be taken back into, and reprocessed inside the self.

7. Where artists need to write and present their thesis in a language that is not their primary means of communication, we can invest time in talking and listening to them as they critique their work and articulate ideas that are formative in its development. This provides practise in giving presence to often quite complex thinking. It also temporarily disconnects their thinking from anxieties about writing. As an extension, at the outset of the inquiry we might consider encouraging students to write a positioning statement that articulates the reason for the thesis, and where it sits in the existing trajectory of their artistic practice. This not only helps them to orient themselves within the inquiry (paradigmatically) but also initiates the development of an authentic scholarly voice.

8. We need to reinforce the need for researchers, when working in potentially dangerous social or physical environments, to enter the field accompanied by another person and, if this is not possible, to ensure that basic information about their intended location and proposed time of engagement is always left with a reliable third party.

9. And finally, we need to be prepared with heuristic inquiries for the research and researcher to experience levels of transformation that are both cognitive and emotional. In such instances it is rare that what was initially embarked upon will be the same as what is completed. To capitalise on the power of

transformative potential, as supervisors we must operate in responsive and insightful ways to changes not only in thesis content, but also to the students' values that shape it.

CONCLUSION

Heuristic inquiry affords a unique approach to land based research because it presupposes a fundamental connection between the researcher and the environment under investigation. In this instance I am reminded of John Muir, the environmental philosopher, who once said, "I went out for a walk and finally concluded to stay out till sundown, for going out, I found, was really going in" (Muir & Wolfe, 1979, p. 439). In this statement he referred to a distinctive state of interior knowing where a dialogue develops between the self and the land one encounters. What is outside and what is inside the body no longer exist as a demarcation, or as Alfred Irving Hallowell has argued, "any inner-outer dichotomy with the human skin as boundary, is psychologically irrelevant" (1955, p. 88). This being "in" and "with" the physical world is integral to how certain artists engage with the environment. It can offer very resonant insights that draw into positive connection intimate lived experience with environments that surround it. By critically considering research approaches that affirm such connections, we have the ability to develop transformative pedagogies that ignite the quest for knowledge and understanding across disciplinary boundaries.

This is no small thing, but it has roots that run very deep into the ways artists respond to and create meaning from the environments they encounter.

REFERENCES

Banfield, J. (2015). Knowing between: Generating boundary understanding through discordant situations in geographic–artistic research. *Cultural Geographies*, 1–15. http://dx.doi.org/10.1177/1474474015591121

Brydon-Miller, M., Berthoin Antal, A., Friedman, V., & Gayá Wicks, P. (2011). The changing landscape of arts and action research. *Action Research, 9,* 3–11. http://dx.doi.org/10.1177/1476750310396405

Burton, R. (2015). *A creative consideration of climate adaptation as a social and ecological palimpsest.* Unpublished MA thesis. AUT University, Auckland, NZ. Retrieved from http://aut.researchgateway.ac.nz/handle/10292/9138

Carter, M. (1992). Training teachers for creative learning experiences. *Exchange, 85,* 38–40.

Connell, R. (1985). How to supervise a PhD. *Vestes, 28*(2), 38–42.

Donop, A.V., Davies, T., Hill, L. (Producers), & Riedelsheimer, T. (Director). (2003). *Andy Goldsworthy rivers and tides - Working with time* [Motion picture]. Munich, Germany: Mediopolis Films, Art and Design.

Douglass B. G., & Moustakas, C. (1985). Heuristic inquiry. *Journal of Humanistic Psychology, 25*(3), 39–55.

Edwards, S. (2013). Spaces of other thought: E kore e pirite uku kit e rino. In A. C. Engels-Schwarzpaul & M. A. Peters (Eds.), *Of other thoughts: Non traditional ways to the doctorate – a guide for candidates and supervisors* (pp. 53–66). Rotterdam, Netherlands: Sense Publishers.

Eisner, E. (1991). *The enlightened eye: Qualitative inquiry and the enhancement of educational practice.* New York, NY: Macmillan.

Ferman, T. (2002). The knowledge needs of doctoral supervisors. Retrieved from http://www.aare.edu.au/02pap/fer02251.htm

Gadamer, H. G. (1975). *Truth and method.* New York, NY: Seabury Press.

Grant, B. (1999). Walking on a rackety bridge: Mapping supervision. HERDSA Annual International Conference, Melbourne. Retrieved from https://www.researchgate.net/profile/Grant_Barbara/publication/228505875 _Walking_on_a_rackety_bridge_mapping_supervision/links/56c4287a08ae6 02342513696.pdf?origin=publication_detail

Guba, E. G., & Lincoln, Y. S. (1989). *Fourth generation evaluation*. Newbury Park, CA: Sage Publications.

Hallowell, A. I. (1955). *Culture and experience*. Philadelphia, PA: University of Pennsylvania Press.

Harmsworth, G. R. (1997). Maori values for land-use planning. *Broadsheet, Newsletter of the New Zealand Association of Resource Management*, 37–52. Retrieved from https://www.researchgate.net/publication/237091789 _Harmsworth_GR_1997_Maori_values_for_land-use_planning_Broadsheet _newsletter_of_the_New_Zealand_Association_of_Resource_Management _February_1997_Pp_37-52MAORI_VALUES_FOR_LAND_USE _PLANNING

Haseman, B. (2006). A Manifesto for Performative Research. *Media International Australia incorporating Culture and Policy, 118,* 98–106.

Hawkins, H. (2011). Dialogues and doings: Sketching the relationships between geography and art. *Geography Compass, 5,* 464–78. http://dx.doi.org/10.1111/j.1749-8198.2011.00429.x

Holden, C. (1987). Creativity and the troubled mind. *Psychology Today, 21*(4), 9–10.

Ingold, T. (2004). Culture on the ground: The world perceived through the feet. *Journal of Material Culture, 9,* 315–340. http://dx.doi.org/10.1177/1359183504046896

Ings, W. (2014). Narcissus and the muse: Supervisory implications of autobiographical, practice-led PhD design theses. *Qualitative Research, 14,* 675–693. http://dx.doi.org/10.1177/1468794113488128

Kenny, G. (2012). An introduction to Moustakas's heuristic method. *Nurse Researcher,19*(3), 6–11. http://dx.doi.org/10.7748/nr2012.04.19.3.6.c9052

King, T. (2003). *The truth about stories.* Toronto, Canada: Anansi Press.

Klein, J. (2010). What is artistic research? Retrieved from https://www.researchcatalogue.net/view/15292/15293

Kleining, G., & Witt, H. (2000). The qualitative heuristic approach: A methodology for discovery in psychology and the social sciences. Rediscovering the method of introspection as an example. Retrieved from http://www.qualitative-research.net/index.php/fqs/article/view/1123/2496

Krauss, R. (1979). Sculpture in the expanded field. *October, 8,* 30–44.

Morganett, L. (1995). Classroom teacher's idea notebook. *Social Education, 59,* 27–28.

Moustakas, C. E. (1990). *Heuristic research: Design, methodology, and applications.* Newbury Park, CA: Sage Publications.

Muir, J., & Wolfe, L. M. (1979). *John of the mountains: The unpublished journals of John Muir.* Madison, WI: The University of Wisconsin Press.

Nepia, M. (2013). *Te Kore: Exploring the Maori concept of the void* (Doctoral thesis, Auckland University of Technology, New Zealand). Retrieved from http://hdl.handle.net/10292/5480

Pearson, M., & Kayrooz, C. (2004). Enabling critical reflection on research supervisory practice. *International Journal for Academic Development, 9,* 99–116. http://dx.doi.org/10.1080/1360144042000296107

Pinchbeck, D. (2006). *2012: The return of Quetzalcoatl.* New York, NY: Jeremy Tarcher/Penguin.

Polanyi, M. (1958). *Personal Knowledge: Towards a post critical philosophy.* Chicago, IL: University of Chicago Press.

Pouwhare, R. (2016). *He iti te manu he nui te korero* (Master's thesis, Auckland University of Technology, New Zealand). Retrieved from http://aut.researchgateway.ac.nz/handle/10292/9776

Rangihau, J. (1992). Being Maori. In M. King (Ed.), *Te ao hurihuri: Aspects of Maoritanga* (pp. 183–190.) Auckland, New Zealand: Reed Publishing.

Rosenberg, T. (2008). New beginnings and monstrous births: Notes toward an appreciation of ideational drawing. In S. Garner (Ed.), *Writing on drawing: Essays on drawing practice and research* (pp. 109–124). Bristol, England: Intellect Books.

Schwandt, T. (1994). Constructivist interpretivist approaches to human inquiry. In N. Denzin, & Y. Lincoln (Eds.), *Handbook of Qualitative Research* (pp. 118–137). Thousand Oaks, CA: Sage Publications.

Sela-Smith, S. (2002). Heuristic research: A review and critique of Moustakas's method. *Journal of Humanistic Psychology, 42*(23), 53–88.

Steagall, M. (2016). *Landspace: An autoethnographic journey between land and image* (Unpublished confirmation of candidature document). Auckland University of Technology, New Zealand.

Stevenson, K. (2013). The river in a landscape of creative practice: Creative river journeys. *Landscapes: the Journal of the International Centre for Landscape and Language, 5*(2). Retrieved from http://ro.ecu.edu.au/landscapes/vol5/iss2/20

Taylor, S. (2006). Thinking of research supervision as a form of teaching. Retrieved from http://www.lancaster.ac.uk/hr/OED/CPD/rsarchive/files/StanTaylor.pdf

Tilley, C. (1994). *A phenomenology of landscape: Places, paths and monuments.* Oxford, UK: Berg.

Tolich, M. (2010). A Critique of current practice: Ten foundational guidelines for autoethnographers. *Qualitative Health Research, 20*(12), 1599–610. http://dx.doi.org/10.1177/1049732310376076

Vilkinas, T., & Cartan, G. (2001). The behavioural control room for managers: The integrator role. *Leadership and Organisation Development Journal, 22,* 175–185. http://dx.doi.org/10.1108/01437730110395079

Whitt, L. A., Roberts, M., Norman, W., & Grieves, V. (2001). *Belonging to land: Indigenous knowledge systems and the natural world*. Oklahoma: Oklahoma City University.

Wilson, R., Wood, L., & Gaff, J. (1974). Social-psychological accessibility and faculty-student interaction beyond the classroom. *Sociology of Education, 47,* 74–92.

Transformative Pedagogies and the Environment

CHAPTER 4

The Whether Project: Transformative "Extra Tertiary" Projects in Tasmania

Lucy Bleach, Wendy Fountain, and John Vella

ABSTRACT

By dominant Australian and OECD yardsticks of educational and economic advancement, Tasmania has languished; its colonial past and resource-related conflicts still palpable. The state's young people typically do not rise to the upper credentials of the Australian Qualifications Framework, yet Tasmania has of late provoked global interest for its transgressive cultural institutions, rarefied wild landscapes and quality production. Tasmanians, young and old, are awakening to a sense of place beyond the literal and local, aided by digital connectivity and pervasive sharing of visual culture. In this context, Lucy Bleach and John Vella have designed, developed and delivered pedagogical projects that target the Tasmanian population across intra-tertiary frameworks, and into the *extra-tertiary* domain. The projects are responsive to their context, and represent a contingent and rhizomatic approach to otherwise well-established pedagogical frameworks. Therefore, the projects have been deemed *Whether* due to their conditional nature, with an intended double entendre to the climate change that they encourage. For example, specific activities introduce *pressure systems* of risk and experimentation, elicit *precipitation* of expressed and tacit knowledge, or establish unique creative *atmospheres* that privilege process, tactility and intuition.

The collective programs engage Tasmania as a lab; a testing ground for national and international responses to regional, environmental, and social challenges framing art as an agent for change, and positioning the tertiary art school as a catalyst node within a network of dynamic social relations. How future programs might be designed with an overt social-ecological systems perspective, and how we might engage participants with ideas of the anthropogenic, as well as art making as an expression of citizenship and ethics, will be addressed. Finally, we reconnect how the surfacing of creative agency through such contextual making intersects with the contemporary discourses of transformative pedagogy with a view to progressing the Tasmanian climate for change.

Introduction to the Whether Projects and the Extra-Tertiary Zone

"The mode of being of the new intellectual can no longer consist of eloquence, which is an exterior and momentary mover of feelings and passions, but in active participation in practical life, as constructor [and] organizer, as 'permanent persuader', not just simple orator" (Gramsci, 1971, pp. 9–10).

Tasmania has of late provoked global interest for its transgressive cultural institutions, rarefied wild landscapes, and quality or crafted production. Tasmanians, young and old, are awakening to a sense of place beyond the literal and local, aided by digital connectivity and pervasive sharing of visual culture. In this context, The "Whether Project," a Tasmanian College of the Arts (TCotA), University of Tasmania, pedagogical project suite, has been developed to target the Tasmanian population across the intra- and extra-tertiary domain.

The intra-tertiary consists of relatively fixed structures and cohorts: a universe of rubrics, assessment tasks, and discursive dialogue and ambition. Within the art school context there are genuine attempts to introduce rhizomatic disruption to defined structures; however, these are conceived in reference, if not deference, to "walls" of policy, bureaucracy, capacity, and efficiency—constructs that manifest as institutional requisites. Walls also exist within the extra-tertiary context; however, their complexity makes them malleable, open to a re-interpretation of their very foundations, and while not unstable, more capable of being destabilized. These walls are more open to the artist/educator as simultaneous infiltrator, catalyst, and agitator.

Whilst the intra-tertiary is increasingly restricted by metrics, the extra-tertiary is a zone of challenging situations and relations characterised by post-industrial landscapes, under-resourced educational systems, and disadvantaged communities. Within these peripheral zones, the art school operates on uncertain ground where the perceived value of tertiary education is increasingly scrutinised. Delivering pedagogy in the extra-tertiary necessitates a shift in thinking, a capacity to speculate and innovate in situ. Consequently, this is also a rich terrain, where an art school can conjure unique and diverse projects whilst establishing complex and enduring relationships with its extended community.

The Whether Projects and Transformative Pedagogy

This chapter presents case studies that evidence impact within this extra-tertiary zone, describing models of engagement involving school students, teachers, the local community, and local industries, as well as tertiary institutions. The pedagogy of the Whether Projects engages social and cultural responses to Tasmania's challenges as a multi-scalar place. In common with Rolling (2013), this pedagogy embraces the arts as a wider system, the dynamics of which can serve as mechanisms for personal and broader human development. Fundamentally, the arts are a "sociobiological imperative through which to aggregate, accommodate, and assimilate ways of thinking not our own, as well as disseminate our own resources to others" (p. 7). Our goal is to foster trajectories of transformation for individuals and collectives, who experience through art-making the kind of "shape-shifting" of self, thoughts, emotions, relationships and world views that Butterwick and Lawrence (2009) suggest leads to a more just society. In Tasmania motivation to engage with the arts is high, as is TCotA's commitment to sharing resources with others beyond the art school.

Transformation resulting from extra-tertiary activities, as experienced by school students, parents, and teachers; for example, is underpinned by "artful learning" that is imaginative, intuitive and soulful in nature (Mantas & Schwind, 2014). Such learning through art making engages and elicits "expressive ways of knowing" (Taylor, 2009), of which learners may have been previously unaware, and can be expanded through ongoing reflection. This results from activities that engage learners in material and interpersonal dialogue, sensitisation to personal and social contexts, relationship and community building, and moments of critical reflection—all core elements of transformative learning (Taylor, 2009). More specifically, the extra-tertiary pedagogical projects welcome and enable differing emphases in the patterns of individuals' transformations, as proposed by Mezirow (2009). Through their art making, learners may; for example, explore new roles, relationships, and potential action, from which they plan and actively acquire new skills. Provisional testing of new, expressive ways of knowing and related roles may in turn develop learners' competence and self-confidence to adopt new roles and relationships beyond their present circumstances (Mezirow, 2009, p.19).

In the extra-tertiary zone, curriculum is even further liberated from the flexible, student-driven "shell curriculum" common to art and design higher education (Orr, Yorke, & Blair, 2014). In response, the pedagogy of the Whether Projects conceives of curriculum as both a focusing frame and a mode of engagement, in which artist-educators are co-learners alongside participants (Reiss & Pringle, 2003). Place-based projects located in communities, such as the Live Site Catalyst case study in Triabunna demand a respectful yet energetic engagement by artist-educators, who may at times find themselves out of their art school comfort zone. According to Cormier (2008), in this respect the community drives the curriculum, and the pedagogical approach intersects transformational learning principles with a rhizomatic model of learning. Originally coining the term "community as curriculum," in the context of online learning, Cormier describes the community as "spontaneously shaping, constructing, and reconstructing itself and the subject of its learning in the same way the rhizome responds to changing environmental conditions," including the weather (para. 13). This whether view of curriculum reinforces the dynamism of the arts as a system in the extra-tertiary zone, and the potential for artful learning by diverse participants therein.

The Whether Projects are framed by experience and impact dilemmas extracted from the definition of the word "whether": whether as a vacillation of commitment between alternatives, whether as a moment through which to express an enquiry, or whether as an indication of defiance. These suggest rich contradictions; an *insecurity* in relation to the quality and eventual impact of engagement, a *wonder* at the capacity for the speculative to evoke unforeseen consequences, combined with a *rebellious* stance in relation to the institutional (intra-tertiary) machine. In combination, these conditions of insecurity, wonder, and rebellion enable a pedagogy based on symbiotic exchange; reactive environments with unique weather patterns, constituencies that together create the curriculum, which in turn impact the original environment.

"The materialist doctrine that men are products of circumstances and upbringing, and that, therefore, changed men are products of other circumstances and changed upbringing, forgets that it is men that change circumstances and that the educator himself needs educating" (Marx K, cited in Levitas, 2012, p. 63).

The perception of an artist as a solo practitioner is increasingly becoming anathema to the contemporary art school. Collaboration, flexibility, and interdisciplinarity have replaced self-dependency as core skills for the art school graduate. The expectation for artists to be communicators, role models, and researchers has increased to a point where they challenge how and what is taught in art schools. In seeking to better understand what we now mean by artists, Pringle describes them as "educators, collaborators, role models, social activists and researchers / enquirers" (Pringle, 2002, p. 8).

In an environment as economically challenged as Tasmania, there is an implicit imperative for the University to engage with the broader concerns of social welfare. This pressure for extra-tertiary engagement is driven by diverse and, at times, conflicting motivations, including both "mercenary" and "missionary" imperatives that may contrast with the traditional roles and responsibilities of tertiary (art) education. At the same time, intra-tertiary institutional requirements to deliver research outputs, meet funding metrics, and address a Federal education agenda further impacts the context in which pedagogy is developed. However, by aligning the "Whether" projects with institutional strategies for local and remote engagement, the art school can instigate meaningful, risk-taking pedagogical systems within economically and geographically disadvantaged regions, while establishing unique and diverse relationships with its extended community.

Each pedagogical case study that follows is described according to its location, cohort, methodology, and duration, followed by a precis of situation and impact (see Tables 4.1 and 4.2). Some of the case studies are also framed alongside specific artworks that inspired or informed the development of the project, or are otherwise aligned with the project's aims.

PRESSURE SYSTEMS AND STORM FRONTS

Table 4.1: Whether Project: MACHINES

Whether Project	MACHINES
Location	Tasmanian College of the Arts, Centre for the Arts (Hobart) and Inveresk (Launceston); and University of Tasmania Cradle Coast (Burnie) campus
Cohort	Year 10 school students/TCotA undergraduate students/TCotA staff
Approach (metaphor and method)	*Pressure systems and storm fronts*: Risk, immersion and materiality
Duration	4-day intensive sessions (inaugural project 2010)

"Reaching the epicenter of the storm, the artist is breathless and almost blinded, yet he encounters a furtive moment of peace that could hint at a new moment of possibility" (Alÿs, n.d, para. 1)

A tornado is a mobile vortex of powerfully rotating winds, advancing beneath a large storm system that lifts heavy and apparently fixed objects as it moves across the ground. In the *Tornado, Milpa Alta 2000–2010* project, Belgian artist Francis Alÿs filmed his repeated attempts to enter the eyes of small-scale tornadoes in regional Mexico. Alÿs considers the dust storm as a metaphor for the destabilising of a system. Beyond the "very primitive relation to the elements," Alys suggests a metaphorical reading of the work. In a time of extreme weather patterns "we've lost control of this planet somewhere. There's an echo in that kind of tornado situation, where you're powerless facing those phenomena" (*Bloomberg*, 2010, para. 12).

This destabilisation is analogous to a Whether Project that extended the university art school into Year 10 of secondary education, engaging school students with undergraduates in a pressure system of change. In 2010, the Tasmanian College of the Arts (TCotA) Whether Project developed a teaching program called "MACHINES," which aimed to stimulate engagement between tertiary art education providers and secondary colleges/high schools. The MACHINES program provided collaborative art-making opportunities for large groups of Year 10 school students, drawn from local and regional areas across the public and private secondary education sector. Over an intensive four-day workshop, MACHINES challenged students to work in experimental and spontaneous ways, providing opportunities to work directly with TCotA staff and facilities, at times exhibiting in professionally esteemed venues. Within this extra-tertiary environment, TCotA sought to deliberately destabilise existing secondary school teaching and learning practices. The purpose was to question the emphasis placed on achievement in secondary education outcomes, mediated by an individual's a priori capacity, on the assumption that this can lead to an overly precious approach to learning, constraining risk taking, and negatively impacting engagement.

In the MACHINES program, this preciousness was relinquished through group learning experiences, shared outcomes, and collaborative engagement. Group-centred learning was core to the program's success, where students from diverse contexts and demographics, work, play, and take risks in collaboration. Throughout the workshop, students worked together in response to staged challenges and events. These approaches were carefully choreographed to enable students to understand and experience teamwork, both as a means to achieving resolved outcomes and as mechanisms for inspiring their individual practice. Here, collaboration became a powerful tool for expanding the possibilities for learning through a social, cooperative, and dynamic network; a place where individuals working together create and experience shared understanding and knowledge.

Figure 4.1: Students Working on "MACHINES," 2013
Source: Photograph by Laura Wilkinson

As a learning ecosystem, MACHINES also generated intra-tertiary learning at various levels. TCotA Visual Communication students were able to engage in real-world learning opportunities through designing bespoke MACHINES catalogues; whilst TCotA Sculpture students supported the school students in the workshops, gaining insights into techniques and processes relevant to their own practice. Reflecting on the opportunity to adapt their expertise to a new educational context, TCotA staff were able to develop their approaches to teaching. In addition, secondary art teachers who attended the workshops found them to be valuable professional learning opportunities, and were able to bring MACHINES-derived knowledge and experience back to their secondary school teaching.

MACHINES participants at all levels experienced educational models liberated from the prescribed activities (and pressures) of their usual curricula. In this extra-tertiary zone, students found themselves in the eye of a pedagogical tornado; the familiar landmarks of art making were erased as they collectively hurtled through non-goal oriented processes, engaging freely in risk-taking without a predetermined outcome.

PRECIPITATION AND SIPHONING

Table 4.2: Whether Project: Artist in Residence Program (AiR)

Whether Project	Artist in Residence Program (AiR)
Location	Tasmanian College of the Arts, Centre for the Arts (Hobart)
Cohort	TCotA Undergraduate, Postgraduate students and staff
Approach (metaphor and method)	*Precipitation and siphoning:* professional artists and practice
Duration	Variable (inaugural project 2014)

Condensation is the process that causes airborne water vapour to transform into liquid water. Precipitation is the release of water from clouds, allowing for the transfer of atmospheric water to the earth. Evaporation changes water from its liquid phase to a gas, or vapour, the important first step in the water cycle generating atmospheric water vapour. To siphon is to draw something (a material, substance, experience) from one location to another.

In the subtly nuanced work "Kreuzberger Pfütze," Kirsten Pieroth (2001) siphoned a rain puddle from the low socio-economic area in Kreuzberg, famous as an area of alternative subcultures, immigrants, and high unemployment to a gallery in the historic and fashionable centre of Berlin (once a low-socio economic area), thereby transforming the small body of precipitated water from its original spatial and socio-political context. In its fluidity, the siphoned puddle is a symbol of border crossing and infinite adaptation. Kreuzberger Pfütze resembles a poetic and scientific experiment, where Pieroth monitors water quality (oxygen, temperature, organic material) and observes the puddle's capacity to adapt and remain local.

In the contemporary context, the provision of traditional resources serves limited aspects of the student experience. These might include developing new approaches to pedagogy as determined by rubrics for learning outcomes, assessment processes, or similar. In contrast, contemporary learning requires a diverse consideration of the traditional merged with the experiential, and here students need to be enabled to become the drivers of their own learning. We have witnessed various scenarios where traditional assessment and engagement has stifled learning, whereas adjunct non-assessable experience has delivered learning that transcends metrics. It is on the threshold between these approaches that we are becoming charged and inspired; the trans-, cross-, and hyper-disciplinary spaces, such as social hubs, work integrated learning contexts, and the parallel resources accessed by stealth that supplement and enhance established pedagogical frameworks. These terrains are defined by terms such as agility, malleability, and opportunity, and are inspired by Nassim Nicolas Taleb's "antifragile" treatise, which identifies a capacity to benefit from threat (Taleb, 2012). This approach could stand in opposition to the traditional university remit, or it could in fact re-position the hierarchy of learning, redefining the "educational" in ways attuned to contemporary and future needs.

Inspired by Pieroth's siphoning, the art school seeks to resource the shape-shifting of self, thoughts, emotions, relationships, and world views within the student cohort. The role of visiting artists is a particular example. Over a number of years, a TCotA studio coordinator "siphoned" visiting artists into the school, invigorating under-utilised facilities and increasing access to professionals, thereby enhancing experiential learning opportunities for students. In response, TCotA developed the invitation-only Artist in Residence (AiR) program, a unique initiative supporting professional practice within the art school. Through this program, professional local, interstate, and international practitioners, as well as outstanding TCotA alumni, have the opportunity to extend their practice whilst positively impacting TCotA's student cohorts and educational culture.

Whilst pursuing their independent projects, the Artists in Residence engage with students both explicitly and implicitly, through presentations, workshops, and one-on-one discussions. By providing meaningful insights into the live, in situ process of professional practice, the program affords tangible links between the structured learning experiences within the institution and the open, responsive, and collaborative models operating in the vibrant local arts community, or access to international networks and models of practice. The AiRs, as they've become known, also provide specialised experience and knowledge that complements core staff expertise.

Transcending established studio territories and allegiances, the AiRs generate a powerful, symbiotic ecosystem of rhizomatic engagement between artists, staff, and students revealing new pedagogical possibilities. AiR is now firmly embedded within TCotA pedagogic practice, continuing to activate and enhance the collective culture and community of practice. This approach shifts the art school from passive fortress to active platform, where visiting artists and designers facilitate new perspectives, their collective incremental contribution applying an extra-tertiary logic on site, transforming the established system from the inside out.

CLIMATIC CHANGE

Table 4.3: Whether Project: Live Site Catalyst

Whether Project	Live Site Catalyst
Location	Triabunna
Cohort	Year 5 & 6 students; Undergraduate and Postgraduate students and TCotA staff
Approach (metaphor and method)	*Climatic change*: mobilising contact and re-seeing community
Duration	On going

The following interview took place between the internationally renowned environment-focused artist Olafur Eliasson and the critic, writer, and curator Hans Ulrich Obrist:

> Olafur Eliasson: The idea of colouring downtown Stockholm became something I just had to do. I bought the pigment in Germany and came back through customs with a real feeling of suspense and excitement; after all, I had enough colorant with me to dye the whole centre of the city. This wasn't an official project; I had to work really fast, so I'd got the planning down pat together with the current and the turbulence in the river, and one Friday at half past one there I was on the bridge with Emile and a bag full of red powder and people starting to stare at us. I hesitated for a moment then emptied the bag out over the parapet and the wind whipped up this enormous red cloud. I could literally feel people in cars slowing down, the cars went all quiet. And there was this cloud, floating over the river like a layer of gas. When it came in contact with the water, all of a sudden the river turned green, it was like a shock wave. There was a crowded bus ten metres a way and everybody was staring at the water . . . my heart started jumping up and down like mad: the whole length of the river was completely green and all these people had stopped to look at it. Next day it was all over the front page of the papers: "The river turned green."

> (Interviewer) Hans Ulrich Obrist: So the idea was to make the city visible for its inhabitants, who no longer take any notice of the way it works or what's special about it. What you did was aimed at challenging their perception of their environment as something changeless and reassuring.

> OE: Right. I wanted to get a fix on how the river is perceived in the city. Is it something dynamic or static? Something real or just a representation? I wanted to make it present again, get people to notice its movement and turbulence. For a few minutes there it was "hyperreal." (Eliasson, 2002, p. 17)

"Live Site Catalyst" (LSC) is a TCotA project, funded by the University of Tasmania's Institute for the Study of Social Change. It focuses on the contested post-industrial coastal landscape and regional community of Triabunna, north east of Hobart, and frames two years of ongoing activities delivered in collaboration with Monash University's *Triabunna Tomorrow* project, led by the architects Ross Brewin and Anna Gilby.

During preliminary research, the project team noticed the care local residents took of their private gardens. The individual tending collectively manifested a nurtured, abundant space that sat in stark contrast to the bleak socio-economic and cultural terrain of this town, impacted by the closure of the local pulp mill some years before. This local growth inspired LSC to visualise new streetscapes: vertical gardens that could operate as unique landmarks as well as industries defined by the propagation of gardens, as opposed to the pulping of trees. This ambitious, long-term project evolved through diverse stakeholder engagement, including with the 2016 *Dark Mofo*, the Tasmanian winter festival delivered by the Museum of Old and New Art (MONA).

Dark Mofo's 2016 theme of *tempest*, set in the darkness of mid-winter, triggered "NIGHT GARDEN," a one-night event geared to activating the township, and the vertical garden concept, through presenting gardens of horror. Over the course of a month-long workshop, Grade 5 and 6 students from Triabunna District School worked with TCotA staff Lucy Bleach and John Vella, and TCotA Sculpture and Moving Image students, to produce their own B-grade horror films of their Triabunna gardens. Workshops involved costume design, mask making, and sculptural body adornment construction that synthesised the students' bodies into plant-human hybrid forms. Students were directly engaged in film making activity—including shooting Super 8 B-grade horror clips of the school vegetable garden, and digital footage shot through a microscope revealing various cross-sections of vegetable and endemic plants. The local community hall was hired to project classic plant horror films, such as *Day of the Triffids*, as well as time-lapse footage of fungal spores, luminescent mushrooms, and carnivorous plants. TCotA students painted the local school students' faces, assisted in choreographing performances, and filmed the students "acting up" to the projected footage.

NIGHT GARDEN was staged in two parts. On June 16, 2016, between 7 and 12 p.m., more than 600 people trailed into an underground basement in Hobart navigating the subterranean city space to experience projected video installations of root systems, fungal spore growth, and the arresting portraits of the school children. On June 24, 2016, between 5 and 9 p.m., the Triabunna streetscape was illuminated with projections of luminescent mushrooms, carnivorous plants, microscopic cellular footage, and botanical B-grade horror films. The projected footage charged the streetscapes of Triabunna, translating multiple narratives of the town through moving images created by the students who live there, reframing the locale by fusing the real with the imaginary. Through the workshops and projected footage, the students explored new roles, relationships, and possibilities for experience and expression. Pedagogy operating in this context again establishes a new territory, one apart from the traditional domain in the classroom or university studio. Situated within the public confines of the local school the project also resonated with students' families; whilst making sets, props, and stages for films it restages the locale; whilst projecting images onto the buildings it is, in effect, *teaching the town*.

Place-based projects located in communities, such as Live Site Catalyst, demand a respectful yet energetic engagement by artist-educators. In this regard, the community drives the curriculum, and the pedagogy merges transformational learning principles with a rhizomatic model of learning (Cormier, 2008). As the antithesis of didactic content dissemination or rubric-affiliated metrics, this pedagogy also revealed new potential for familiar terrains. NIGHT GARDEN delivered a Whether event, the raw Besser block architecture and post-industrial landscape of the town translated into armatures for the imagination, and a hyperreal trellis for dreaming.

TEMPERATURE AND TOWN TEACHER

That afternoon the wind carried the sound of fire sirens from the expressway to the coast. From our hill the western sky was a thick bruised cloud fading to yellow. The eucalypts around the house suddenly began to peel. The hot winds had dried and cracked their bark and given the trees a strange mottled look. … Now the bloodwoods and peppermints and angophoras were peeling and shedding fast in the wind, dropping sheets of bark all around us, changing colour and shape before our eyes. Some trees revealed themselves as orange, others were pink, yellow, even purple underneath. All of them seemed moist and vulnerable, membrane instead of wood. They looked as if they'd shiver if you touched them. (Drewe, 1993, pp. 23–24)

For Elliason, the dramatic moment of reveal triggered by the red pigment contacting the river's surface afforded the city an opportunity to reacquaint itself with a dynamic system that had become stagnant in their consciousness. In a previous iteration of *Dark Mofo* (2015), the site of the art school itself was similarly re-activated as a town teacher, this time located at the centre of Hobart's waterfront. The artwork "Radiant Heat," by artist and TCotA staff member Lucy Bleach employed localised thermal heat, literally and metaphorically, thereby substituting Elliason's river for the crackling, thermal current of contemporary art education.

Radiant Heat comprised thermal imaging video footage of the interior spaces and pedagogic exchanges of the art school rear projected for ten nights onto select windows of the façade of Hobart's Centre for the Arts during the festival *Dark Mofo 2015*. Radiant Heat revealed to the public the invisible heat generated by learning and teaching, as well as the latent heat stored within the building. The projected footage pulsed intermittently across the building's façade, presenting a charged manifestation of heat as exhaust and creative energy, emitted through architectural apertures and radiating into the night and the city. The thermal footage, generated by people, activities, and equipment, blushed across the building's skin.

Figure 4.2: Lucy Bleach, Radiant Heat, as Part of *Dark Mofo 2015*
Source: Photograph by Peter Mathew

Proposing the art school as a pulsing, radiant force extending its reach visually into the local community, in effect turning it inside out, we draw on Helguera's performative act of education as a collective and participatory as a tool for coming to know the world (Helguera, 2011). Here the very act of pedagogical exchange taking place within the art school (the intra-tertiary) is reperformed, translated and projected into the extra-tertiary terrain.

CONCLUSION

Is it still possible to believe, as Antonio Gramsci did, in the artist as an organic intellectual whose role is not to act subordinate but to be a critically independent voice that negotiates civil society? In some ways. But it is most important not to fall into the trap of considering any of the … players or institutions as fixed entities. This constant flux, this shift of what outside and inside even are, makes it possible to open a space in education for rethinking values and judgements and to develop new critical practices. The biggest challenge may not be the pressure of the art market, but the willingness of the academy to challenge itself. (Bauer, 2009, p. 226)

The traditional art school mission has shifted from one of educating students to become artists or designers, to catalysing creative experience across multiple and diverse communities and contexts. Through extra-tertiary models, we now have an opportunity to facilitate creative transformation beyond the academy. Art schools are forced to respond to dramatic shifts in making methodologies (across both digital and analogue streams); the need to expand their capacity to address wicked problems, such as the social and environmental challenges found in Tasmania, in addition to developing graduates suitably equipped for the twenty-first century. At this time of change, learning manifests symbiotically in surprising and exciting ways.

In *Education for Socially Engaged Art: A Materials and Techniques Handbook*, Paulo Helguera states, "traditional pedagogy fails to recognise three things: first, the creative performativity of the act of education; second, the fact that the collective construction of an art milieu, with artworks and ideas, is a collective construction of knowledge; and third, the fact that knowledge of art does not end in knowing the artwork but is a tool for understanding the world" (Helguera, 2011, p. 80).

With a focus on transformational outcomes, the Whether Projects apply diverse and often unorthodox methodologies, targeting increased engagement. They are fluid and malleable, developed in response to a specific locale, cognisant of existing histories and ecosystems. The Whether Project identifies and activates an extra-tertiary domain, by positively impacting on a changing climate of learning.

Engagement with communities, individuals, or teaching the town is driven by listening and observing, framed by indeterminacy. This requires an adaptive approach to deploying pedagogic expertise, propelled by empathy and sensitivity to existing frameworks. In the way that Eliasson makes visible the turbulence of the river, TCotA aspires to understand how the community perceives education: is it dynamic or static? rhetorical or discursive? singular or multiple? The Whether Project allows people to feel turbulence and the capacity for change, challenging their perception of pedagogy as something stagnant and imposed.

Reflecting on the possibility that an exhaled Tasmanian breath can be in China in two weeks, we constantly collaborate to create our atmosphere. Such climate control is a function of the things that transpire through action and in reaction to collectively determined intentions, movements, and expressions. Integrating community engaged contextual making with transformative approaches to pedagogy, the ongoing Whether Project offers an opportunity to consider, question and ultimately progress a Tasmanian pedagogical climate for change.

REFERENCES

Alÿs, F. (n.d). *A Story of deception: Room guide, tornado*. Retrieved from: http://www.tate.org.uk/whats-on/tate-modern/exhibition/francis-alys/francis-alys-story-deception-room-guide/francis-alys-6

Bloomberg. (2010). *Tornado artist defies deadly twisters for video show* [Interview]. Retrieved from http://www.bloomberg.com/news/articles/2010-07-05/tornado-artist-alys-defies-deadly-twisters-for-tate-video-show-interview

Bauer, U. M. (2009). Under pressure. In S.H. Madoff (Ed.), *Art school: Propositions for the 21st century* (pp. 219–26). Cambridge, MA: MIT Press.

Butterwick, S., & Lawrence, R. L. (2009). Creating alternative realities: Arts-based approaches to transformative learning. In J. Mezirow & E. W. Taylor (Eds.),

Transformative learning in practice: Insights from community, workplace and higher education (pp. 35–45). San Francisco, CA: Jossey-Bass.

Cormier, D. (2008). Rhizomatic education: Community as curriculum. *Innovate: Journal of Online Education, 4*(5), Article 2. Retrieved from http://nsuworks.nova.edu/innovate/vol4/iss5/2

Drewe, R. (1993). Radiant Heat. In R. Drewe (Ed.), *The Picador book of the beach* (pp. 23–24). Sydney, Australia: Picador.

Eliasson, O. (2002). Chaque matin je me sens différent. Chaque soir je me sens le meme (J. Tittensor, Trans.). In J. Jacquet (Ed.), *Exhibition catalogue* (pp. 17–37). Paris, France: Musée d'Art Moderne de la Ville de Paris.

Gramsci, A. (1971). *Selections from the prison notebooks.* New York, NY: International.

Helguera, P. (2011). *Education for socially engaged art: A materials and techniques handbook.* New York, NY: Jorge Pinto.

Levitas, M. (2012). *Marxist perspectives in the sociology of education.* New York, NY: Routledge.

Mantas, K., & Schwind, J. K. (2014). Fostering transformative learning through cocreative artmaking processes and emerging artful forms: Two educators reflect on and dialogue about a shared arts-based workshop experience. *Journal of Transformative Education, 12,* 74–94. http://dx.doi.org/10.1177/1541344614541327

Mezirow, J. (2009). Transformative learning theory. In J. Mezirow & E. W. Taylor (Eds.), *Transformative learning in practice: Insights from community, workplace and higher education* (pp. 18–31). San Francisco, CA: Jossey-Bass.

Orr, S., Yorke, M., & Blair, B. (2014). 'The answer is brought about from within you': A student-centred perspective on pedagogy in art and design. *International Journal of Art and Design Education, 33,* 32–45. doi:10.1111/j.1476-8070.2014.12008.x

Pieroth, K. (2001). *Kreuzberger Pfütze* [Installation]. Retrieved from http://www.sparwasserhq.de/Index/HTMLjanuar/HTMLEngA.htm

Pringle, E. (2002). *"We did stir things up." The role of the artist in sites for learning.* London: Arts Council of England.

Reiss, V. & Pringle, E. (2003). The role of the artist in sites for learning. *International Journal of Art and Design Education, 22,* 215–221. http://dx.doi.org/10.1111/1468-5949.00356

Rolling, J. H., Jr., (2013). Art as social response and responsibility: Reframing critical thinking in art education as a basis for altruistic intent. *Art Education, March,* 6–12. Retrieved from https://www.academia.edu/2622702/Art_as _Social_Response_and_Responsibility_Reframing_Critical_Thinking_in _Art_Education_as_a_Basis_for_Altruistic_Intent

Taleb, N. N. (2012). *Antifragile: how to live in a world we don't understand* (Vol. 3). London, England: Allen Lane.

Taylor, E. W. (2009). Fostering transformative learning. In J. Mezirow & E. W. Taylor (Eds.), *Transformative learning in practice: Insights from community, workplace and higher education* (pp. 3–17). San Francisco, CA: Jossey-Bass.

Transformative Pedagogies and the Environment

CHAPTER 5

Truly, Madly, Deeply: Sharing Story on the Bundian Way

Denise Ferris, Amanda Stuart, and Amelia Zaraftis

ABSTRACT

The Bundian Way led me on a journey; I travelled from a state of profound ignorance about the nature of Aboriginal occupation and land-use to a point where I now acknowledge a sophisticated agricultural people with a wealth of knowledge to offer contemporary Australia. I have tried to express this journey in a new body of work. (Joanna Harris-MacNeil, Master's Student, Balawan Winter Intensive 2015)

This chapter examines the pedagogy and its transformative influence on students and staff participating in the Balawan Elective, a field-based research course for making visual art. The course is unique to the Australian National University (ANU) School of Art & Design Environment Studio, which offers supervised field research and related studio development. The field research concentrates on the formulation of ideas, the gathering of materials, and visual imagery, or the undertaking of site-specific work. Data gathered in the field inform the studio development of a folio of artwork.

The course feedback that was received positions the Balawan Elective as being an agent of significant change through the educational process, fostering histo-cultural awareness and initiating greater understanding through new knowledge. Through feedback received, the field-based studio research was reported to have driven changes to students' methodologies and approaches, exemplifying a distinctive learning opportunity.

In this chapter, we use Paul Ramsden's principles of effective teaching, from his seminal book *Learning to Teach in Higher Education*, as a framework to articulate the success of the educational processes of the Balawan Elective (Ramsden, 1992). Through alignment with Ramsden's tenets identifying effective teaching and learning in higher education we reveal the course's transformative qualities. Additionally, the value of student and teacher relationships experienced during the course delivery are recognised through consideration of Ramsden's principles.

The impact of learning about *Country* from Indigenous communities throughout this field elective is a key contribution to the pedagogical success and knowledge impact of this course, noting that Aboriginal language usage of the word Country is much broader than standard English. The high value ascribed to the Indigenous community involvement is mentioned throughout the student feedback; however, this aspect has not yet been subject to specific scrutiny. It is nevertheless acknowledged and respected.

INTRODUCTION

The Bundian Way is a shared history pathway between Targangal (Mount Kosciuszko) and Bilgalera (Fisheries Beach) that connects the highest part of the Australian continent and the coast. On its way to the coast, the Bundian Way crosses the Snowy River and passes through some of the wildest, most rugged and yet beautiful countryside in Australia. In many parts the influence of Aboriginal land management in its landscapes is still obvious. It is the first Aboriginal pathway to be listed on the NSW State Heritage Register (Eden Local Aboriginal Land Council, n.d.).

The Balawan Elective is an ANU School of Art & Design (SOA&D) course conducted largely in the field at sites along the Bundian Way. Balawan is the local Yuin name for Mount Imlay, one of three spiritually significant mountains to the region's Indigenous people. Within a structure of weekly classes and debriefings held on site at the SOA&D in Canberra, the course's two- and five-day field trips are conducted on site, a few hours away from the School by road. The course represents an educational partnership between the SOA&D and Indigenous communities along the Bundian Way. These communities, their organisations, and individuals are aware of the route's significance as a rare surviving ancient pathway used by Aboriginal people over thousands of years, and they are striving to improve access to and promote understanding of the *Way* (NSW Government Office of Environment and Heritage, n.d.).

There are two overarching pedagogical features of the Balawan elective course that align with Ramsden's "six principles of effective teaching in higher education" (1992). These predominant features are evidenced by verifiable changes to practice as well as observed transformation, with respect to both the student and the staff experience. These two characteristics, along with other teaching and learning actions outlined in this chapter, will be addressed by utilising examples of the course feedback from students.

The first distinctive feature, a crucial starting point, is that the pedagogy and learning methods utilised foreground the student's experience and deeply consider the student's perspective. Claiming this perspective as the fundamental pedagogic approach is significant. It is not that students are in the lead when undertaking the tutorials or field trips—quite the reverse. The course structure is heavily prescribed; structured to involve academic staff, Aboriginal Elders, stakeholders, and community members in guiding student participants in the field. However, every consideration through the teaching and learning process in and out of the field is deliberated from the perspective of the student experience. That experience is influenced by fieldwork instrumental to change and transformation, according to the student feedback received. The Balawan experience alters student perceptions of learning, how they learn, as well as what they learn. Recognition of learning is evident both as a result of the profound nature of the subject itself—the transporting, intense effect of firsthand encounters with Aboriginal Australia—as well the student-centred focus encouraging a deep approach to learning.

In analysing the context of learning, Ramsden describes characteristic approaches that are deep, or surface. Active and long-term engagement with learning tasks is one contributing indicator of a deep approach to learning. According to Ramsden, such an approach is achieved through "stimulating and considerate teaching, especially teaching which demonstrates the lecturer's personal commitment to the subject matter, and stresses its meaning and relevance to students" (1992, p. 81).

The change and impact on the staff is the course's second marked feature of distinctive pedagogy, understandably not recognised in the student feedback and course evaluations but communicated by the staff involved, including two of the co-authors of this chapter. Transformation is evident in the staff's facilitation and negotiation of changes to the teaching modes of the course. This occurs particularly in first hand experiences in the field, as teachers encounter and respond to their own new understanding and that of students, and to the intricacies of cultural differences. In the field, staff members maintain their capacity for flexibility, holding on to uncertainty in the process and recognising in this complex opportunity the relative nature of learning. They cultivate and maintain a culture of reciprocity for all contributors, which encourages a flow of dialogue and maximises communication opportunities across cultures, age groups, teachers, and learners.

We argue the Balawan Elective course, through its constituent parts, offers deep learning experiences for students and staff. The lecturers working with students in the field demonstrate a commitment that is powerful in engaging all participants. The community participants who give this course significant context are the voluntary Elders, Aboriginal artists and others associated with the Bundian Way, who embody and reinforce Ramsden's call for meaningful, relevant learning for all participants.

THE BUNDIAN WAY ARTS INITIATIVE:
THE CONTEXT FOR BUILDING THE BALAWAN ELECTIVE

John Blay is a writer and inveterate walker with a strong personal and professional commitment to the Bundian Way. Alumna of SOA&D, Amanda Stuart, originally raised the prospect of the SOA&D connecting with John Blay, who was a key research informant for her PhD thesis. Blay initially contributed to the 2011 Eden Project Field Study, a previous field-based course for which he briefed the SOA&D students about the Bundian Way and the research associated with his book (Blay, 2015). In the spring of 2013 a slow burning conversation about collaboration and the Bundian Way commenced at the SOA&D. This conversation united key individuals with diverse expertise and a common interest in the Way. Principally, these were Denise Ferris, artist and Head of School; John Blay; and John Reid, artist and architect of the SOA&D Environment Studio's Field Studies program. When joined by freelance writer Chris Freudenstein, and artist/educators Heike Qualitz, Amelia

Zaraftis, and Amanda Stuart, the Bundian Way Arts Initiative (BWAI) was established with the aim to progress active relationships between our respective cultural communities.

Figure 5.1: Writer, naturalist and avid bushwalker John Blay interprets the culturally significant country around Bilgalera (Fisheries Beach, southeast NSW) to students and staff of the ANU School of Art & Design Environment Studio Balawan Elective, April 2016. The region is abundant with signs of ancient and continued Aboriginal use and heritage.
Source: Photograph by Amanda Stuart

From the School's perspective, the establishment of the BWAI offered an opportunity to connect with a nearby community of Aboriginal Australians, adding to the School's existing relationships with Indigenous Australians in the more distant states. BWAI members embraced the vital foci of respect, exchange, and sharing in finding a way forward, acknowledging that our partnership possibilities were founded on hopes rather than expectations. The close proximity of the Bundian Way to Canberra presented an ideal prospect for the SOA&D to develop a deeper appreciation of Aboriginal culture and heritage in places familiar to many ACT residents and ANU students. Further, the BWAI provided a prized opportunity to actively engage with this living and evolving culture; to build respectful relationships and affirm the relevance and continuity of Australia's first peoples in an area that was, and continues to be, heavily impacted upon by white colonising culture.

The SOA&D's early connections with the Bundian Way quickly revealed the dedication and tireless networking of John Blay, showing just how vital the community Elders, members of the Eden Local Aboriginal Land Council, Franz Peters of the NSW Department of Environment, and others from the region would be to the Balawan Elective course. Many of those whose efforts enabled the route to gain Heritage status in NSW, including Aboriginal Elders B. J. and Ossie Cruse, Darren Mongta, and Lee Cruse, as well as John Blay, pledged their support for the development of a tertiary visual arts field program, offering to assist with field planning and coordination, and to share their expert knowledge with students in the field. Local associated land management agencies were likewise willingly involved, and the input of individuals such as Franz Peters proved significant in gaining an understanding of the region. This sharing is central to the endeavour's quality and key to the impact on the staff and student participants.

The Way's indigenous communities were central not just to the operation of the course, but to its integral content, cultural insights, historical contribution, and cultural framework. Their traditional and contemporary understandings of this ancient route made it clear that the Bundian Way was hugely important, not only as a shared historic pathway, but also as an entity with enormous cultural significance for present and future generations of Australians. Within the diverse matrix of connections and initiatives comprehensively known as the Bundian Way Project, the BWAI conceived the Balawan Elective. At the heart of this initiative was the aim of sharing knowledge.

BWAI TO BALAWAN ELECTIVE 2015: A PILOT PROGRAM

The Balawan Elective that was established drew on not only the lecturers' cultural concerns and foci as artists and educators, but more importantly, on their desire to facilitate an outstanding shared experience and exchange of creative ideas between cultures, both on Country and at the SOA&D. Central to this exchange was the reciprocal nature of being hosted by Aboriginal artists on Country and in turn, hosting these artists at the SOA&D. Familiar to many initiatives that are incredibly exciting, this proposal came with a non-existent budget. The SOA&D pledged the funding necessary to staff a pilot program including on-campus residencies for the visiting indigenous artists. The Bundian Way then demonstrated its allure and power in its often-observed capacity to "generate its own path," as noted in personal communication between John Blay and Amanda Stuart in 2013. ANU students revealed their inclination to participate in such a course with unprecedented enrolment numbers. The Balawan Elective simply, and suddenly, gained traction.

The first Balawan Elective course was offered through the Environment Studio in Semester 1, 2015, reuniting Heike Qualitz, Amelia Zaraftis, and Amanda Stuart as a field teaching team from the 2011 Eden Project Field Study. Guided by John Reid this successful Field Study rehearsed the methods, practicalities, and possibilities for the Balawan Elective. Building on the established foundations of their experiences with the SOA&D Environment Studio's Field Studies program (Reid, Lamberts, Young, & Tambiah, 2010, p. 3), these three ANU sculpture alumnae incorporated field-learning approaches they had experienced during residencies in the University of New Mexico's *Land Arts of the American West* program, particularly in developing and refining course objectives. Strategies to carefully foster a collaborative group dynamic (e.g., shared meals, discussion circles) were introduced, and subject-specific readings outside of the field of visual arts were incorporated. In addition, an ANU online Indigenous Cultural Awareness module called ANU Pulse was included, special guest lecturers were invited, and a reflective writing component was embedded in the elective matrix as a valuable learning tool.

The Balawan Elective was envisaged as a means to provide workshop, field-based visual art engagement opportunities with all aspects of the Bundian Way. Students travelled together and learned firsthand from informed individuals, representatives, and artists from the local Aboriginal communities, who voluntarily participated in the program to enhance student understanding of cultural relationships with Country. Field trips were designed to enable the collection and synthesis of materials and imagery, as well as providing locations for undertaking site-specific work. These trips were reinforced by ongoing tutorial sessions both on site and back on campus, which further informed the secondary studio development of a folio of artwork.

Figure 5.2: Balawan Elective student Roseanna Parkes collecting imagery of Balawan (Mount Imlay) as part of field research undertaken during the Balawan Elective, 2015
Source: Photograph by Heike Qualitz

As visitors to the regional area, students were able to reflect upon the notion of connection to Country in a region that has been severely impacted upon by white settlement. Powerful dialogues were opened and maintained even beyond the course, based on respect for different cultures. It can be confronting and challenging for participants as they absorb the subject matter, both broad and from first person accounts, and acknowledge the consequences of the colonising culture. Relationships were formed with the local Indigenous community, Elders, and artists, and the sustained impact is recorded in feedback.

COURSE FRAMEWORK: THE BALAWAN EXPERIENCE

In the elective, the students are liberated from the confines of a conventional studio practice and from the familiar making processes of their discipline majors. Students enrol from various degrees, including others at ANU external to the SOA&D.

Students are also encouraged to explore other aspects of visual art research. As an example, ceramicists have cultivated their drawing and painting strategies; gold and silver smithing students have experimented with textile approaches and, in so doing, pushed previously unexplored avenues of practice. These outcomes are significantly enhanced by the cross-discipline exposure and discussion evident in tutorial sessions, which prompts heightened critical awareness of alternative strategies, including spatial and material awareness, ephemeral mark making, installation practices, and documentation.

Students develop their individual work proposals (IWP) from field-based encounters, and this proposed work can vary substantially from their previous methods, materials, approaches, and outcomes. In the Balawan Elective, students are encouraged to explore new avenues of visual art research and initiate changes to their practice. The embodied, on-site experience is basic to the field research process. For some students, this is encountered within their visual art studies for the first time, as is the potential for collaboration. Collaborative and peer learning processes are encouraged in all aspects of the course, and tutorial sessions are also designed in and out of the field to capitalise on those learning processes. Supporting one another's learning is strongly encouraged.

COURSE PRACTICALITIES: STAFF AND STRUCTURE

For cost effectiveness, a minimum of eight students is required to conduct a field research elective. Because of logistics and WHS requirements, two staff working together in the field is optimal. The course is structured over thirteen teaching weeks and involves two field trips, the first a short orientation of two days and nights early in the elective, and the second a longer five-day field trip. The short field trip enables orientation, as well as fundamental sensory, physical, and cultural inputs that inform the students' methodology and rationale for the longer field trip. Two tutorial sessions are scheduled prior to the first field trip. In these, staff elicit student hopes for the course and their reasons for enrolling. The course structure is clarified, and the field research locations and specifics are communicated in relation to weather, supplies, and amenities.

Risk assessments are conducted and the field library of resources is introduced. Students are encouraged to read the first recommended course readings and to complete the online Indigenous Cultural Awareness ANU Pulse module. Students have an opportunity to share any apprehensions, to pool resources, and form cooking teams for the shared evening meals. Students learn of one another's disciplines and are asked to start thinking about how they might approach field research (e.g., using cameras, doing drawings, writing notes, and assessing methods or strategies they may wish to test). The students are not expected to draft an IWP until after the first trip. The IWP is written to establish a broad area of interest and intent for the work, so the proposals are malleable and subject to significant change as the course unfolds.

Trip 1: Reconnaissance—In the Field

Two vehicles and a large trailer with weather resistant luggage depart Canberra on Friday afternoon and make the four-hour journey to the field location; campsites vary from course to course, season to season. Travelling in the lowest possible number of vehicles assists group cohesion. On arrival, camp is established and generally everyone has an early night. In the field, meetings are held with John Blay, Franz Peters, Eden Local Aboriginal Land Council, Elders and staff at Jigamy Farm, hosts, and visiting artists. In 2015 the Eden community nominated two Yuin artists for involvement, Darren Mongta and Lee Cruse. In 2016, the students worked alongside Narooma based Yuin woman and painter Natalie Bateman. Where possible, the nominated artists contribute works to the final exhibitions associated with the Balawan Elective. Students interact with these field experts, listen, and ask questions.

As mentioned previously, stories shared are often very striking in personal historical content—the fears of the Aboriginal Protection Board and avoiding being stolen, experiences of racism and colonisation, as well as local history. Ongoing grievances against unjust treatment by government authorities are also raised; for example, the frustration held by Aboriginal people being denied access to traditional food sources, such as abalone. These are current debates and part of the political landscape for all Australians. Both in tutorials and in the field, the story heard is reflected on in association with relevant current events. This raises the students' level of engagement in the national discourse about our nation's history and, in particular, to the voices of Indigenous Australians in the media.

Indigenous contributors share knowledge of Country, including a nuanced understanding of immediate plants and animals, as well as Aboriginal and local customs. Pride and respect for culture through deep knowledge are imparted from both local and visiting community members. This process of generously imparting knowledge is humbling and brings out the best in the gathered people who recognise this exchange of knowledge as a gift. Staff take students to a few main field locations each day and there is a sense of locating and scouting the environment. At Jigamy Farm, there are hot showers, flushing toilets, access to power, and fresh water on site. It is ten-minute drive to Eden, with its cafes, dollar shops, museums, and local art and craft venues. Swimming, walking, lying in the sun, sitting and observing, and listening all add to the experience of immersion and to the physical activity of being on Country.

Trip 2: Making Work in the Field

Having had time to investigate and reflect on the areas visited, the students approach Trip 2 with methodologies that focus on their IWPs. There is extended time for experimentation, making and testing work ideas on site. Students have a midweek personal tutorial feedback session with the lecturers for 30–45 minutes each, which provides the opportunity to discuss their intended projects in terms of progress, challenges, and ideas. Communal meals are prepared by cooking teams so no individual has to cook every night. Food is shared, and reflecting on the day around the fire each evening is an important ritual. Fireside reading discussions are an indispensable part of the field trip. The group also observes all local protocols in relation to camping respectfully.

Working Away from the Field

On campus, weekly tutorial sessions on Monday afternoons build on the academic requirements of course outlines. For example, the background to the Balawan Elective course is discussed, including its origins and the context for field-based work on Country resulting in studio output. Definitions of field-based research are offered and discussed, in particular, how this approach is different to studio based practice; learning outcomes, and assessment breakdowns and weightings are identified to account for their difference to course/studio based work. Cultural concerns and protocols are clarified, and the logistics and aspects of remote camping, and learning in a collaborative environment (including WHS travel concerns) are reinforced.

The preparation of the IWP is discussed, as well as the requirements for the exhibition at the end of the course. The required artist statements and titles for the exhibition and the documentation of work are noted. Time is spent talking about effective reflective writing and the importance of the visual diary and journal keeping. The testaments previous students have made about the usefulness of these reflective journals are extremely helpful, and reinforced throughout the course. Readings and literature can be discussed; work in progress tutorials and opportunities for peer and lecturer feedback as well as critique sessions are scheduled.

The evaluation and tutorial processes support the principal aims of development through field-based enquiry strategies and the resultant visual language. The students' development and its articulation draw heavily on the increased cultural awareness and personal transformation imparted by this elective. Reviews of work in progress are held after Trip 2 to enable maximum engagement with, and reflection on, the field trip content. These reviews of work and the students' sense of achievement toward assessment and exhibition represent another valuable learning opportunity. They present, talk to, and refine secondary studio work, identifying any issues arising from test ideas, and contextualise their work. Throughout the course, they are encouraged to drive the process and seek creative pathways based on personal response, observation, and reflection. After the final semester's assessment, the students refine their artist's statements and continue working in preparation for the course exhibition.

Post-Assessment: The Balawan Elective Exhibition

Held at the SOA&D after assessment, the *Beyond Balawan* 2015 exhibition galvanised students, staff, and visiting Aboriginal artists Darren Mongta and Lee Cruse, by showcasing a comprehensive aesthetic and cultural response to the Bundian Way. The exhibition was held in unison and support of the official ACT launch of John Blay's book *On Track: Searching Out the Bundian Way*, a pivotal text for Balawan Elective students.

Elders from the Eden Local Aboriginal Land Council attended and esteemed Elder, Ossie Cruse, gave an Acknowledgement of Country and shared aspects of his story with an audience of 180 people. Academic historian and author Mark McKenna addressed the audience and John Blay opened the exhibition. A catalogue was produced, supported by a student-sourced grant. The exhibition encompassed a range of media, scale, and practices, including furniture, ceramics, sculpture, print media, painting, gold and silversmithing, glass, textiles, digital media, photomedia. Students gained useful experience in mounting, installing, and promoting a catalogued public exhibition. Students also wrote an article for the *ANU Reporter*, as well as initiating and organising a satellite exhibition at Eden.

In August 2016, *Beside Balawan* was the second Balawan Elective exhibition that showcased the work of students, alongside an Aboriginal artist mentor. Yuin woman Natalie Bateman had met with students and shared her story at Jigamy Farm, and accompanied the field group to areas significant to the Bundian Way. *Beside Balawan* was held in the SOA&D Foyer Gallery, and also included work by Emeritus Fellow John Reid, artist and initiator of the SOA&D Environment Studio, who mentored students in the development of their studio practice.

COURSE EVALUATIONS AND FEEDBACK FROM STUDENTS: EVIDENCE OF HIGHLY EFFECTIVE TEACHING AND LEARNING

The student feedback about their individual learning experience in the Balawan elective course was captured by formal evaluations and also through unsolicited feedback. In this section the feedback is mapped onto the six principles that Ramsden suggests evidence effective teaching in higher education. The feedback cited reveals teaching and learning actions in the Balawan Elective that are highly successful. The first and last of the pedagogical principles we discuss were mentioned at this chapter's beginning—the approach by staff to the student learners and the identification by staff as themselves journeying learners in the Balawan Elective.

1. Interest and Explanation

Students consistently commented on the deep involvement by the staff in the field, observing their passion for guiding the students to experience the subject. Staff showed an entrenched interest in the idea of sharing stories, steering greater awareness of Aboriginal Australia, and facilitating work that responded to the impact of exposure to the course. The personal commitment displayed by the teaching staff was based on their fervent investment in exploring colonial and post-colonial relationships between white settler culture and Aboriginal communities. The facilitator's strong interest in the subject, communicating the process of understanding to the student participants, reinforced the importance of the course being taught.

Student Evaluation of Teaching and Learning (SELT) formal questionnaires, which generate data from generic questions and open-ended feedback, showed that students recognised the high levels of interest, curiosity and concern generated by the staff: The lecturers worked tirelessly to allow for the students to experiences as many things as possible, whilst still allowing for personal and art making time. There was a real sense of community involved in this planning and allowed for every individual voice to be heard.

The unsolicited feedback received was exceptional. This feedback supported the importance of fulsome explanation during the course, detailing how elements fitted into the entire picture and connected seemingly minor tasks to the larger endeavour of producing work for exhibition. Responses noted project managing and producing artwork off site were helpful to learning. Post-Graduate, Master's Coursework email feedback included:

> This is the first time I have:
> - seen a structure for an IWP, had it explained to me, and been given the chance to refine it with input from lecturers;
> - discussed the importance of a title for work and been given concrete examples of how one works toward a Title;
> - discussed the importance of an Artist statement, and been given samples and a chance to write and rewrite with guidance;
> - been shown the usefulness of reflective writing; and
> - most importantly, been guided through the process of material thinking so that I can make well thought out decisions about my making.
> - I feel as a result of this elective that I can begin to engage fully with my making in a way that I have never been able to do before.
> - I really cannot express how grateful I am and how useful this has been.

The Aboriginal facilitators, and those in Bundian Way communities, communicated to students their deep emotional and historical investment in Country, and the value of coming to an understanding of that investment. These community participants were teaching and explaining the significance of place through story. Feedback from students included:

> *Student A:* Having stories told to us first hand was a remarkable experience. It's one thing just to be told stories by other white folk, but to have an Aboriginal tell you their own stories is completely different and much more powerful.

> *Student B:* Direct Indigenous contact was invaluable on a personal and educational learning level. It was a rare opportunity to have.

2. Concern and Respect

Staff erred on the side of generosity with fieldwork students, and with sustained flexibility, allowed the time and thinking space to develop the expected work. Student feedback acknowledged scaffolding of the learning experience and noted an environment that facilitated risk. Nevertheless, staff persistently challenged students to experiment with materials or forms with trust acting as the conduit to supporting learners. Within that safe space, students were encouraged to expand and extend their current experience, to take risks in the work, including the possibility of failure to realise work that met their own expectations.

The entire team, students, staff, and facilitators moved into the field optimistically, philosophical about the challenges and with increasing flexibility; students also noticed they developed far greater resilience. The trust and hopefulness comprising the core of the fieldwork continued through to the making of the final exhibition work. Similarly, student access to field expertise was modelled on mutual respect and aspirations for student learning. Students commented that all staff were approachable, lent assistance, and guided students as individuals.

> *Student A:* [Staff] genuinely wanted to get to know us, not just our work but who we were.

> *Student B:* Facilities were superb—comfortable & beautiful! The trips to sites were excellent to swiftly orientate us to the area. Lecturers were unwaveringly flexible, approachable & available before, during & after the field trip.

3. Appropriate Assessment and Feedback

The Learning Outcomes, while representing relatively standard expectations, aligned with the information delivered to students throughout. The Course Overview & Learning Outcomes included:

1. Develop a basic method for field-based enquiry based on observations made in the field and create a body of artwork that reflects this methodology.
2. Demonstrate a basic capacity, in the field and studio, to apply creative processes to primary research materials collected.
3. Reflect critically on your own work and articulate key concerns and reference points.
4. Show basic awareness of the environmental, cultural, and social issues informing field research and associated creative processes.

The assessment weighting was acutely relevant to the objectives of the course. The folio constituted 50 percent of the mark, which was a weighting aimed at ensuring enough pressure on active learning through making in the field. There was weighting on aspects such as participation; for example, being active in discussion, group dynamics, and overall contribution. Ongoing research, documentation, and professional development tasks, such as the artist statement, were also considered in the total mark.

The reflective space given to students offered an opportunity to reactivate the learning experience, where students importantly recognise their own agency in the process of learning and making. Approaching the subject as informed art practitioners, as well as field facilitators, the lecturers consistently interacted with the students' methodologies and processes, and responded to outcomes in tactical ways. Typically for practice disciplines, critique sessions were a source of feedback, and the multi-disciplinary cohort was invaluable to the diversity in these sessions, making methodology explicit rather than implied. Staff gave written feedback on all draft assessment items, such as artist statements, steering the work toward assessment expectations. The very evident structure and clarity regarding expectations and requirements was seen as a notable strength of the course.

Feedback indicated that students recognised the possibilities in their developing agency while understanding the support framework:

> *Student A:* We were given our own choice to how to go about the field trip, it wasn't set into a rubric

> *Student B:* [Lecturers] promoted that they were willing to give any extra support/feedback if anyone so desired, and to simply approach them about it.

4. Clear Goals and Intellectual Challenge

The students had the imperative of the exhibition providing an objective; this expectation motivated the testing of outcomes and further development. Significant professional development resulted from the rigorous standards required to exhibit, and to engage directly with the public and community. Apart from obtaining substantial experience in the field, the progression of the practice from the field to exhibition was a transformative challenge. The lofty goal of exhibition-standard work was supported by continually offering occasions for feedback or openings to talk with lecturers, guest artists, and specialists in the field.

There was a considerable amount of tutorial time spent on critique sessions and student presentations. The sequencing of tutorials to meet student needs, and the targeted activities within them such as reflective journals, writing tasks, and artist statements created the structure for engaged hardworking students to succeed. Indeed, these activities by their very nature invited students to incrementally engage. Students responded to the apparent freedom of the structure but also appreciated the group ethos, sensing the assembly of others on similar journeys. They appreciated access to both group and supervisory advice:

> *Student A:* Meetings with the supervisors after the first Field Trip, during the Second Field trip and subsequent to this trip, along with presentations to the tutorial helped refine my work for the elective. The Supervisors challenged and helped refine my concept.

> *Student B:* The supervision allowed for each individual to be very autonomous. The trust that was given and ability to be by [oneself] meant that each person could have as little or as much involvement with the group. Surprisingly the majority of people enjoyed congregating and assisting each other, yet when someone needed time by their self, it was encouraged and

never questioned as to why. The supervision aspect for this course I believe was one of its strong points.

5. Independence, Control, and Engagement

Throughout the Balawan Elective course students were encouraged to drive the process and seek creative pathways based on personal response, observation, and reflection. Providing the space to develop through reflective learning, with sufficient structure to promote engagement, facilitated Independence. By iteratively considering developments within their work, the students' understanding of their progress incited deeper engagement in the learning process.

Students acknowledged how successful the structuring of the learning journey was. The course was established to offer exceptional encounters with the place and people, which maximised student experience and involvement in a measured situation while leaving room for taking independent decisions. The exposure to novel situations and encounters with different modes of thinking was managed in an environment of enjoyment and fun.

> *Student A:* We were given all the time to do our own thing, while having the time to talk.

> *Student B:* I was encouraged to experiment and let the field-work experience form the rationale for a work/s of art.

> *Student C:* It [the incorporation of Indigenous contacts] was so important. The conversations we had particularly with Darren, but also John Blay putting Indigenous past and present into context. The generosity of Darren Mongta was incredible. Walking through the landscape with him was a privilege.

6. Learning from Students

While responsibility was given to students to take risks, to shift, to adapt, and to be open to the process in the field, teachers in the course were also responsive to the uncertainties, with the changing circumstances of learning acknowledged. This reiterates Ramsden's "teacher as learner" (1992). These teachers responded to their teaching's effect on the students, and adapted that teaching delivery to what was needed, engaging individually with each learner. The diversity of student skills and approaches, due in part to the mixed cohort from different making backgrounds, drove negotiation of individual approaches. This diversity in turn informed the staff members in their own teaching and practice.

The marker of truly effective high quality teaching and learning is recognising the reciprocity between student and teacher. Teachers in the Balawan course all have previous experience as undergraduate or postgraduate Field Studies participants. As early visual arts researchers, they had personally experienced the field research process as transformative for their own practice and methodology, and, as it transpired, were now teaching fieldwork in their practice as teachers, so could bring that experience to bear. The teachers were influenced by the students' responses to their teaching and acknowledged they were learning along with students—which the students noticed:

> *Student A:* From lecturers, to guest speaker and artist, I could not think of a better teaching team for such a subject.

> *Student B:* Also to be able to make discoveries alongside your lecturers and get immediate feedback is very helpful.

EVIDENCE OF TRANSFORMATIVE TEACHING AND LEARNING

Undertaking field research had a transformative impact on the participants, both students and staff. In this section, students reflect on their impressions of that impact. Questions to students were asked focusing on the main pedagogical tools of the Balawan Elective. Some questions with related responses follow:

> *Question:* Do you think the field research component of the trip will have a lasting impact on your practice?

> *Student A:* I think that I will always consider taking a more hands on approach to my research.

> *Student B:* If not my practice, it will leave a lasting impact on me personally. Such amazing scenery, land and experiences. It will drive my ability to reflect and write for my work, and process experience and information differently.

> *Student C:* I cannot stress YES enough. Apart from having many ideas I would like to explore more, directly relating to the Balawan elective— creating art responding to discovery of landscape/area & community is incredibly nourishing, satisfying & enjoyable.

The reflective writing tasks were set up to ensure there was deep and adequate thinking on the process of making. Students could evaluate the opportunity this reflection offered to their future methodology. It guided direction, identifying themes of interest, and generated a self-awareness that fed the working process.

> *Question:* Was the reflective writing useful or relevant to your learning and/or making process in this course?

> *Student A:* I think I need to write more. I think it's a wonderful way to tap into understanding your subconscious decisions as well as themes in your

work. I don't like being forced to write, but whenever I do, I feel like I learn a lot.

Student B: Very useful. In previous work I had played with reflective writing, however this pushed me to do it often and reflect on many aspects of learning, process, making and experience.

Student C: It cleared out the clutter in my mind that comes with avalanches of thought & ideas in a very short time frame. It was great to reread & pick up threads to carry on with.

The preparation for the fieldwork, debriefings and readings, optimised the immersion into the subject for the students and led to deeper learning.

Question: Did you read some or all of the articles and if so, were the articles useful to your experience of the Elective and development of your work? Note articles you found most useful (and why).

Student A: Yes. My favourite was the "cultural matters" excerpt from John Blay. I think it opened my eyes quite a bit about the differences in western culture to Aboriginal culture. My favourite was the bit at the end talking about sacred sites.

Student B: I read all the recommended readings. Time restricted reading further posted or stored readings, unfortunately. But recommended reading allowed better use of camping time.

Student C: All articles were relevant, interesting and enlightening. Again due to the short time frame, it was wonderful to have such carefully selected readings (esp. McKenna & Blay) to ground and immerse us into the landscape and issues surrounding Far [NSW] South Coast & Bundian Way.

The writing was both reflective and instrumental, as habits of thinking and writing were combined with the production of an artist's statement for the exhibition. The latter was a very relevant exercise for the final production of the work, and was supported by the teaching staff, who had expertise with writing for this purpose.

Question: Were the artist statement/title exercises useful?

Student A: Talking to another person and having them write what you say down is fantastic. I always have an easier time speaking than I do writing.

Student B: I had never had to write proper title or artist statement before. Title exercises helped get ideas flowing.

Student C: It was an area I struggles with—so having a time to start this process and talk about it with the group was excellent. Then, receiving personal feedback on the artist statement was so helpful—it gave me time to edit and refine. Incredibly useful.

Open-ended questions also formed part of the survey to students on the course.

Question: Do you have any other comments for future students considering enrolling in an Environment Studio elective?

Student A: Write your heart out and document everything and anything that interests you. You never know what turns your ideas may take. BEST COURSE I HAVE TAKEN AT UNI.

Student B: I would love to do it again. Amazing to get out of studio and set workshop, to experience something and make different work.

Student C: Do it! Wonderful spending time with people who respond to things creatively but who work/think in different ways from you. You get to see/experience different parts of Australia—nudges you out of your comfort zone. The support & advice from the lecturers … is unparalleled.

Of course, there were learning aspects in the course that could be strengthened. Student feedback informed the understanding of issues by teaching staff, creating an iterative process of change to the course over time. For example, the Indigenous Training Module was identified as generic, and not very relevant in terms of making art or encountering community participants. However, the student's recognition of considering issues that are complex and perhaps unresolvable is also a significant transformation, as this student noted: "This is perhaps the stand out course for me in my Visual Arts degree program because it deals with perhaps one of the most sensitive and unresolved issues facing contemporary Australia."

CONCLUSION

The highly effective teaching and learning in the Balawan Elective course was successful for an enriched and transformative student experience. The structure of the course was a key component to its success, specifically in that its design included engagement with community members, and those with specific expertise, in a format that was responsive to their input. Additionally, those who taught from their own experience of transformative fieldwork were able to impart what they themselves had learned, particularly in relation to studio practice, and were pivotal to the creation of a trustful, safe environment. Students were given both structure and flexibility, and tasks and reflective time to consider their learning, while being supported toward an exhibition outcome. Throughout, the student experience was underpinned by team teaching. The continuity and number of staff involved is perhaps one of the elements that will be most challenged in the future, as the logistical and financial support required for fieldwork is often questioned in times when courses are being rationalised.

Following a successful collaboration in 2015, the 2016 Balawan field electives brought together the Eden Local Aboriginal Land Council and the ANU School of Art & Design as partners in the Bundian Way Project. In future, this partnership will primarily facilitate Aboriginal and non-Aboriginal visual artists to undertake field research together on parts of the Bundian Way, and be interspersed with associated studio development for visiting indigenous artists at the ANU School of Art & Design. Ultimately the ongoing collaboration will produce fine art for public exhibition that aesthetically characterises the Bundian Way, and most importantly, the experience of engaging with its significant value to Aboriginal people, and fostering cultural understanding, as well as personal and professional growth.

REFERENCES

Blay, J., (2015). *On track: Searching out the Bundian Way*. Sydney, Australia: NewSouth Publishing.

Eden Local Aboriginal Land Council. (n.d.). *The Bundian Way*. Retrieved July 11, 2016, from http://www.bundianway.com.au

NSW Government Office of Environment and Heritage. (n.d.). *Bundian Way*. Retrieved July 11, 2016, from http://www.environment.nsw.gov.au /heritageapp/ViewHeritageItemDetails.aspx?ID=506015

Ramsden, P. (1992). *Learning to teach in higher education*. London, England: Routledge.

Reid, J., Lamberts, R., Young, C., & Tambiah, C. (2010). *Engaging visions: Engaging artists with the community about the environment*. Canberra, Australia: The Australian National University.

CHAPTER 6

Transformative Participation and Collaborative Practice-Led Design Research

Dr. Helen Norrie

ABSTRACT

In *Future Practice: Conversations from the Edge of Architecture*, Rory Hyde (2012) speculates on a range of trajectories for architectural practice from the "environmental medic" to the "near future inventor." These profiles imagine roles that span disciplines from architecture and urban design, to sociology, politics and the creative arts, highlighting the increasing interdisciplinarity of design practices. This reflects a diverse range of emergent creative and spatial practices in the fields of research and design that are increasingly central to design practice and pedagogy.

Although the design studio has traditionally formed the key domain of architectural practice, increasingly, "design research" is emerging as a specific mode of creative engagement. Design research provides a form of "critical spatial practice," that can be both collaborative and transformative (Rendell, 2013, p. 119). In contrast to traditional modes of design or research that explore defined problems with the aim of producing solutions, Peter Downton (2003) notes that design research is "a way of inquiring, a way of producing knowing and knowledge" (p. 1).

This paper explores collaborative practice-led design research that engages with real world issues through research-based teaching, promoting open-ended exploration and enquiry. Rather than focusing on architecture as a process of problem solving that aims to produce built formal or spatial solutions, this paper explores the field of "*dispositif*-architecture," which is "made out of relations and…generates relations" (Dascălu, 2013, p. 208). It explores collaborative practice-led design research projects that engage local communities through strategic design, which according to Brian Boyer (as cited in Hyde, 2012, p. 138) "gives shape to decisions rather than objects or buildings." Drawing on Jeremy Till's ideal of "transformative participation," which provides a catalyst for new modes of practice that "expos[e] the limits of normative architectural methods," the paper considers how collaborative practice-led design research can recast the architect as an "urban curator," facilitating collaboration to address a range of urban spatial issues in diverse ways (Till, 2005, p. 11).

INTRODUCTION

Beyond the bounds of traditional practice, architecture is engaged with myriad interwoven issues, conditions, and relationships that impact on, or are impacted by, the built and natural environments. Although essentially spatial in nature, architectural practice also engages with the physical, conceptual, social, and temporal contexts of the built and natural environments. Attending to this broader field of practice extends the ways that the skills and knowledge of architects can be employed. In *Future Practice: Conversations from the Edge of Architecture*, Rory Hyde (2012) highlights divergent trajectories that map out the expanding field of architectural practice. From the "double agent" to the "environmental medic" or "near future inventor," Hyde profiles practices that span disciplines from building and urban design, to sociology, politics, and the creative arts. These new guises of architectural practice include engagement in diverse aspects of context, through collaboration and co-opting methods and techniques from other disciplines, to produce a diverse range of emergent creative and spatial practices that are central to both practice and pedagogy.

Traditionally, architectural practice is positioned as a process of problem solving, casting the architect in the role of expert who identifies and resolves problems through formal built solutions or propositions. However, Jane Rendell (2013, pp. 119–120) suggests that the "reflexive nature" of architecture can also create "critical spatial practices" that incorporate the spatial, the temporal, and the social, expanding the domain of architecture beyond problem solving. The profiles that Hyde presents provide evidence of this shift, illustrating Rendell's assertion that "projects that put forward questions as the central tenet of the research, instead of, or as well as solving or resolving problems, tend to produce objects that critically rethink the parameters of the problem itself" (Rendell, 2004, p. 145).

Considering the possibilities of reflexive critical spatial practices, and questioning the position of architect as problem-solver, offers opportunities to examine the broader context of practice, highlighting issues that are politically, socially, or culturally positioned. This paper explores how design research contrasts with conventional design processes, offering possibilities to reconsider the limits of practice. In particular, it considers how collaborative practice-led design research can recast the architect as an "urban curator," engaging in "strategic design" to facilitate interaction and collaboration in urban spatial issues (Hyde, 2012, p. 138).

DESIGN RESEARCH AS TRANSFORMATIVE PRACTICE

Design research is increasingly shifting from the margins to the centre of architectural practice, providing a framework that is transforming both practice and pedagogy in myriad ways. In contrast to design-as-problem-solving, design research employs a diverse range of methods, strategies, and tactics to examine the broader context of design issues, often resulting in the production of questions rather than answers or solutions to problems. Research is generally characterised by the development of new knowledge, and design research, in particular, seeks to address specific issues through an open-ended process that is both projective and speculative. Engaging in design research facilitates new ways of understanding design and architecture, expanding fields of investigation across traditional disciplinary boundaries (Norrie & Abell, 2016, p. 3).

Distinctions can be made between traditional design practices and design research in relation to characteristics of research as a systematic process of investigation, advancing knowledge for the broader field and dissemination of findings (Griffiths, 2004, p. 714). Design research offers ways of drawing connections an expanded context, or the "set of immediate general conditions that help to situate meaning," providing new ways of understanding a wide range of issues, from within and beyond particular disciplinary boundaries (Isenstadt, 2005, p. 157).

Design research involves multiple processes that utilise both established and emergent methodologies. In contrast to traditional modes of research that explore defined problems, design research may be both open-ended and speculative. Peter Downton (2003) observes that rather than adhering to a "dogma-driven set of methods," design research processes involve a kind of "cheerful eclecticism" (p. 13). Design research is "a way of inquiring, a way of producing knowing and knowledge" (p. 1), that utilises a "collection of methods, approaches, ideas and practices," as well "ideas from outside design, [which] need to be discussed to elucidate and elaborate ideas about design research" (p. 13).

Research through the medium of design provides a process of iterative thinking, which Rendell suggests can bring together different modes of research that are often kept separate: natural sciences, social science/humanities, history/theory, and design/practice-led research (2004, p. 145). Rendell observes that design research does not require any kind of linear relationship between each stage; in fact, it frequently reverses the traditional order by generating questions rather than seeking to solve problems, with both the research processes and outcomes evolving throughout the life of the project (2004, pp. 143–144).

Christopher Frayling's article "Research in Art and Design" (1993) has become a touchstone for the discussion of design research. Frayling's differentiation of research *into*, *for*, and *through* design is frequently used as a basis for discussing design research methods. Frayling's model is speculative rather than rigorously constituted; it was presented as a theoretical framework, rather than a set of prescriptive methodologies. However, it provides a useful scaffold that differentiates modes of enquiry within and between disciplines. This tripartite description can be understood in various ways, and for the basis of this discussion is interpreted in the following manner: Research *into* design focuses on the advancement of new scholarship in design through historical and theoretical interpretations of design and the "site," or context, in the broadest terms. Research *for* design involves investigations into fields outside of design, conducted with a design application in mind and encompassing studies driven by the perceived needs of the sector, including the development of new materials and technologies. Research *through* design takes design processes to constitute the research methodology itself, a form of practice-led research that may focus on product or process (Norrie & Owen, 2013, p. 227).

In contrast to traditional architecture and design problem solving processes, design research allows for an engagement with diverse issues, particularly with context: physical, social, cultural, political, and temporal, which allows for the exploration of diverse agendas, information, and expertise. This facilitates the expansion of architectural endeavour, which in turn necessitates the development of new modes of engagement with a broad range of issues. The varying modes of research design (*into*, *for*, and *through*) reposition design as a practice of exploration. In particular, research *for* design expands disciplinary boundaries, by considering how knowledge from outside of the design discipline can impact on design thinking. Research *into* design highlights the value of context; for example, highlighting the transformative potential of understanding past and present conditions for informing future ideas. Processes of research *into* or *for* design may produce insights that can directly inform design, or lead to speculative investigation via research *through* design, presenting propositions for future scenarios.

RESEARCH THROUGH SPECULATIVE DESIGN

Research *through* design involves speculation to test boundaries and present questions that may subvert or illuminate the field of enquiry, rather than merely presenting solutions to design problems. Murray Fraser suggests that while speculation and imagination are important to the scientist, the social scientist, or the historian, the creative aspect becomes the "dominant part of the investigation" of design research, introducing "its own ideas of testing and evaluating, even in rather lateral or unexpected ways." Furthermore, he notes that a key characteristic of design research is the "creative leaps and lateral thinking," that can develop through "a kind of improvisation, inventing and testing" of newly devised strategies, which challenge or subvert traditional processes (2013, p. 2). The unknown is embraced as part of the process: trying out an idea to see what comes of it, reflecting on this, and then establishing ways to represent what has been discovered (Norrie & Abell, 2016, p. 12). This produces a form of critical design, which presents "a form of critique and speculation within disciplinary, scientific and societal frames ... challeng[ing] established discourse, institution, episteme, and present alternative roles for product design to those driven by technological and fiscal concerns" (Malpass, 2013, p. 333).

Design research processes, particularly research *through* design, produce a reflexive criticality that allows questioning of conditions, and engagement with context in a broad range of guises. In *Educating the Reflective Practitioner* (1987), Donald A. Schön describes the process of "reflection-in-action" as iterative, generative or propositional processes that are experimental and involve the trial and error of testing, producing an outcome to then be reflected upon rather than a finite solution. Schön observes,

> [W]e think critically about the thinking that got us into this fix or this opportunity; and we may, in the process, restructure strategies of action, understandings of phenomena, or ways of framing problems. . . Reflection gives rise to on-the-spot experiment. We think up and try out new actions intended to explore the newly observed phenomena, test out our tentative

understandings of them, or affirm the moves we have invented to change things for the better. (Schön, 1987, p. 28)

Critical spatial practices, or critical design, that engages in speculation, rather than design as problem solving may question or redefine parameters. Fraser (2013, p. 4) notes that design research often involves "projective undertakings equally rooted in uncertainty and contingency, and thus needing to oscillate between past, present and future conditions." Speculative design is not necessarily confined to fictitious or imagined scenarios; it can be employed as part of practice-led design research that investigates real-world issues to expand an understanding of existing conditions and future possibilities. This can be understood through the work of US-based architecture practice, Dunne and Raby (2001), who engage in critical spatial practices that are deliberately transformative and future oriented, to provide ways of "operating outside the tight constraints of the service industry" (p. 59). Furthermore, Dunne and Raby (2007) suggest that critical design employs "speculative design proposals to challenge narrow assumptions, preconceptions, and givens about the role [designed works] play in everyday life." Reflecting on Dunne and Raby's approach, Brad Tober notes that

> critical design is explorative, experimental, and does not serve an end-user (or consumer) audience in the same way that commercial design work might. Speculative design asks questions and proposes answers (which may or may not be correct), but does not attempt to identify or prescribe singular solutions. (Tober, 2016, p. 3)

COLLABORATIVE PRACTICE-LED DESIGN RESEARCH AS TRANSFORMATIVE PEDAGOGY

Within the broad field of design research, practice-led design research provides a particular avenue of exploration, drawing on diverse conceptual and theoretical approaches that bridge the divide between theory and practice. Collaborative practice-led design research can be used to reconceptualise the scope of research, and reposition both design and design research within broader social, temporal, and disciplinary contexts, thus facilitating diverse modes of collaboration, between and within disciplines, and also with the community, including industry and government, providing unique models of engagement and impact.

As a form of pedagogy, collaborative practice-based design research engages students with live projects and local communities, offering ways to reconceptualise and reposition both teaching and research by engaging with the teaching-research nexus in varying ways. Ron Griffiths identifies four models of engagement between teaching and research. He suggests that *research-oriented* teaching involves the understanding of research processes, whereas *research-led* teaching develops the content of the curriculum based on specialist knowledge. In contrast, *research-based* teaching builds the curriculum based around research inquiry, while *research-informed* teaching is based on inquiry into the teaching and learning process, or pedagogy (Griffiths, 2004, p. 722).

Griffiths suggests that these models offer different relationships between the academic and the student, which can be understood as being on a spectrum from "weak" to "strong". At the weak end of the spectrum, the research experience is "diffuse," research knowledge is located at the periphery of the learning experience and the flow of knowledge from academic to student is unidirectional; for example, *research-oriented* and *research-led*. At the strong end of the spectrum students engage in *research-based* enquiry that is directed by academic staff, where the research shapes the learning task and there is a perceived "two-way" relationship between academic and student (Griffiths, 2004, p. 722). From this perspective, research not only serves to enrich the content of the curriculum and learning experience for students, but also provides academics with the opportunity to place their work in a wider intellectual context to gain feedback from students and to provide a testing ground for research ideas (Norrie & Owen, 2013, p. 226). Research-based teaching provides opportunities for diverse models of Workplace Integrated Learning (WIL), with the students gaining an understanding of both academic practices and disciplinary knowledge of the field of enquiry under investigation.

Design research can also transform pedagogy though the fostering of collaborative and cross-disciplinary engagement. Frayling's tripartite model of research *into*, *for*, and *through* design highlights how design research can both emphasise and erode disciplinary boundaries. Using the definitions cited above, research *into* design can be understood as enquiry that focuses specifically *within* the field of design, while research *for* design can be understood as research *from* fields beyond design that can inform design thinking, or reposition the design investigation. Facilitating different modes of engagement between and within disciplines fosters the development of diverse research methods and processes. Understanding different multi- and inter-disciplinary processes allows for the "production of complex forms of research that are at once self-reflective and propositional," Rendell highlights the distinction between multidisciplinary research, which involves each discipline "maintain[ing] their own distinct identities and ways of doing things," and interdisciplinary processes in which "individuals operate at the edge and in between disciplines and in doing so question the ways in which they usually work" (2004, pp. 145–146).

TRANSFORMATIVE PEDAGOGY CASE STUDY: REGIONAL URBAN STUDIES LABORATORY

These ideas are examined through the Regional Urban Studies Laboratory (RUSL, pronounced Russell), a collaborative practice-led design research project within the School of Architecture & Design at the University of Tasmania, which engages directly with local communities and government authorities to examine urban issues in small towns and cities. RUSL engages in collaborative practice-led design research, which employs research-based teaching as a mode of transformative pedagogy. Projects explore physical, spatial, social, cultural, and temporal contexts of urban settlements, collating and communicating information about historic and current conditions as a way of building a dialogue that poses questions, and presents speculative scenarios for urban futures. Projects employ diverse processes of research *into, for,* or *through* design to generate speculative design research, which allows for the investigation of ideas that are at the periphery of day-to-day practice. This leads to productive ways of reinterpreting local issues, which are essentially spatial, but also impact on and are impacted by a range of issues related to the broader physical, social, or cultural context.

RUSL engages in various modes of collaboration. Projects are developed as part of the Advanced Design Research (ADR) unit of the Masters of Architecture, which draws on the research interests of academic staff to facilitate research-based teaching. First, students collaborate with academic staff, becoming research assistants in ongoing projects that span several cohorts, drawing on the findings of previous studies to inform both processes and knowledge acquisition. Research methods embed a strong engagement with the teaching-research nexus, providing new insights into both teaching and research practices, and into the field of enquiry itself. Second, projects are developed in collaboration with local councils, with direct engagement between university and council shaping research questions, and leading to new ways of understanding particular urban issues within regional municipalities. Third, projects are extended through internships with the councils, with students supervised jointly by council staff and academics; outputs are generally focused on practical outcomes. Fourth, projects engage directly with community, providing an understanding of the physical and social context, and facilitating a forum for discussion and development of speculative ideas. Fifth, cross-disciplinary engagement is central to the research methods, with processes of research *for* design drawing on knowledge from a broad range of fields to inform the development of projects. Some projects also involve cross-institutional engagement, providing a sixth mode of collaboration (Norrie & Brewin, 2015, pp. 239–240).

RUSL engages in "live" urban *practice-led* design research that bridges the divide between theory and practice. Projects employ open-ended processes that are both projective and speculative: examining, analysing, and hypothesising in various ways, in order to generate discussions that extend the current understanding of particular urban issues. While these projects can be understood as practice-led, as they engage with real world issues, they also expose students to alternative forms of architectural practice whereby the architect/designer is an active participant in the development of the project scope and field of enquiry, rather than mirroring the traditional model of consultancy, where the architect is instructed to carry out a specific design task. Projects aim to "stretch" traditional modes of practice, finding and filling gaps in and between these conventional processes. They question the constraints of planning policy and processes that are traditionally focused on defining boundaries or limits, which can be a very blunt or ineffective tool for instigating positive change. Projects also expose the limits of the terms of reference of traditional design consultancies and building procurement practices, with their particularly tight timeframes that can be un-engaging and disempowering for the community, and lead to limited outcomes (Norrie & Brewin, 2015, p. 242).

Engaging with situated and community-based projects provides a range of benefits for council, community, and university. First, complementary agendas are foundational to the collaboration, mediating between the desire for deliverable projects and understanding the value of speculative ideas that promote longer term strategic thinking and critical spatial practices. Second, the university is positioned as a collaborative research partner working together with the council in a relatively open-ended process, rather than as a consultant who is constrained to delivering a fixed outcome. The collaborative processes employed in these projects are "future focused" and ideas driven, and aim to assist councils and communities to develop briefs for future professional consultancies. Third, the semester- or year-long projects allow for a slower, repeated interaction with the council and community than can be afforded within the temporal and financial constraints of traditional consultancies; this highlights issues and ideas that may not have come to the fore otherwise. The duration of the projects enables an iterative process that allows the teams to spend time on site, and the open-ended process results in a stronger "people focus" than produced by traditional professional consultancies. Fourth, direct engagement with the council and the community through the consultation meetings and ongoing conversations fosters "transformative participation," as discussed in detail below (Norrie & Brewin, 2015, p. 242).

RUSL COLLABORATIVE PRACTICE-LED DESIGN RESEARCH: METHODS AND TACTICS

RUSL employs diverse design research methods to engage with a range of critical spatial practices. The process is open ended, posing questions through projective thinking and speculation, illustrating Downton's belief that design, and particularly design research "is not normally intended to produce a fully pre-conceived outcome, rather it is expected to produce change in the existing situation and hopefully offer fresh surprise and delight" (Downton, 2003, p. 5).

While projects are situated in local communities, they engage with various aspects of the broader context to reveal ways to question limits and reveal alternative possibilities. Research aims to be productive, exploring the broader context from historical to current conditions, to present speculative propositions that suggest potential future scenarios or morphologies. At the simplest level, context can be understood as the physical characteristics of the immediate environment—the formal structure, the physical and visual setting. However, shifting the focus beyond the immediate conditions, particularly the constraints of a specific bounded plot of land, allows a consideration of the broader physical, temporal, and philosophical context. This highlights the wide web of spatial and cultural fields in which architecture and design is situated (Norrie, 2013, p. 3).

RUSL projects draw on contemporary "site practices," as discussed by Carol Burns, Andrea Kahn, Sandy Isenstadt, Elizabeth Meyer, Mark Wigley, and others, which highlight a multiplicity of ways of understanding context, from "built form to implied meaning to underlying ideology" (Isenstadt, 2005, p. 158). Burns and Kahn assert that, beyond the bounds of the physical conditions, the notion of "site" also includes the terrain of "temporal, cultural, ideological, perceptual, scalar, and ontological dimensions" (2005, p. xiii). Meyer notes that the site or context may encompass conceptual ideas or associations with the broader cultural landscape, evoking connections to social and ecological histories (2005, p. 94). She believes sites are "found as well as invented," and design process can provide ways to "read" and "imagine" sites, which may be spaces that are "as much between disciplines as they are between surfaces, membranes, and operations" (Meyer, 2005, p. 121). For Burns and Kahn, the "site" is neither singular, nor static; engaging with a gamut of site concerns involves an "exchange between the real and the representational, the extrinsic and the intrinsic," and they advocate for a process of "site thinking" that involves a process in which the "site and designer engage in dialogic interaction" (2005, p. xv).

By engaging with diverse interpretations of site and context, RUSL examines issues beyond the constraints or usual limits of architectural practice, acknowledging the impact of the physical, cultural, temporal, and ontological context. This provides new ways of understanding possible futures, illuminating scenarios that might be out of reach of normal day-to-day objectives, budgets, or processes, and generating ideas that may be enabled through speculative design that is aimed to facilitate broader long-term strategic thinking. Tober observes that

> speculative design is particularly forward-looking, as it must anticipate upcoming trends and engage with them in a way that prepares them for use by other designers in a timely fashion. This conceptualization of speculative design frames the critical practitioner as one who develops a base framework for practice that other designers can develop further, mirroring the way in which a scientist might conduct pure (or basic) research to establish a foundation for other scientists to subsequently build upon. (Tober, 2016, p. 3)

RUSL Projects employ reflexive practices that engage in the interplay between different methods, drawing on Frayling's tripartite definition of research *into, for,* or *through* design to develop processes that are interconnected and iterative, rather than singular and linear. The diversity of the modes of engagement and collaboration requires the development of various ways to investigate projects, and particular ways of communicating with and between students, academics, professionals, and the community. Looking beyond design-as-problem-solving, and the service delivery traditional consultancies, RUSL projects employ a range of design research processes that allow speculation and testing of ideas, which can be understood through terminology developed by the Monash School of Art, Design and Architecture (MADA). MADA highlights key design research methods or tactics as: *study*, *sample*, *illustrate*, *image*, *narrative*, or *manifesto* (MADA, 2014). Each involves documentation of existing conditions, utilising creative processes to test ideas that are both speculative and indeterminate, but also productive. These processes encompass a shift from architectural design traditions that focus on the production of "things," to design research that involves an exploration of "issues," investigating site and context in the broadest sense (Norrie & Abell, 2016, p. 9).

For RUSL, the processes of *study*, *sample*, *illustrate*, *image*, *narrative*, and *manifesto* allow the curation of ideas and scenarios, or "projective future morphologies," that interpret historical contexts and question current conditions. *Study* includes documenting and analysing spatial conditions, patterns of use, and occupation, drawing together socio-economic and demographic data and examining social, temporal, and spatial urban issues. This may include research and mapping of the built and natural landscape past and present, uncovering connections and relationships between places, and highlighting patterns of use and connectivity to reveal new opportunities. *Studies* may also include aspects of the broader cultural landscape: social and cultural activities, values and events that provide an understanding of context in the broadest sense, and engaging in research *into* or *for* design (Norrie & Abell, 2016, p. 9).

Projective and speculative processes that involve *sampling*, *illustrating*, and *imaging* provide ways of visually testing ideas, engaging in research *through* design in a range of ways. *Sampling* involves processes similar to those used in music, in which parts of other projects are coopted into a new context, which may include grafting of examples or precedents on to new sites as a way to test or speculate on particular spatial or formal ideas. *Illustrating* may also involve the "use of examples or comparisons" drawing on precedents to demonstrate ideas, but it focuses on visualising strategic ideas through three-dimensional diagrams and drawings to demonstrate a unique response to a design problem. *Imaging*, or developing "physical likeness or representation" translates strategic ideas into visualisations, which can demonstrate possible spatial and social opportunities through the use of montages or other photo realistic representations, as shown in Figure 6.1 (MADA, 2014).

Speculative and conceptual ideas may also be examined through a *manifesto* or the generation of *narratives*. A *manifesto*, or "declaration of the intentions, motives, or views" provides a "broad vision of ideas for exploration, which steps outside of the practical constraints." *Narratives* presents a "story or account of events, experience, or the like, whether true or fictitious" (MADA, 2014). This allows for the development of scenarios, or "future morphologies" that are both speculative and projective (Norrie & Abell, 2016, p. 9).

Figure 6.1: Imagining Speculative Urban Narratives through Collage and Montage
Source: Image by Elizabeth Walsh, 2012, for RUSL CAPITheticAL competition

RUSL THEORETICAL CONTEXT

RUSL draws on a range of theoretical and practical ideas that inform the research process: reflection, analysis, questioning, reinterpreting, and projecting future narratives. Contemporary urban and landscape theories provide a scaffold for thinking, highlighting the importance of "networks of inter-relationships," and considering the value of engaging with collaboration and diverse interpretations of context as core aspects of urban research (Corner, 2006, p. 30). Projects are underpinned by the belief that "the projection of new possibilities for future urbanism must derive less from an understanding of form and more from an understanding of process—how things work in space and time" (Corner, 2006, p. 29).

According to Brian Boyer, accommodating diverse modes of collaboration is key, and this requires the orchestration of the dynamics of interaction, drawing on "strategic design" to facilitate processes that "give shape to decisions" rather than "objects or spaces" (as cited in Hyde, 2012, p. 138). Hyde observes that strategic design "seems to sit at the intersection of the spatial and the bureaucratic and explores how the combination of knowledge can allow us to make more informed decisions" (2012, p. 139). Strategic design highlights the importance of designing relationships as a core part of the process, particularly the way relational connections can facilitate the potential of cross-disciplinary and community engagement. This reiterates the focus on "networks of inter-relationships" that is central to landscape urbanism, and highlights the importance of context as a core aspect of urban research (Corner, 2006, p. 30).

RUSL also draws on ideas of "transformative participation" and "spatial agency," as discussed by Jeremy Till, which also focus on connection and inter-relationships, and the design of processes of interaction, collaboration, and engagement, rather than the creation of objects as the primary outcome (Till, 2005; Schneider & Till, 2009). Till describes "spatial agency" as a process that is both enabling and disruptive, "pro-active instead of re-active … working in alternative ways on alternative" projects (Schneider & Till 2009, p. 99). The spatial agent is "one who effects change through the empowerment of others, acting with intent and purpose," advocating strategies of appropriation, dissemination, empowerment, networking and subversion (Schneider & Till, 2009, p. 99).

Transformative participation is described by Till as "forward thinking," projecting a "shadow of the future" in the process of actively engaging community and creating a shift from "problem solving" to the "negotiation of hope" (2005, p. 9). To facilitate this, Till advocates for processes that subvert traditions of design-as-problem-solving and the architect-as-expert, believing that focusing on problems looks "determinedly backward," whereas "hope projects ambiguously forward" (2005, p. 9). Till acknowledges the importance of context, drawing on John Forester's idea of "sense making" which recognises "the contested social situation in which the design process is first initiated and … the contingent social world in which buildings and their users will eventually be situated" (Till, 2005, p. 10). This resonates with the notion of "site thinking," advocated by Burns and Kahn, highlighting the importance of engaging with broad conceptions of site and context to expand the parameters of the project, and the specific field of investigation.

Till contests that shifting focus from the architect as "expert" problem-solver is necessary in order to facilitate spatial agency, believing that focusing on design-as-problem-solving privileges the architect-as-expert who "assumes authority over the layperson." This limits the scope of practice and risks, relegating engagement and participation to a placatory process that seeks to elicit a consensus to ratify ideas. Till believes that the architect as expert or "mere facilitator" is "unable to re-imagine their knowledge from the perspective of the user," and, as a consequence, their skills are used instrumentally rather than transformatively, citing Gillian Rose's observation through this process "the architect is demoted; the people do not accede to power" (as cited in Till, 2005, p. 6). Till notes that the "technical know-how of the expert is not enough to help users to develop new spatial visions; the user is given nothing to enable them to expand on their nascent but unarticulated desires, and so these remain at the level of the lowest common denominator" (Till, 2005, p. 6).

The development of modes of engagement that address the traditional power hierarchy between architect and layperson are essential to facilitating the skills and knowledge of both parties transformatively. Participation relies on all parties having access to "requisite knowledge" and "transparent channels of communication," particularly between the expert and non-expert (Till, 2005, p. 3). Till asserts that architects tend to "cling to the certainty of what they know rather than expose themselves to the uncertainty of what others may know" (2005, p. 7). Transformative participation disrupts this process by focusing on the development of knowledge as internal to the collaborative process, rather than "as an abstraction from the outside," facilitating opportunities for the user to "actively transform the knowledge of the architect" (Till, 2005, p. 7).

Central to the building of transformative participation and spatial agency is the fostering of social capital, which can be understood as the "network of relationships based on trust and reciprocity between individuals" (Dascălu, 2013, p. 204). Till (2005) advocates for the strategic rearrangement of the dynamics between participants and the reformation of knowledge through the development of complementary roles of "citizen expert" and "expert citizen." This involves the architect (as citizen expert) allowing the knowledge of the community (expert citizens) to transform understanding (p. 8). In order to create this shift, architects must "project themselves into the spatial, physical and social context, of the user" to become "an activist working on behalf of and as a dweller," rather than "fixating on the building and user as objects" (p. 7).

Like Till, Drago Dascălu also observes that the "perceived difference of knowledge and expertise between the agents involved" presents an impediment to the sense of equity required to promote reciprocity. Highlighting the link between knowledge and empowerment, Dascălu echoes Till's call for the reciprocal relationships of "expert citizen" and "citizen expert," as central to transformative participation. Dascălu (2013) advocates for a process of *dispositif* architecture, a relational architecture that is "made out of relations and it generates relations" (p. 208). This process engages with "norms, laws, use, function process, practice" to highlight how design process can provide ways of seeding community engagement and building social capacity (p. 204). Key to *dispositif* architecture is the "network of relationships based on trust and reciprocity between individuals," to create a "tool for building trust", and "simulating social capital" (pp. 204–209).

Dascălu (2013) asserts that trust is dependent on the "empowerment of individuals, social equality, level of information and knowledge and the quality of previous cooperative experiences;" furthermore, he suggests that if we "consider architecture only as object or space, then it cannot have any role in building trust based relationships" (p. 209). Differentiating between personalised and generalised trust, Dascălu highlights the importance of personal engagement of the architect or the designer, and the importance of presenting themselves as individuals, rather than as a representative of an institution, in order to create "empathy and understanding" (p. 211). This reinforces Till's argument that promoting a two-way process builds trust and addresses inequality.

Furthermore, Dascălu suggests that successful collaboration can be facilitated by the initiation of "very small actions" as "empowerment exercises," with small successes acting as agents in trust building between participants. Also, he advocates for "intervening in the everyday space of the user" highlighting the processes of the tactical urbanism movement as key examples of successful collaborative interventions (2013, p. 214). Identifying the initiating projects requires direct engagement with community, particularly the *strategic design* of processes of engagement, rather than the presentation of completed design proposals for places and spaces. Hyde supports this view, suggesting, "when objectives are reframed to target a specific issue, even the most minimal of interventions can lead to immense results" (2012, p. 105).

RUSL: DESIGN RESEARCH—SHIFTING FROM PROBLEM-SOLVER TO URBAN CURATOR

Engaging in critical spatial practices that focus on the broader urban context and the strategic design of relationships offers the potential to transform the architect or designer from an expert problem-solver to an "urban curator," who examines issues through research and documentation, facilitating the development of speculative ideas and questions that are communicated through various means.

In the role of urban curator, RUSL develops speculative narratives as a framework to present scenarios for projective future morphologies. In particular, civic or urban narratives are developed to address particular contemporary urban issues. The term "civic" refers to the notion of *belonging* to the city, which implies a sense of connectedness, and highlights the importance of relationships between people and places, and across time (Norrie, 2013, p. 1). The development of civic and urban narratives is explored through various themes, via hybrid design research processes that employ various methods and tactics to facilitate the crossover between disciplines. Projects are specifically designed to address the typical challenges for regional councils that operate within limited budgetary means. Although speculative propositions presented are freed from specific budgetary constraints, the limits of funding are acknowledged, through projects exploring maximised inherent value via the development of staged propositions, or the continual refinement of projects to reduce complexity while optimising performativity (Norrie & Brewin, 2015, p. 241).

Drawing on the specific expertise of the RUSL team, the focus is on particular issues, notably urban amenity and urban legibility, which is examined in a range of ways—physically, visually, and conceptually—and at various scales. The examples below highlight the scope of some of the RUSL projects. The scope of projects is curated through a dynamic process of engagement, shaping, and presenting specific civic and urban narratives that suggest future scenarios with the aim to provoke questions and discussion. The strategic design of interaction that underpins collaborative engagement in these projects requires an understanding of social networks, and research confirms that the "complex ways in which [we] interact can only be developed through a willingness to engage with the community" (Simpson, Wood, & Daws, 2003, p. 260). Social mapping provides ways of scoping out the various parties, identifying specific interests and concerns, and understanding the relationships to other organisations; this is a key element of the curation of projects. It highlights the potential spatial agency of groups and individuals, and is carried out through research into organisations, and via direct involvement and conversations with key people to identify leaders and design champions.

At the broadest level, the theme "City vs Landscape" examines the relationship between urban settlement patterns and the natural landscape, highlighting ways to reinforce, rather than erode, this connection through future development. This is particularly significant in the regional towns and cities that are central to RUSL research, as the scale of these settlements allows the relationship to the natural condition to be easily read, offering ways that future development at a range of scales could engage with this physical, ecological, and cultural context. This is not merely about the provision of green spaces, but also involves an understanding of the natural landforms and ecology, both past and present. Projects speculate on future scenarios for individual sites, drawing on both localised precedents and examples of city-wide strategies and urban theories to identify opportunities, which are developed through multiple processes of study, sample, illustrate, image, narrative, or manifesto, as part of research *into, for*, or *through* design (see Figure 6.2).

The development of urban character inherent to the "City vs Landscape" projects is also examined in other ways. For example, collaborative projects with Gehl Architects involved mapping and analysing of the "public space" and "public life" of the city to understand current spatial and social conditions, which reveals patterns that both support and undermine urban legibility and character, and this informs visualizations that speculate on future scenarios. Central to this process is the idea of providing "places for people," which includes developing more mixed uses in the city to facilitate a diversity engagement of a broad range of people, and to promote an equitable and inhabitable city (Gehl, 2010).

Drawing on the ideas learnt from the collaborative projects with Gehl Architects, a series of projects that considered the "City as …" explored a range of different scenarios that could shape urban narratives. "City as Campus," "City as Culture," and "City as Urban Playground" explored a series of complementary narratives through mapping, analysis, and speculation. In these projects, research *into* design processes highlights the historical development of places, illuminating cultural and urban morphology to reveal founding or enduring patterns, both spatial and relational.

Focusing on the relationship between past, present, and future shapes, the formation of urban narratives can be used to underpin design briefs facilitating an engagement with temporal, cultural, and social aspects of sites and architectural programs.

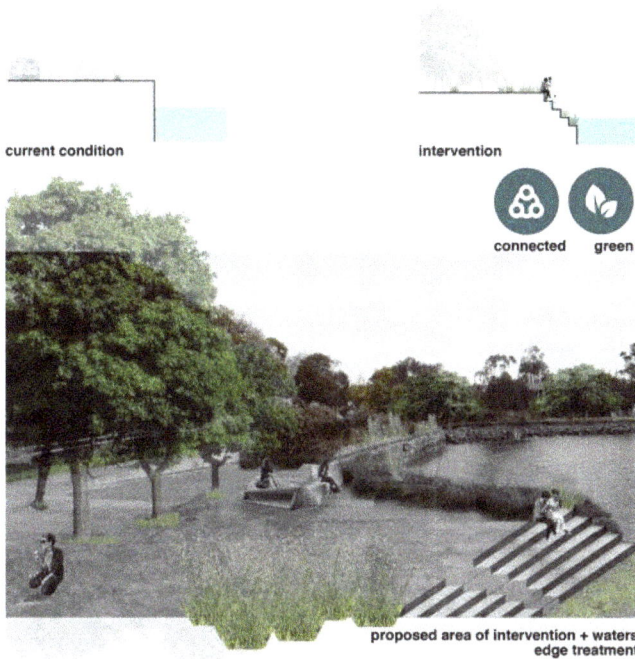

Figure 6.2: Imagining Speculative Urban Narratives through Collage and Montage
Source: Image by Camilla McBeath 2015 for RUSL "City vs Landscape"

An exploration of the theme or narrative "City as Culture" involves speculating on ways that art and culture can lead the development of urban narratives, promoting the city as a site for various modes of performance and cultural engagement. Similarly, the movement of the university into urban sites underpins the "City as Campus" explorations, which poses the question of how the university could be positioned as a civic player, through active collaborative engagement with the local councils and communities at both a conceptual and practical level. This involves exploring the notion of *campus* across time and in other places, and examining the relationship between the university's cultural aspirations and the future civic visions. In other projects, processes of research *for* design examine aspects of context that address cross-disciplinary fields, including sociology, health, technology, philosophy, and science. Developing an understanding of these associated fields shifts the spatial agency of design practice to intervene in a broader cross-disciplinary domain. For example, introducing knowledge drawn from sociological research into play theory informs the development of the "City as an Urban Playground" narrative, exploring parameters for the design of flexible play spaces that can used by all age groups and demographics, at different times of the day and year (see Figure 6.3).

The various processes of research *into*, *for*, and *through* design are mapped through diagrams that visually illustrate the similarities and differences between the inherent methods and techniques used for each project, highlighting the points of critical discovery that have led to a change in research process or method. This allows all project participants to understand the research process, offering research models for consideration in future projects. These diagrams are particularly useful in assisting external parties to engage in projects, and to allow individual team members to understand the role of particular activities in the overall research task (see Figure 6.4).

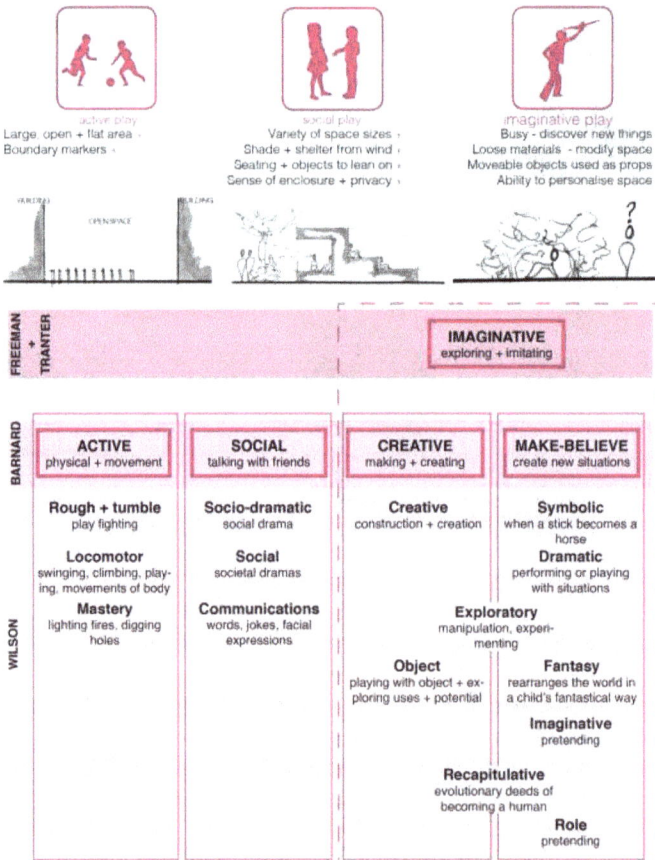

Figure 6.3: Research *for* Design, Drawing on Sociological Play Theory
Source: Image by Katherine O'Byrne 2013 for RUSL "City as Urban playground"

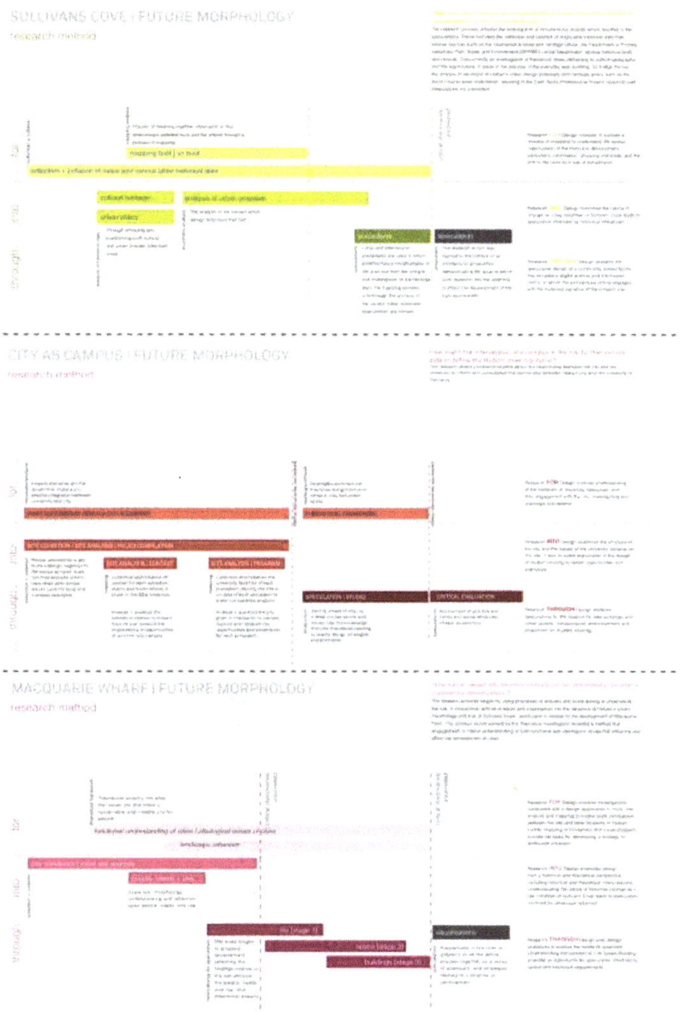

Figure 6.4: Mapping Research Methods for Three RUSL Projects, 2012–2016

CONCLUSION

As the research landscape within tertiary education continues to shift, increasingly, value is placed on engagement and impact requires the participation of a range of collaborators, including research partners, industry, and the community. Engaging students in research-based teaching provides productive opportunities, highlighting possibilities for cross-disciplinary practices and transformative pedagogies. Pursuing collaborative engagement with local councils and communities provides a creative field of exploration that engages productively with the research-teaching nexus in architecture and design, and allied disciplines. Collaborative design research provides ways to shift the role of the architect from expert problem-solver, offering new ways of engaging with urban issues and questioning traditional practices.

Collaborative practice-led research allows an engagement in pragmatic issues in alternative ways, subverting traditional approaches and reinforcing connections between theory and practice. The process of speculation produces ideas that can be seen as either idealistic provocations or realistic propositions for future development that may be more immediately viable. The process is simultaneously productive, yet indeterminate. Collaboration between the university, the council, and the community spans the divide characterised by Schön as the *high ground* in which "manageable problems lend themselves to application of research-based theory and technique" and the *swamp* where "messy confusing problems defy technical solution" (Schön, 1987, p. 3). It allows everyday and messy problems to be informed through theoretical research, which expands conceptual understanding and provides a broader engagement that enlightens these issues (Norrie & Abell, 2016, p. 13).

Each of the RUSL Projects involves different modes of dissemination and communication to diverse audiences, as wells as addressing the demands of the structured target-driven outputs required by the university framework. Research and speculative explorations are presented graphically, exploring inclusive modes of interaction in which the council and community are able to begin to project themselves into the speculative and future orientated propositions. Knowledge gained about projects in site-specific locations is presented in a way that allows these findings to be understood in a more generalised manner, opening the possibilities for localised projects to act as case studies for other places. Engaging with a range of regional urban issues in different locations is allowing the compilation of a diverse set of knowledge and ideas that can then be used as part of a process of sampling for other projects.

Research is also disseminated in academic journals, and via academic and industry-specific conferences, via outputs that both record and critically reflect on processes. Presenting projects and research processes for critical review encourages more detailed description of projects, particularly in theoretical terms. Critical reflection on research questions, methods, contexts, and speculative ideas highlights the hybrid processes of research *into*, *for*, or *through* design, providing a feedback loop, critically reflecting on both the research outcomes (which may be questions) and the research processes themselves (Norrie & Abell, 2016; Norrie, 2015; Norrie & Brewin, 2015; Norrie & Owen, 2013; Marjela & Norrie, 2013; O'Byrne & Norrie, 2013). This allows for research *about* design, which "enquires into what takes place when design is undertaken, and then seeks to find methods to improve or refine the observed activity" (Murray, 2013, p. 95).

While collaboration between students and academic supervisors through practice-led research-based teaching produces transformative pedagogies that bridge the research-teaching nexus, it also presents some complexities. First, the very nature of design research requires that the process is not necessarily clear; the questions and research processes are iterative rather than linear, and engagement with other collaborative partners further expands the open-ended processes. As a consequence, it can be difficult to communicate in advance the scope of work required within the framework of assessment tasks, which are not limited by a simple measure of word count. As this process is counter to the increasing expectations of providing clear frameworks for assessment, a certain amount of trust must be invested in the supervisor to successfully guide students through this messy process. This is essential to allow the research to produce unexpected, but productive, directions that are not reflected in the "contract" of the assignment outline and assessment rubric (Norrie & Owen, 2013, p. 233).

Second, the process shifts the roles of teacher and student to supervisor and assistant, eroding traditional hierarchies. While this is commonly promoted as one of the key opportunities of the teaching-research nexus, aspects of this relationship require careful negotiating (Brew, 2001; Griffiths, 2004, pp. 714–718). There is a need to destabilise the collaborative relationship in the context of assessment, and Angela Brew argues that this may require substantive transformations to assessment practices emphasising formative rather than summative assessment (Brew, 2001, p. 153). For the academic, this also requires the shift from immersive collaborator to objective assessor. Within RUSL projects, engaging other supervisors from parallel research studios in the Advanced Design Research (ADR) stream, as "external examiners," mitigates this difficulty. However, each of these issues has implications for workload, and presents risks that the emphasis will shift to documenting for the assessment process, rather than focusing on outputs that best serve the research (Norrie & Owen, 2013, p. 233).

Third, as the projects involve group work, negotiating the diverse capabilities of the student cohort presents complexities for both the research processes and the modes of engagement with collaborators. As the objective of research-based teaching is to immerse the student fully as a collaborator, it is important that they participate in the framing of research questions rather than merely working as research assistants on clearly defined and/or repetitive tasks. This is challenging for some students, and there is a need to create open-ended scaffolds for research collaboration at the start of the project, which are then continually reviewed as students' interests and abilities develop (Norrie & Owen, 2013, p. 234).

RUSL's Modes of collaborative engagement with local councils and communities provides new ways of engaging with urban issues, transforming practice and pedagogy. This is a work in progress, which involves the continual collation of ideas, methods, and theories and constant critical reflection on processes and outcomes. Modes of collaborative engagement with communities are relatively nascent, involving consultation through community meetings and ongoing conversations. Future projects will continue to investigate similar locales, working with overlapping community groups and individuals to build stronger collaborative links. The repeated engagement in projects across several cohorts of students is essential to trust building, with both the community and the local government council. This allows for the development of knowledge and skills in parallel, as RUSL finds more diverse ways to communicate, explore, and expand urban narratives that inform future morphologies at a level of broader conceptual site thinking, and through influencing the development of site-specific briefs that engage with value-based agendas.

RUSL draws on Deyan Sudjic's proposition that the future of our cities can be understood and managed through collaboration between three groups: policymakers, builders, and theorists (2007, p. 36). The practice-led design research conducted by RUSL links the academy (as theorists) within the tripartite collaborative with the local government (the policymakers) and the city builders; the development of links between the disciplines of architecture, planning, sociology, and economics provides fertile ground for research investigations. Collaborative practice-led design research provides a scaffold for collaborative engagement and transformative participation (Norrie & Abell, 2016, p. 1).

ACKNOWLEDGEMENTS

The process of collaboration central to the RUSL has involved a number of key academic colleagues, project partners, and research assistants. Founding of RUSL was in collaboration with local councils in Hobart, Launceston, Meander Valley, Bright, and Spring Bay, and the Tasmanian Office of the State Architect (OSA). Research assistant Alysia Bennett, who was part of the initial research team, continues to be a key interlocutor in ongoing conversations. Colleagues at the University of Tasmania, Judith Abell and Dr. Ceridwen Owen, and Ross Brewin of MADA, have provided key input and critical reflection. Ideas and research processes have been developed and refined with several cohorts of Masters of Architecture students, who have assisted in developing the theoretical framework of research, and testing through projects and critical reflection. The participation of all parties is acknowledged in the development of this paper.

REFERENCES

Brew, A. (2001). *The nature of research: inquiry in academic contexts*. London, England: Routledge.

Burns, C. J., & Kahn, A. (2005). Why site matters. In C. J. Burns & A. Kahn (Eds.), *Site matters: Design concepts, histories and strategies* (pp. i–xxix). London, England: Routledge.

Corner, J. (2006). Terra fluxus. In C. Waldheim (Ed.), *The landscape urbanism reader* (pp. 21–33). New York, NY: Princeton Architectural Press.

Dascălu, D. (2013). Architecture as tool for building social capital. *Acta Technia Napocensis: Civil Engineering & Architecture, 56*, 204–20.

Downton, P. (2003). *Design research*. Melbourne: RMIT University Press.

Dunne, A., & Raby, F. (2001). *Design noir: The secret life of electronic objects*. Basel, Switzerland: Birkhäuser.

Dunne, A., & Raby, F. (2007). *Critical design FAQ*. Retrieved from http://www.dunneandraby.co.uk/content/bydandr/13/0

Fraser, M. (2013). *Design research in architecture: An overview.* Farnham, England: Ashgate.

Frayling, C. (1993/4) Research in art and design. *Royal College of Art Research Papers*, *1*(1), 1–5. Retrieved from http://researchonline.rca.ac.uk/384/3 /frayling_research_in_art_and_design_1993.pdf

Gehl Architects. (2010) Public space, public life: A city with people in mind. Copenhagen, Denmark: Gehl Architects.

Griffiths, R. (2004). Knowledge production and the research-teaching nexus: The case of the built environment disciplines. *Studies in Higher Education*, *29,* 709–26. http://dx.doi.org/10.1080/0307507042000287212

Hyde, R. (2012). *Future practice: Conversations from the edge of architecture.* London, England: Routledge.

Isenstadt, S. (2005). Contested context. In C. J. Burns & A. Kahn (Eds.), *Site matters: Design concepts, histories and strategies* (pp. 157–84). London, England: Routledge.

Malpass, M. (2013). Between wit and reason: Defining associative, speculative, and critical design in practice. *Design and Culture*, *5,* 333–56. http://dx.doi.org/10.2752/175470813X13705953612200

Marelja, M., & Norrie, H. (2013). Teenagers and the city. In (Unknown Eds.), UrbanAgiNation: Proceedings of the 6th International Urban Design Conference (pp. 105–20). Nerang, Australia: Urban Design Australia.

Meyer, E. (2005). Site citations: The grounds of modern landscape architecture. In C. J. Burns & A. Kahn (Eds.), *Site matters: Design concepts, histories and strategies* (pp. 93–130). London, England: Routledge.

Monash Art Design and Architecture (MADA). (2014, April 4). Architecture PhD workshop: what is design research? Monash University, Caulfield, Australia.

Murray, S. (2013). Design research: Translating theory into practice. In M. Fraser (Ed.), *Design research in architecture: An overview* (pp. 95–116). Farnham, England: Ashgate.

Norrie, H. (2013). *Urban narratives: Museums and the city.* (Doctoral thesis, University of Melbourne, Australia). Retrieved from https://minerva-access .unimelb.edu.au/handle/11343/122134

Norrie, H. (2015). Regional urban studies laboratory: Engaging in collaborative research with policy makers. In J. Moloney, J. Smitheram, & S. Twose

(Eds.), *Perspectives on Architectural Design Research* (pp. 54–56). Baunach, Germany: Art Architecture Design Research.

Norrie, H., & Abell, J. (2016). Collaborative design research: Linking universities with government policy-makers. *Networking Knowledge: Journal of the MeCCSA Postgraduate Network*, *9*(3). Retrieved from http://ojs.meccsa.org.uk/index.php/netknow/article/view/436

Norrie, H., & Brewin, R. (2015). Urban collaborations. In D. K. Brown, M. Manfredini, P. McPherson, A. Pretty, U. Rieger, & M. Southcombe (Eds.), *Applied collaborations: Proceedings of the 8th International Conference and Exhibition of the Association of Architecture Schools of Australasia* (pp. 239–245). Retrieved from http://aasa.butterpaper.com/AASA-2015 -proceedings.pdf

Norrie, H., & Owen, C. (2013). Advanced design research: Exploring the teaching research nexus. In D. Ramirez-Lovering, J. Alexander, & A. Fairley (Eds.), *Design / Education: Proceedings of the 7th Annual Conference of the Association of Architecture Schools of Australia* (pp. 222–37). Retrieved from http://www.artdes.monash.edu.au/docs/aasa2013-proceedings.pdf

O'Byrne, K., & Norrie, H. (2013). The City as an Urban Playground. In (Unknown Eds.), *UrbanAgiNation: Proceedings of the 6th Annual International Urban Design Conference* (pp. 143–53). Nerang, Australia: Urban Design Australia.

Rendell, J. (2004). Architectural research and disciplinarity. *Architectural Research Quarterly, 8,* 141–47. http://dx.doi.org/10.1017/S135913550400017X

Rendell, J. (2013). A way with words: feminists writing architectural design research. In M. Fraser (Ed.), *Design research in architecture: An overview* (pp. 117–36). Farnham, England: Ashgate.

Schneider, T., & Till, J. (2009, Spring). Beyond discourse: Notes on spatial agency. *Footprint*, (4), 97–111. http://dx.doi.org/10.7480/footprint.3.1.702

Schön, D. A. (1987). *Educating the Reflective Practitioner*. San Francisco, CA: Jossey-Bass.

Simpson, L., Wood, L., & Daws, L. (2003). Community capacity building: Starting with people not projects. *Community Development Journal, 38,* 277–86. http://dx.doi.org/10.1093/cdj/38.4.277

Sudjic, D. (2007). Cities: The urbanization of the world. In R. Burdett & D. Sudjic (Eds.), *The endless city: The urban age project by the London School of*

Economics and Deutsche Bank's Alfred Herrhausen Society (pp. 32–52). London, England: Phaidon Press.

Till, J. (2005). The negotiation of hope. In P. Blundell-Jones, D. Petrescu, & J. Till (Eds.), *Architecture and participation* (pp. 19–40). New York, NY: Spon Press.

Tober, B. (2016). Envisioning design futures via practice-led speculative design research. *Networking Knowledge: Journal of the MeCCSA Postgraduate Network, 9*(3). Retrieved from http://ojs.meccsa.org.uk/index.php/netknow /article/view/442

Transformative Pedagogies and the Environment

CHAPTER 7

The Humanist Don Quixote and the Windmills of Sustainability: How Innovative Pedagogy Can Help Support Classical Subjects for a Sustainable Future

Doina Carter

ABSTRACT

This chapter looks at how innovative pedagogy transformed a humanities subject to make the module more immediately relevant to architectural education, the profession, and society, while improving engagement of an increasingly diverse student population. This was achieved through didactic shifts: from word to image; from individual passive study to social, active, participatory, experiential, and interdisciplinary learning; and from pure theory to practical applications of theory.

Militating for the survival of humanities subjects challenges the current societal (and pedagogical) trope that by concentrating on "sustainability" subjects, Architecture schools will produce perfectly trained new generations of specialists able to create a sustainable future. The aim of any educational environment, tertiary education in particular, as professional springboard is to create responsive individuals, unafraid of the unknown, but also unafraid of knowledge, capable of finding it with intentionality and sifting through it in order to deal with problems of varied complexity.

In today's politico-economic climate it would be financially unfeasible to provide a classical architectural education based on the pedagogical algorithm developed in the nineteenth century by L'Ecole des Beaux Arts in Paris—the model employed in many European countries over the last decades. Compulsory subjects that were part of such courses (e.g., philosophy, aesthetics, history of art, architecture, and urban and landscape design, theory of architecture) are now separate specialist degrees. However, for architecture to maintain the artistic, humanistic, and social aspects of the craft, architectural education has to be divergent enough to provide at least an awareness of these subjects.

"Providing awareness" is the remit of the humanities vein within the architecture course at the University of Lincoln, taught as one module in each of the three undergraduate years. Even such frugality has been proving onerous in recent years because of changes in Higher Education and the diversification of student profiles.

It is the author's conviction that professionals with multi-nodal cognitive nets are more adaptable and, in consequence, more prepared to address complexity, regardless of what the problem is—sustainability being only one of them.

PREMISE

In 2011, I was asked to coordinate the *History and Theory of Architecture and Design* module, one of the core subjects taught in the first year of the BArch (Hons) undergraduate Architecture course at the University of Lincoln, United Kingdom.

The *History and Theory* module is part of the humanities strand running from the first to the sixth year of the architectural training in our school. For students this module is usually the introduction to the scope of an architect's professional remit and also an outline of the architecture's place in society. The *History of Architecture* component covers significant architectural styles in chronological order, from antiquity to contemporary architecture, in an attempt to explain philosophical and societal context triggers for formal and functional changes in architecture. The *Theory of Architecture* aspect articulates knowledge acquired in the *History* lectures to prime students for their first incursions into subject specific critical thinking—the finest instrument to be used in design.

Significantly, this is the subject that starts revealing to the neophyte the difference between *building* and *architecture*, a fundamental distinction in the intellectual workings of an aspiring architect. As Pevsner (2009, p. 10) asserts, a "bicycle shed is a building; Lincoln cathedral is a piece of architecture"—although one could argue that even a bicycle shed can be architecture. This distinction is not an explicit, discrete piece of knowledge; it is a "threshold concept" (Meyer & Land, 2003), which is comprehended and assimilated in time as part of each student's understanding of what design is, and the role of an architect. Architectural *apprentices* need to start seeing that a construction, which merely shelters and stands up, is not necessarily architecture. For instance, while gothic cathedrals keep out the elements and successfully deal with gravity, they also materially express the theology of light, as physical manifestations of medieval thinking that light is the embodiment of spirit. The remit of architecture as a discipline means that the reverse is also true: a construction which has aesthetic and symbolic qualities, but is precarious or is not purposeful cannot be considered architecture.

This necessity for an architect to master a wide, and significantly different, range of skills was acknowledged from antiquity. The roman architect Vitruvius postulated that architecture has to exhibit three qualities: *firmitas*, *utilitas*, and *venustas*—that is, it must be solid, useful, and beautiful (Vitruvius, 1998). Therefore, architects ought to master disciplines which inform these characteristics. While solidity and usefulness are more objective, quantifiable, and therefore more teachable subjects, the beauty or sublimity of a building result from a humanistic and artistic sensitivity augmented by training. For architecture to attempt to engage the psyche and at the same time answer specific requirements, architects have to operate in the conceptual world of artistic idea(l)s while simultaneously complying with a myriad of physical, material, and structural constraints, and legislation that covers building and planning issues. The corollary of Vitruvius' definition of architecture is that an architect cannot be a technocrat or an aesthete, but has to be a melange of the two. This duality is at times difficult to reconcile in an individual as well as in a teaching environment.

In recent years, pressures placed on Higher Education coupled with policies regarding the building industry have affected the equilibrium within the curriculum, manifested in a disinterest in supporting humanities studies, while the sustainability and *green* agendas are actively promoted. While this is a strategic response to the world's perceived immediate needs, a renunciation of the *venustas* discourse in architectural education would eviscerate it, as its outcome would be different types of specialists, not architects. Practitioners know that a good designer is able to respond to constraints of any nature—architects constantly deal with a variety of them (among others, ecological and environmental) through a variety of methods, such as aesthetic judgement *and* technical competence. There is a lot of talk about "sustainable architecture." For a sustainable *architecture* and not only sustainable *buildings*, including buildings that are energy efficient, self-sufficient, or built out of renewable materials, architectural education has to ensure the *sustainability of the profession* by continuing to produce *architects.*

This chapter looks at how innovative pedagogy transformed a theoretical humanities subject to challenge its perceived stagnation in the past and make it more immediately relevant to architectural education, the profession, and society, while also improving engagement of a diverse student population. This was achieved by changing assessment along with making a theoretical subject become more a part of the design studio culture.

It is rarely in one individual's power to influence simultaneously the environment of an institution before students start learning, *presage* (Gibbs, 2010), *process* (what goes on as students learn) and the quality of the *product* (outcomes of that learning), as these indicators represent involvement at different hierarchical levels of management and policy making. However, intentional, well-constructed episodes of teaching and learning can be transformative at *product* (student) level during *process* (classroom) experience, to affect *presage*.

ARCHITECTURAL EDUCATION

The purpose of architectural education is learning to design (the ultimate aim being to design complex entities, such as buildings), and it could be argued that *design* is the fundamental threshold concept within our discipline. Threshold concepts are more easily identifiable within areas where the body of knowledge can be readily ascertained, such as mathematics, physics, and medicine, but *"ways of thinking and practicing"* are also considered to be "a crucial threshold function in leading to a transformed understanding" (Meyer & Land, 2003, p. 9). In his "Lectures on Architecture" John Soane (1753–1837), an architect of great ingenuity, said he believed that architecture is "an Art purely of Invention and Invention is the most painful and the most difficult exercise of the human mind" (as cited in Russell et al., 1983, p. 77). However, the mind needs educating before being required to perform such exercises. "The difference between education and training is the development of the mind so that practitioners do not simply follow rules but decide wisely among a variety of ways" (Fish, 1996, as cited in Ryan, 2001). Reflecting on how one learns to design, within the framework provided by Bloom's taxonomy of the cognitive domain (Anderson & Krathwohl, 2001), it becomes apparent that a student in architecture has to start *creating* while *understanding*, thus having to operate at the top and the base of the pyramid at the same time. In architecture schools, *education* and *training* happen concomitantly, in lectures and studio, opening the way to *understanding* in order to enable *creating*. According to Palmer (2001), this simultaneous leap in understanding and starting to function as a designer is the "quicksilver flash of insight" which marks a transformed world view, a necessary metamorphosis in a student. The added difficulty in architecture is that the ability to think conceptually is not sufficient, unlike in other artistic milieus. Students with an art background find the incipient stages of an architecture project easier, as this is the period of speculative investigation, which aims to teach how to "attack a problem with a set of contrivances foregrounding not the solution, but the poetic tropes applied to the solution" (Deamer, 2005). Students without such previous experience often struggle longer in this first phase. The rationality of the next step, however, having to draw or build—physically or virtually—is easier to grasp and therefore it is easier to teach. That is why the Beaux Arts school in Paris required an impeccable drawing technique of classical ornamentation and the Bauhaus taught practical skills in specific workshops: teaching *mechanical* skills associated with the profession was seen as a gateway into teaching how to *design*.

The defining environment for European and North American architectural education, the studio, has been derived from the pedagogical *algorithm* employed in L'Ecole des Beaux Arts in Paris in the nineteenth century and the apprentice system practiced at the Bauhaus, Dessau, in the 1930s. "The Beaux Arts teaching system relied heavily on brilliant teachers and learning-by-doing" (Lackney, 1999, p. 2), while solving a design problem. Crucially it introduced "crits" (critiques), a review method still used in architecture schools. At the beginning of the 20th century, the Bauhaus changed the attitude to design, considering that it "was neither an intellectual nor a material affair, but simply an integral part of modern concepts of mass production and modern technology" (Lackney, 1999, p. 3); students had to acquire technical skills and undergo aesthetic training to employ those skills. Bauhaus challenged the status architecture had within the world of design, for instance, architecture was seen as fundamentally no different from product design, but the principle of the studio based teaching and learning model remained unaltered.

Importantly, studio work was supported by extensive theoretical study, which included philosophy, aesthetics, and the histories of art, architecture, urban and landscape design, the theory of architecture, traditional and modern detailing, and structures. These subjects formed the canon for any traditionally educated architect.

In the last ten years, however, architectural education has been under a lot of pressure to change; a paper on what academics write about in the disciplines of Art, Design, and Architecture (de la Harpe & Peterson, 2008) identified the most concerning topics as the studio reform and thinking in art and design. The educational space (intellectual and physical) represented by studio has been irreversibly eroded in the years I have been teaching. The recently introduced Key Information Set (KIS) forced all programs to assess the number of contact hours, "most institutions are having some issues, and the really substantial issue seems to be around contact hours: what they mean and how you collect the information and make it auditable, from the point of view of the reliability, transparency and accessibility" (Hitchcock, 2012). Seen through the prism of KIS criteria, studio teaching could be perceived as inefficient: numerous contact hours spent in one to one dialogues, punctuated by frequent intermediate (formative) day-long crits; studio teaching is also demanding in terms of accommodation—space, wall area, and furniture—which is occasionally used day and night, making hot-desking problematic. What is difficult to quantify, or replace for that matter, is the qualitative dimension of the teaching and learning experience, especially in the first year when, ideally, the "transformative leap" should start taking place.

The reality is that while several years back students worked in studio most of the time and, during timetabled tutorials, individual dialogues lasted as long as necessary. Today a studio session assumes ten to fifteen minutes contact time per student. At the same time, subjects intrinsic to classical architectural education, which supported students' intellectual development, ensured a broad exposure to specialist, relevant knowledge, and conferred meaning to studio work, have become different degrees. Only condensed versions of these subjects remain, grouped under the headings of *Humanities* and *Technical Studies*.

Academics are caught between the "investment-cost" paradigm shift affecting higher education—changes in funding means that universities are "operated from an economic rationalist platform" (Lawrence, 2001, p. 5)—and the pressures exerted by validating bodies, quality assurance agencies, various surveys, along with their own moral responsibility as teachers to equip students with at least a "professional survival kit."

FIRST YEAR CURRICULUM

The most important activity throughout architectural education is studio (or design) work. At the University of Lincoln, this is reflected in the number of modules dedicated entirely to it. In first year, for instance, two modules are purely design work delivered in studio through individual tutorials (materialised in design projects); one is technical studies (delivered through supporting lectures and in studio, resulting in a design project) and the other a humanities module, *History and Theory of Architecture and Design* (delivered through lectures and assessed via essays). For the first year architecture students, project based work, with which studio teaching is concerned, can be difficult to engage with; it requires a degree of autonomy students might not be accustomed to, or comfortable with, especially in an unfamiliar learning environment. The majority of students arrive at University from a teacher-centred, exam-driven school environment, with learning strategies that do not seem relevant. School teaching is often, in effect, *problem solving* (Savin-Baden, 2000), while any design exercise is *problem based*: it requires students to have a sound understanding of the knowledge they have researched and explored, and an ability to critique information, to involve life experience, engage *with* complexity, and see and manage ambiguity (Savin-Baden, 2000). Devising the curriculum for this formative and transformative period is a dilemma, as tutors try to find a balance between elements, such as prior experience and new knowledge, conceptual and formal dexterity, material manipulation and cultural awareness, and urban context and functional necessities. Deamer (2005) considers that it is the "entire net of relationships of the studio teaching—the critic (tutor), the program, the object (project) and the student" which determines if the course will produce a "person interested in contributing to civic life via her/his skills as an architect," an "architectural citizen."

Lawrence (2001) talks about the change in nature and purpose of higher education due to "elite – mass" and "investment – cost" paradigm shifts. The effect is felt routinely in class, affecting didactic approaches; however, the aim to produce "architectural citizens" is not merely a mirage chased by idealistic pedagogues. As the professional accrediting body for architecture schools in the UK, the Royal Institute of British Architects (RIBA) responds to pressure from practitioners who feel that the *actual* vocational education happens in the office, an unsustainable state of affairs, especially in a recession. Statistics show that "only 30% of those embarking on a first degree in Architecture eventually succeed at Part 3" (Robinson, 2013). The reasons are multiple, some can be extrapolated or inferred from RIBA statistical data (2012; 2014), but lack of relevant skills in a competitive and over-populated profession would undoubtedly be one of them.

While studio has been losing timetabled contact time and space allocation, the necessity to teach students how to design remains. Creative curriculum design and development can assist by using all other subjects to explicitly support studio teaching.

FIRST YEAR HUMANITIES: HISTORY AND THEORY OF ARCHITECTURE AND DESIGN

Didactically, the *History and Theory* module operates more or less according to the knowledge structures described by Bloom's taxonomy of the cognitive domain. It is delivered in two lectures every week in both Semester A and B and assessed via essays throughout the year.

In 2011, departmental reshuffling was seen as a propitious moment to rethink how humanities subjects could support design modules across undergraduate and postgraduate courses. A radical solution involving vertical restructuring over the six years was ultimately not implemented because of, amongst other issues, the logistics of delivering modules shared horizontally and vertically by three different programs, which is the case with the *History and Theory of Architecture and Design*. Nevertheless, this reflective pause in our academic routine formed a rare intellectual space for us to debate the aim and direction of the humanities modules; it also highlighted the potential for improvement of teaching and assessment, and it increased individual awareness of how one's discrete contribution related to the subject continuum. Gibbs (2010, p. 6) notes that the "extent to which teaching is valued, talked about and developed" is one of the "process variables" (what goes on while students learn) that is difficult to quantify, but seems to surface in "studies of the characteristics of institutions and departments that have been found to be outstanding in terms of valid dimensions of educational quality," such as Oxford and the Open University.

The outcome of these departmental discussions for the Year 1 *History and Theory* module was a shift in the emphasis placed on what was worth knowing and why. While the content and mode of delivery were to stay more or less the same, our efforts focused on changing the types of assessment and assessment criteria.

ASSESSMENT OF HISTORY AND THEORY OF ARCHITECTURE AND DESIGN

The traditional method of assessing humanities subjects has been the essay, and our first year students produced four. As summations of episodes of independent study considered to be "the most useful way of assessing deep learning" (Brown, Bull, & Pendelbury, 1997, p. 59), in our experience, essays were increasingly less apt in achieving and proving "deep active approach of searching and constructing meaning" (Brown, Bull, & Pendlebury, 1997, p. 24).

This situation was a result of steady, incremental changes in first year student intakes over the last decade:

- The liberalisation of Higher Education in the UK means that students arrive with varied abilities, one of them being academic writing. Pickford and Brown (2006) comment that it should not be surprising that with approaching 50% of the 18–30 population in higher education, a significant proportion of students do not have well developed skills relating to academic reading or writing; in 1990 Gee (as cited in Beasley, 1997, p. 182) goes further by emphasising that higher education represents an unfamiliar world which favours certain "ways of writing, knowing and valuing" to which students need to adjust;

- James (2003) reported a higher proportion of dyslexic students in creative arts and design (5.59%) compared to the overall undergraduate student population in the UK (1.97%). More recent data from the Equality Challenge Unit (2015) shows that 15.3% of undergraduates who declare a specific learning difficulty are studying creative arts and design, representing 10% of all art and design students;

- New entrants have increasingly varied educational and cultural backgrounds: only around 60% of the first year intake come via University and Colleges Admissions Services (UCAS), the rest are mature students, from vocational courses, or international students. International students account for 31% in an upward trend—the biggest increase has been of students from outside the EU—although Europe has been providing the most significant numbers until recently (RIBA, 2012, p. 7). The last review notes "the largest source of entrants is now Asia" (RIBA, 2015, p. 3).

Interestingly for me, as an academic coming from practice and mainly involved in studio tutoring, written work exposed the variability of student profiles more starkly than design (studio work). Kalantzis & Cope found in 1993 that apart from the subject specific learning explicitly evaluated, what surfaced in essays were identity markers, such as language, dialect, and register (as cited in The New London Group, 1996) which offered fragments of insight into students' previous core life and educational experiences. While an interesting observation, this pointed to the fact that essays had become a deficit mode of assessment in first year.

I became responsible for coordination of the *History and Theory of Architecture and Design* module at this particular turning point when the decision was made to challenge the assessment status quo by focusing on a different set of skills with every submission. This was seen as a way of making a Western-centric module more accessible and its assessment fairer. Pluralism in assessment resonates with The New London Group's *multiliteracy* paradigm, which encourages the usage of "modes of representation much broader than language alone", intended to replace traditional language-based academic discourses (The New London Group, 1996). Since adequate time cannot be given to prepare our diverse students to function in the new *culture* Universities represent, we have to allow their background to support this transition without penalising the "un-matchingness"; differences are not deficiencies. Empowering students to use aptitudes, skills, and interests that made them enrol in the Architecture course in the first place, was a way to promote engagement as a vital aspect of retention, especially in their first semester in tertiary education.

The module descriptor for *History and Theory* was generous in terms of how submissions could be structured. Thus it presented the opportunity not only to diversify assessment, but at the same time associate it with studio teaching. Requirements set in the new assignments linked the module's modus operandi with studio praxis, thus, in effect, contributing to studio teaching time and making explicit the applicability of this theoretical module to architectural education and practice. In consequence, the new types of assignments had a manifest dual purpose: to answer module specific requirements (assess knowledge of history and theory of architecture) and to teach or rehearse skills usually employed in studio (including sketching, organisation of graphical information on a page, development of explicit and succinct title blocks, architectural annotation, construction of physical models, design with style constraints, and use of light, colour and texture to convey meaning).

The Higher Education Academy's (HEA) report regarding the National Student Survey (NSS) findings in design disciplines for 2012 (HEA, 2012) conclude that the most important factor affecting student satisfaction is the quality of learning and teaching, followed by personal development, organisation and management, academic support, and assessment and feedback, with learning resources being last. Quality of teaching is one aspect of an academic's job that is most in one's control regardless of institutional or policy background. A coordination role extends pedagogical intentionality to curriculum design to influence the scope, the breadth, and the profundity and relevance of learning, given the ultimate aim: the forming of "architectural citizens." In my view, "architectural citizen" does not necessarily mean a qualified professional, but somebody with a heightened awareness and discernment, with work-life experiences and options, who is knowledgeable or unafraid of knowledge. The *History and Theory* module is a good platform to start this attitude development: the subject itself is broad and while it would be suitable for many art related disciplines, for architects and designers it tends to have a more focused approach.

Taking on the *History and Theory* module at a moment of transition was, for me, an opportunity not to be missed. A keen interest in the subject, a reasonable knowledge of practice and the profession, an increased self-awareness as an educator, and recent exposure to pedagogical theory (as a student on my way to becoming an HEA Teaching Fellow), meant that I saw the potential these changes could have as "emancipatory strategies" for our students (McGlinn, 2009, p. 35). The coordination role meant that my involvement was evolving from the "technician" in the classroom to a "decision maker, consultant, curriculum developer, analyst, activist, school leader," which in 1999, Cochran-Smith & Lytle (as cited in McGlinn, 2009, p. 34) considered characteristic of educational researchers. Modifying assessment in *History and Theory* became action research rather than having started with this ambition, and over three years it developed the shifting, but recognisable rhythm of planning, acting and observing, reflection, and re-planning.

The changes proposed for the *History and Theory* module triggered a reflection on how we evaluate work in architectural education. In studio, design is appraised in formative and summative crits, which answer a lot of current desiderata for assessment: they are dialogical, often interdisciplinary, improvisational, and oriented towards the future of the work. Crits sit well within the constructivist paradigm as they incorporate social interaction and knowledge sharing; they are a scene for implicit peer assessment and peer learning and allow for immediate and interactive feedback. The outcome of reconsidering assessment was that I began to acknowledge it as a bi-directional connection in a conversational framework between student and teacher, as theorised by Laurillard (2002), rather than reductively equating it with marking. This bi-directional connection is obvious in design work evaluation (crits), but is seldom self-evident with written work.

Learning from what was successful in studio and transferring it to a theoretical subject meaningfully could help diversify assessment. In practical didactic terms, the newly introduced submissions incrementally climbed through Bloom's taxonomy of the cognitive domain (Anderson & Krathwohl, 2001) and had an intentional dual purpose of testing theoretical knowledge of history of architecture and practical skills associated with studio work. The emphasis in the first two assignments was on the *process of learning*, in the spirit of experiential learning theories (Kolb, 1984), while only the last one was an essay, as a necessary introduction to academic writing.

The new assessments revolved less around how much students would know if they absorbed the *deposits* of information *banked* with them in lectures (Freire, 1972), and more on the learning modus operandi to improve engagement, to "create educational experiences for students that are challenging, enriching and expand their academic abilities" (Zepke & Leach, 2010, p. 171). In other words the planning of the module's narrative throughout the academic year "was not simply [about] a sequence of ideas," it considered "consequence" (Dewey, 1910, p. 5).

FIRST ASSIGNMENT: BUILDINGS IN CONTEXT

In the first semester, the module lectures cover the *History of Architecture* from antiquity to the present day. The first assignment consisted of six hand drawings: it asked students to walk around Lincoln to identify and hand draw three pre-20th century buildings of different styles; therefore, representing different historic periods (see Figures 7.1 and 7.2).

Figure 7.1: Gothic Revival in Lincoln,
Buildings in Context Assignment
Source: Drawing by Lyndsy Hutchinson, 2014

Figure 7.2: Gothic Revival in Oxford,
Buildings in Context Assignment
Source: Drawing by Lyndsy Hutchinson, 2014

This exercise was to be followed by scholarly research of trying to find three corresponding examples from the same periods in books of history of architecture. The implicit and explicit requirements of the brief were a reflection of this submission's dual purpose of:

1. **evaluating subject specific knowledge**—by asking students to extract from the urban fabric continuum only relevant historic buildings, and to reinforce this understanding by consulting books of history of architecture; and

2. **assisting studio tuition**—the assignment had to be hand-drawn. Hand drawing is a skill necessary in studio but undervalued and undermined because of the urgency for students to become literate in computer aided design, a fundamental architect's tool-kit skill; however, the ability to sketch is appreciated in practice as an effective way of conveying ideas, and researchers have concluded that competence in drawing is developed over time, in much the same way as other areas of expertise (Chamberlain et al., 2011).

From the pedagogical point of view, this assignment was devised based on the conscious decision to re-contextualise theory, because as theorists posit "human knowledge is initially developed not as 'general and abstract', but as embedded in social, cultural and material contexts" (The New London Group, 1996). Lincoln, with its Roman remains, allows history of architecture lectures to become relevant quite early in the academic year and the chronology of the subject. Lincoln's rich past as a significant trading centre in the Middle Ages means that there are also good examples of Romanesque (Norman), Gothic, and Neo-classical architecture. Confining the physical area of enquiry to Lincoln limited the possible viable examples to a manageable number, so the process of selection was dependent only on knowledge acquired in lectures, thus making the quality of information gathered and submitted dependent only on individual level of engagement with the subject.

Methodologically, the brief for the first assignment was intended to be what Prince and Felder (2006) define as "structured inquiry learning," where students are given a problem with clear guidelines on how to solve it, and also an attempt to employ "learning-cycle based instruction" (pp. 126–27). The act of walking the city with a sketchbook or camera in hand, while mentally trying to sort vast amounts of recently acquired knowledge and make sense of it, was vital as a first step into the cycle of learning. Also, these purposeful wanderings were a surrogate for the educational pilgrimage to ancient sites architects used to embark on, at the beginning of their careers, to develop their draughtsmanship and understanding of Vitruvian rules of proportion and symmetry—rules developed by the ancient Greeks, later adopted by the Romans, and catalogued by the Roman architect Vitruvius during the first century BC. Sketching ancient ruins in situ had been a formative activity employed by Italian architects, painters, and sculptors since the Renaissance, but it was still considered relevant by architects such as Le Corbusier, Tadao Ando, and Rem Koolhaas. This methodology could be considered "situated learning" (Lave & Wenger, 1991), where *doing* knowledge is how unqualified people who are potentially part of a learning community acquire it. Learning through drawing was formalised to become a didactic method in classical architectural education by L'Ecole des Beaux Arts (Lackney, 1999).

The second part of the assignment involved visits to the library in a quest for other national or international examples of the same historic styles discovered in Lincoln, and relied on a modest understanding of stylistic characteristics and historic chronology (see Figure 7.3).

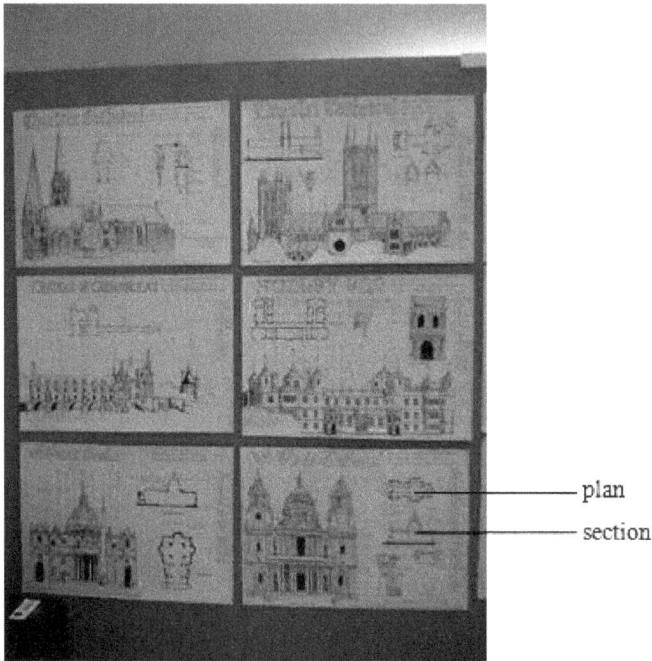

Figure 7.3: A Full Submission: *Buildings in Context* Exhibition
Source: Drawings by Joseph Istance, 2015

The assessment criteria acknowledged the dual purpose of the assignment by evaluating both content and presentation, thus rewarding engagement as evidenced by quality of research and/or comprehensive illustration. As a consequence, the accuracy of the students' conclusions was not primary, albeit important. As an educator, in general, I agree with Piajet's stance that "learning is an emergent process whose outcomes represent only historical record, not knowledge of the future" (as cited in Kolb, 1984, p. 26), so the fundamental aim was to engage students and thus enable them to start assuming responsibility for their instruction.

In contrast to the previous year's first submission for the *History and Theory* module, an essay, the *Buildings in Context* assignment relied on a pre-existing ability to draw (a likely skill for architecture students), for the "most important single factor influencing learning is what the learner knows already" (Ausubel, Novak, & Hanesian, 1978). Also, in respect of the intended democratisation of assessment, hand drawing required only individual application and basic tools; its product, the drawing, is comparable and does not discriminate between international and local students, and studies have shown that dyslexia does not affect accuracy of drawings (Chamberlain et al., 2011).

The first *History and Theory* assignment created the environment for hand drawings to be celebrated, exhibited, and talked about (See Figure 7.3). Submission time saw febrile activity in studio, with all students present, pinning up their work and analysing their colleagues' efforts, in an impromptu but valuable peer assessment, especially for first year students who need to gauge their ranking in the new "pack." The resulting exhibition became an ad hoc event, enjoyed by staff and students alike—especially post graduates who slalomed through the boards to admire the hand drawings on the way to their studio, with the comment "they are good, we wish we did this instead of the essay!"

The sociability of this assignment was not limited to the way students worked to compile and submit it, but also to the way we assessed it, as a collective, which allowed us to appraise a range of aptitudes within our cohort—something impossible to do with essays, which are marked in isolation and moderated afterwards. The work in the exhibition indicated representation techniques, which could have benefited from attention in studio. Observations gathered at this point, before plans and sections became a requirement (see Figure 7.1), also informed subsequent iterations of this assignment, introduced to make the submissions look less like life drawing and more about architectural graphical presentation. Thus the assessment of a theoretical subject managed to become the bi-directional connection in a conversational framework between student and teacher, postulated by Laurillard (2002). The brief developed to be more specific and prescriptive about the drawn components and drawing conventions in order to cement the students' understanding of architectural graphics; the façades drawn in situ or from books were to be accompanied by labelled plans and sections for a more comprehensive description of each building with annotated plans and sections (see Figure 7.4).

SECOND ASSIGNMENT: ROOM IN A BOX

Depending on each student's level of engagement, the first assignment operated in the lower levels of *Remembering* and *Understanding* with incursions into *Applying* and *Analysing* from Bloom's taxonomy of the cognitive domain as modified by Anderson and Krathwohl (2001). The second assignment moved into the top categories, of *Evaluating* and *Creating*. The brief required the design of a historically accurate interior and the construction of a physical model—a room in a box. The brief stipulated only the dimensions of the room, allowing students to choose the style and type of room (e.g., library, drawing room, bedroom). To achieve this, they had to synthetise knowledge of history of architecture to extract characteristics of the style they were going to emulate in order to design (create) a period room. Pedagogically, this task represented an increase in complexity and was conceived as an episode of deep learning, which according to Kuhn et al., was "shown to promote student engagement" (as cited in Zepke & Leach, 2010, p. 171). Although this assignment represented a leap in comprehension, the educated response to its requirements built on the knowledge acquired during the previous one. As suggested by Bruner, instruction should be "spirally organized" (as cited in Prince & Felder, 2006, p. 125). As a self-directed, more challenging academic undertaking, this assignment was also appropriate for group work, which enabled interaction and dialogue, and enhanced collaborative skills and accountability—aspects which define "cooperative learning," shown to increase individual student performance if well conducted (Felder & Brent, 2007).

Again the brief had the dual purpose of evaluating the cohort's understanding of the history of architecture and supporting studio teaching and learning:

1. **evaluating subject specific knowledge**—designing in a certain style required fine understanding of subtleties that defined it, such as structure, materials, ornamentation and decoration, composition, proportions, employment of artificial and natural light; and

2. **supporting studio teaching**—the studio skill *rehearsed* in the second assignment was model making for a domestic interior design, an unusual scale for architects.

Furthermore, creating a convincing ambience of a historic style room gave students the awareness of, and the option to pursue an interest in, a professional niche market: while the majority arrives to study architecture wishing to design technologically daring buildings, in the last few years a rising (and surprising) number of our graduates sought employment in practices specialising in renovation and listed buildings. Having proof in one's portfolio of an experiment in classical design could be helpful in such job interviews, only made possible by photographing the models. Without the time or resources to teach the basics of photography, the idea of collaborating with a colleague from Contemporary Lens Media (CLM) was born; this was to become the **[light/box] project**, a piece of action research conducted in the spirit of the "student as producer" (Neary, 2012) ethos of the University of Lincoln.

Tuckman and Jensen (1977) consider that groups attempting to work together experience a few stages they named "Storming, Forming, Norming, Performing and Adjourning." Architecture students *stormed*, *formed*, and *normed* independently at different rates and intensities, depending on the dynamics of the group, but they micro-managed the process entirely from the start, deciding on style and function of the room, model making techniques, materials, the division of labour, and so on. The concluding effort of the groups, their *performing* and *adjourning*, was to happen over a daylong workshop in studio, a potent active learning environment, when the components of the model were to be brought together (see Figure 7.4).

Figure 7.4: A *Room in a Box* Model Being Constructed in Studio
Source: Photograph by Adam Verity (Ex-CLM Program Leader), 2013

When my CLM colleague agreed to the collaboration, we were a couple of weeks into the project. During the workshop the whole cohort of over a hundred students gathered in studio, and it became the time when the photography students got involved. Each architecture group was to be joined by two CLM students in the afternoon to set up and photograph the models. This increased the level of organisational complexity and required adaptability from the students to go tentatively through all five stages of group morphing, so for a brief time the teams were extended and inter-disciplinary.

In order to create the models, students had to design individual walls, ceilings, and floors (see Figure 7.4), decide on the proportions of the room and all components within, from functional elements (doors, windows, stairs) to structural (columns, beams, domes) and decorative elements (textures, colours, mouldings). This could be achieved through superficial mimicry or a deeper understanding of the style, but the process of deconstructing all components before laying them out and assembling them required intentionality, precision, and cohesion in a group setting. The model making exercise is always challenging because of the need to ascertain how desired effects can be achieved when scaling down; for instance, thin window frames accurately scaled down might become too feeble to support their own weight—increasing the width is not an option as they would appear unrefined, so an educated decision has to be made about what material can be used—this is a problem encountered in practice when choosing building materials. The final models were the result of social learning, skill sharing, teamwork, and meaningful intra-team (and often inter-team) discussions. Researched, designed and collated in studio, the environment for completing this assignment was very different to what it would have been if it were an essay (see Figure 7.5).

Figure 7.5: Atelier Buzz, *Room in a Box* Submission Day
Source: Photograph by Adam Verity, 2013

The collaborative **[light/box] project** was an immersive exercise, which gave the architecture and photography students the experience of working with a professional partner pursuing the common goal of a good picture of the models (see Figure 7.6).

Figure 7.6: The **[light/box] project.** The *Room in a Box* Model
Source: Photographs by the Author (top) and CLM Students (bottom), 2013

CONCLUSION

A Bauhaus or Beaux-Arts educated architect would be consternated by the tug-of-war which seems to characterise discussions between educators in some architecture schools today. The rhetoric surrounding what we need to teach cannot be reduced to resemble a fight between an outmoded, idealistic Don Quixote (humanities) and the currently more in favour, clean-energy-providing windmills (technical/environmental studies). Both artistic and technical aspects define architecture as a subject. It is an unhelpful situation when humanities subjects appear to be an indulgence perpetuated only by a generosity of spirit now unaffordable due to the investment-cost paradigm shift in higher education. However, the effort to preserve and deliver essential subjects is not nostalgia, it is a necessity. As argued in the beginning of the chapter, for architecture to contribute to a sustainable future, architectural education must be able to supply the framework of knowledge that defines the profession.

Modifying the assessment of a theoretical module, which is described here, was in response to a continuously changing environment in higher education in general, and architectural education in particular. It was the change in the student population profile that meant that new arrivals did not engage well with traditional assessment methods, thus triggering the necessity for different approaches to assignments. But the module modification was refined intentionally to become a more active component in the greater sphere of architectural pedagogy to address the loss of studio teaching time and space. In the case of the *History and Theory* module, what has been achieved has been transformative.

In terms of the personal development of students, the new assignments assist their transition into higher education: from school leavers, with a predilection for a problem-solving approach to learning, to architecture students, capable of developing individual informed responses to *problem-based* tasks. This is reflected in the type and complexity of the submissions. The first submission is almost mechanical; the selection process of viable examples relies on subject specific knowledge, narrowed by the limited choice in Lincoln, with the result being almost arithmetic—the answers are generally either right or wrong. The second semester assignment relies on strategies learned in studio, because it requires developing an individual brief, researching relevant characteristics to enable a meaningful response, understanding complex relationships, and applying the rules discovered with intent. However, unlike studio projects, here, innovation is not of the essence; the level of ambition in a *Room in a Box* design is evidenced by its stylistic coherence, as the result of synthesis of knowledge accumulated during research. As such, the outcome is rarely right or wrong; rather it sits on a scale of refinement.

By focusing each assignment on a palette of skills architecture students are likely to have, such as drawing and model-making, the depth and accuracy of knowledge was illustrated by images rather than words, thus equalising the mode of expression within a varied student population, making it independent of language. In this way, the changes also addressed the urgent need for a traditional, language based subject to operate in a more internationalised, democratised, and culturally diverse tertiary education environment, as it can no longer rely for its delivery and assessment on a set of academic skills that a few decades ago were mastered by all prospective students.

The *History and Theory* module has changed to become more interactive; while subject specific knowledge is still imparted through lectures, its assessment managed to form nets of relationships between the lecturer, the subject, the object (project), and the student, which Deamer (2005) defined and considers essential for any chance of developing responsible learners and, ultimately, professionals.

By intention, studio teaching was a beneficiary of the way briefs for *History and Theory* were devised. In the first assignment hand drawing was the medium through which students externalised their knowledge and understanding, an important lesson that architects *must* express thoughts graphically. Moreover, the ability to draw was honed for architectural illustration, which requires a certain discipline, not necessarily one of fine art hand drawing. By prescribing the drawn components, the first assignment reiterated the idea of a complete set of drawings as the way buildings are described graphically—something architects have to do in practice. This was part of the process of generic hand drawing *specialising* to become architectural drawing. With the second assignment, more subject specific and studio skills were employed, such as model making, designing in a coherent stylistic language, group work, and inter-disciplinary collaboration. The assignments encouraged social learning and peer review for the students, and also facilitated dialogue and collaboration between assessors.

It is possible for the changes within the module to go even further. Its structure and delivery have yet to be reconsidered. Furthermore, its relationship with other subjects could be re-evaluated; a more integrative approach to their teaching would go a long way to demonstrating their inter-dependence.

Although illustrated by a specific case study, the suggestion made here is more general; constraints within the curriculum, funding, staffing, and so on, can be tackled in the classroom by innovative pedagogies. Of course, there are limits to how far *unsupported* innovative pedagogues can go. But hopefully, our experience shows that innovative pedagogies can enhance and revitalise the way we teach, to engage both students and academics.

REFERENCES

Anderson, L. W., & Krathwohl, D. R. (2001). *A Taxonomy for learning, teaching, and assessing: A revision of Bloom's taxonomy of educational objectives*. New York, NY: Longman.

Ausubel, D. P., Novak, J. D., & Hanesian, H. (1978). *Educational psychology: A cognitive view* (2nd ed.). New York, NY: Holt, Rinehart & Winston.

Beasley, V. (1997). *Democratic education: An examination of access and equity in Australian higher education* (Doctoral thesis, University of South Australia).

Brown, G., Bull, J., & Pendlebury, M. (1997). *Assessing student learning in higher education*. London, England: Routledge.

Chamberlain, R., Riley, H., McManus, C., Rankin, Q., & Brunswick, N. (2011). *The Perceptual Foundations of Drawing Ability*. Paper in Thinking through Drawing conference, Columbia University, New York, October 2011. Retrieved from https://www.ucl.ac.uk/medical-education/publications/aesthetics-publications/edit/Reprints2012/2012-ChamberlainRileyEtAl-PerceptualFoundationsOfDrawing-Columbia.pdf

Deamer, P. (2005). First year: the fictions of studio design. In M. McCleary & J. Silbert (Eds.), *The Yale Architectural Journal, Perspecta 36 "Juxtapositions"* (pp. 1–7). Cambridge, MA: The MIT Press.

de la Harpe, B., & Peterson, J. F. (2008). Through the learning and teaching looking glass: What do academics in art, design and architecture publish about the most? *Art, Design & Communication in Higher Education, 7,* 135–154. http://dx.doi.org/10.1386/adch.7.3.135_1

Dewey, J. (1910). *How we think* [Online version: HTML]. Retrieved from http://www.gutenberg.org/ebooks/37423

Equality Challenge Unit. (2015). *Equality in higher education: statistical report 2015*. Retrieved from http://www.ecu.ac.uk/publications/equality-higher-education-statistical-report-2015

Felder, R. M., & Brent, R. (2007). Cooperative Learning. In P. A. Mabrouk (Ed.), *Active Learning: Models from the analytical sciences* (pp. 34–53). Washington, D.C.: American Chemical Society.

Freire, P. (1972). *Pedagogy of the oppressed*. Harmondsworth, England: Penguin Books.

Gibbs, G. (2010). *Dimensions of quality*. York, England: The Higher Education Academy. Retrieved from https://www.heacademy.ac.uk/system/files /dimensions_of_quality.pdf

The Higher Education Academy (HEA). (2012). *National student survey discipline report – art and design*. Retrieved from https://www.heacademy.ac.uk /system/files/resources/art_and_design_nss_discipline_report_final.pdf

———. (2016). *The Higher Education Academy strategic plan 2012 – 2016*. Retrieved from https://www.heacademy.ac.uk/system/files/downloads /strategic-plan-2012-16.pdf

Hitchcock, G. (2012). *Lincoln University plans for data KIS*. Retrieved from http://www.governmentcomputing.com/features/2012/jan/05/lincoln -university-key-information-sets

James, A. (2003). *What Subjects Do Dyslexic Students Study at University?* http://dx.doi.org/10.13140/RG.2.2.18470.73286

Kolb, D. A. (1984). *Experiential learning: experience as the source of learning and development*. Englewood Cliffs, NJ: Prentice Hall.

Lackney, J. (1999). *A History of the Studio-based Learning Model*. Retrieved from http://www.edi.msstate.edu/work/pdf/history_studio_based_learning.pdf

Laurillard, D. (2002). *Rethinking University teaching: a conversational framework for the effective use of learning technologies* (2nd ed.). London, England: Routledge Falmer.

Lave, J., & Wenger, E. (1991). *Situated learning: Legitimate peripheral participation*. Cambridge, England: Cambridge University Press.

Lawrence, J. (2001). Academics and first-year students: collaborating to access success in an unfamiliar university culture. *Widening participation and lifelong learning, 3*(3), 4–14. Retrieved from https://eprints.usq.edu.au /5475/1/Lawrence_Acadmics_and_first-year_students_PV.pdf

McGlinn Manfra, M. (2009). Action Research: exploring the theoretical divide between practical and critical approaches. *Journal of Curriculum and Instruction, 3*(1), 32–46. Retrieved from http://www.joci.ecu.edu/index.php /JoCI/article/view/28/46

Meyer, J., & Land, R. (2003). Threshold concepts and troublesome knowledge: Linkages to ways of thinking and practicing within the disciplines.

Enhancing Teaching-Learning Environments in Undergraduate Courses Project, Occasional report 4. Universities of Edinburgh, Coventry and Durham, England. Retrieved from http://www.etl.tla.ed.ac.uk//docs /ETLreport4.pdf

Neary, M. (2012). Student as producer: An institution of the common? [or how to recover communist/revolutionary science]. *Enhancing Learning in the Social Sciences, Guest Paper.* York, England: The Higher Education Academy. Retrieved from http://studentasproducer.lincoln.ac.uk/files/2014/03 /ELiSS0403A_Guest_paper.pdf

Palmer, R. E. (2001). *The liminality of Hermes and the meaning of hermeneutics.* Retrieved from https://www.mac.edu/faculty/richardpalmer/relevance.html

Pevsner, N. (2009). *An outline of European architecture.* London, England: Thames & Hudson.

Pickford, R., & Brown, S. (2006). *Assessing skills and practice.* London, England: Routledge.

Prince, M. J., & Felder, R. M. (2006). Inductive teaching and learning methods: Definitions, comparisons and research bases. *J. Engr. Education, 95,* 123–138. http://dx.doi.org/10.1002/j.2168-9830.2006.tb00884.x

Royal Institute of British Architects, Education Department. (2012). *Education Statistics 2011–2012.* Retrieved from https://www.architecture.com/Files /RIBAProfessionalServices/Education/Validation/EducationStatistics2011 -12.pdf

Royal Institute of British Architects, Education Department. (2015). *Education Statistics 2014–2015.* Retrieved from https://www.architecture.com/Files /RIBAProfessionalServices/Education/2015/EducationStatistics2014-15.pdf

Robinson, D. (2013, February). Wider horizons. *RIBA Journal,* p. 21.

Russell, F., Summerson, J. N., Tilman-Mellinghoff, G., & Watkin, D. (Eds.). (1983). *Architectural Monographs: John Sloane.* London, UK: Academy Editions.

Ryan, S. (2001, July). *Succeeding despite the odds: A narrative of hurdles obstructing lifelong learning pathways.* Paper presented at the 31st Annual Conference of SCUTREA, University of East London, England.

Savin-Baden, M. (2000). *Problem based learning in higher education: untold stories.* Buckingham, England: SRHE & Open University Press. Retrieved from https://www.mheducation.co.uk/openup/chapters/033520337X.pdf

The New London Group. (1996). A pedagogy of multiliteracies: designing social futures. *Harvard Educational Review, 66,* 60–93. http://dx.doi.org/10.17763/haer.66.1.17370n67v22j160u

Tuckman, B. W., & Jensen, M. A. C. (1977). Stages of small-group development revisited. *Group and Organization Studies, 2,* 419–427. http://dx.doi.org/10.1177/105960117700200404

Vitruvius. (1998). *The ten books on architecture* (M. H. Morgan, Trans.). New York, NY: Dover Publications.

Zepke, N., & Leach, L. (2010). Improving student engagement: Ten proposals for action. *Active Learning in Higher Education, 11,* 167–177. http://dx.doi.org/10.1177/1469787410379680

Chapter **8**

Submersion Subversion: Re-Thinking the Anthropocene as a Pedagogical Platform for Disruption and Discovery

Charity Edwards and Kate Tregloan

Abstract

Submersion Subversion was an Interior Architecture design studio, focusing on a Melbourne beachside location during 2015. The studio focused on immersive fluid materialities as both context and content of project development. Students considered the occupation, representation and sensations of water environments, engaging with critical systems thinking about water environments and the cumulative climate change impacts of global warming, rising seas levels, and ocean acidification.

The studio questioned an assumed anthropocentric environmental context, and instead sought to foreground the experience of non-humans in a collective more-than-human relationship with water, simultaneously highlighting the need for empathy as a key element in a "designerly" skillset. Students explored a popular site of beachside recreation, and extended their understanding of the context through an intense investigation of a non-human "client." By subverting the typical category distinctions and power relationships between human and non-human, and client and designer, students were required to undertake a radical re-imagining of their own position in an ecological system—and to discover and perform alternative practices in response to the studio imperatives and anticipated professional roles.

The notion of the Anthropocene may well be considered a conflicted platform for pedagogy, but the contested nature of ecological crisis can also provide great transformative potential within the design studio. By embedding discovery and disruption in subject matter, and pursuing unlikely re-imaginings, alternative representations, and performed practices within studio, we can offer students new engagements with their creative agency, and point towards a necessary but radical re-thinking and re-making of the political in design.

Introduction

This chapter examines an Interior Architecture design studio at the Faculty of Art Design & Architecture (MADA), Monash University, Australia, during the second semester of 2015. The studio, entitled *Submersion Subversion*, encouraged students to question the usual anthropocentric approach to the design of environments by foregrounding non-humans within our collective *more-than-human* relationship with water. This focus highlighted empathy as a key element in a "designerly" skillset. The studio was delivered through a combination of both physical and digital engagement, and raises challenges for studio teaching in shifting pedagogical conditions.

The studio focused on immersive and fluid materialities as both the context and content of project development. Students considered the occupation, representation, and sensations of water environments, engaging with critical systems thinking about water environments and cumulative climate change impacts of global warming, rising seas levels, and ocean acidification. The studio questioned the privileging of humans in what has become popularly understood as the age of the Anthropocene (Baskin, 2014; Malm & Hornborg, 2014; Slaughter, 2012). The studio argued that our planet—and its natural forces such as water—could no longer be considered only as objective units of scientific analysis, lacking in agency. Instead, as Bruno Latour reminds us, in this age of the Anthropocene we are liberated from "technoscientific" divisions between nature and society. Our agency is held in *common*; that is, shared and entangled with non-humans and planetary forces alike in a new political arena (Latour, 2014).

Submersion Subversion was devised to encourage students to engage with many kinds of agency in the challenging conditions of the Anthropocene. In this chapter, we consider agency operating at the level of the *designer* (the student) and by the *designer on behalf of the client*. There is also a third kind that might be termed "latent": the agency of the *environment*. The studio provided opportunities for students to uncover a previously untapped more-than-human capacity for action through their investigations, experiments, and proposals during the teaching semester. Students were pushed to discover the agency of their non-human clients and the changing ecological conditions that those other organisms inhabit. The studio aimed to support students to develop their own perspectives on how to act or practise in the Anthropocene—and to be conscious about this. These actions shift the designer from a traditional client-patron model to a model of design practice based on advocacy. In this capacity, the tutor acted as a seeder of epiphany, framing the studio environment and its values through early exercises and relaying representational approaches to assist in responding to these challenges.

For the tutor, this experience prompted questions of the nature of learning and teaching in emerging digital spaces and those physical environments increasingly disrupted by the unevenly experienced impacts of climate change and other planetary transformations. What is the role and the agency of the tutor in these new spaces of learning and learnt experience? And, if both "normal" ecological conditions and disciplinary boundaries are dissolving, what kind of agency can the student designer harness now with a view to likely future turbulence after graduation? The chapter that follows investigates these issues through the discussion of the *Submersion Subversion* studio. It considers the provocations and challenges of the studio, and sets out an overview of studio activities as well as the implications for transforming pedagogies.

Subsection titles highlight the overlap of studio focus, framing, and perspective through the qualities of the wet volumes it explored.

THE STUDIO AS A PROVOCATION

The *Submersion Subversion* studio challenged both students and other contributors with a key question: *How might designers create and practice in an age of discovery and disruption?* Dramatic new contexts for living, resulting from climate change, call for professionals such as designers to map new perspectives, to make unlikely connections, and to propose specific, circumscribed responses to emerging and perhaps unexpected conditions. And yet, if destabilisation and disorder have become the "new normal," what might a designer contribute to such a world? This question must be understood in wider political, and indeed *planetary*, contexts. Many have argued that the term Anthropocene itself has become sanitised and voided of critical enquiry; avoiding the mutual implication of human and non-human actors, and framing ecological concerns either as a type of global humanitarian effort or as technoscientific management of nature, rather than a call for fundamental transformations in theorising culture, power, and unevenly distributed planet-wide relations (Beck, 1996; Brenner & Schmid, 2015; Ernstson & Swyngedouw, 2015; Malm & Hornborg, 2014; Mentz, 2015). Alongside a potentially limited conceptualisation of environmental change, it is suggested that those within the design academy possess a fear of directly engaging with nature, or present themselves as only spatial practice professionals who suggest these conditions are best left to scientists or engineers. This reluctance may become an act of depoliticisation, masking the potential for environments as "a political project that fully endorses human/non-human entanglements and takes responsibility for their nurturing" (Ernstson & Swyngedouw, 2015).

Submersion Subversion embedded this provocation within the title of its studio. *Submersion* was taken at its most literal: to sink out of (our anthropocentric) sight, to immerse in liquid, to plunge into (the unknown), and to be engulfed in (or by) something. *Subversion* aimed to prompt new learning in relation to the Anthropocene. While students were aware of the term's connection to challenging the power and authority of existing institutions, they were less familiar with its Latin root *subvertere*—importantly, the conjunction of *sub* meaning "from below" and *vertere*, meaning "to turn." Students were asked to take the opportunity to rethink their assumptions in the context of rising temperatures, increased ocean acidification, and more frequent and damaging storm surges, and to leverage these new perspectives for those most vulnerable to change, the "more-than-human" inhabitants of liquid environments. Implicit in this framing is the argument that representations of context, and indeed climate change, are not neutral but socially produced and politically charged, and may "aestheticise or paralyse thinking" (Luke, 2015, p. 280). Privilege in the *Submersion Subversion* studio was given over to the literal and metaphorical "from below"—the very creatures below the surface of the water—and both problems and proposals were considered in response to this new understanding. This moved the studio beyond traditional disciplinary boundaries and challenged the conventional position of the interior as a prepared architectural box waiting to be filled in.

Fluid

Throughout the semester, students focused on working with water as a basic material. This foundation established the context and content of all group and individual projects students would pursue through the teaching weeks. "Categories of fluidity" prompted students to:

1. Explore the immersive material qualities of water,
2. consider how it may be experienced and/or articulated through and by the (human and non-human) body,
3. experiment with representations of the occupation(s) and sensation(s) of water environments, and
4. reconcile critical and cumulative impacts of climate change and thinking about global warming, rising sea levels, and ocean acidification through design in these contexts.

Historically viewed as a flat overlay or landscape, large bodies of water are often represented with an apparently voided character. In terms of Western conceptualisations of modernity they may lack the spatial or material characteristics intrinsic to the *landed* experience. By contrast, deep water such as the ocean may instead be understood as a dynamic and emergent space of "relational becoming" (Peters & Steinberg, 2014). The studio suggested that this space could also act as a critical lens for reflexive thinking and designing, liberating us from a long-held landscape surface bias of spatial projects.

The studio reconsidered water as an entity, and the Anthropocene as a contested arena in which to situate these debates. The notion of the Anthropocene is a slippery one, and should not be used without caution. Increasingly used to describe our current era, this age signals a progression from the geologically determined Holocene period that began roughly 10,000 years ago. There is little consensus, however, as to when this new epoch begins, with some suggesting an 18th century Industrial Revolution start date, or even the early 17th-century Western era of exploration, slave trade, and colonisation (Malm & Hornborg, 2014; Mentz, 2015). Others dispute these claims as a function of an Age of Man bias, which ascribes too much to human agency as a species-specific driver for permanent planetary change (Malm & Hornborg, 2014). However, while troubling in itself, this concern is not without its own merit; contestation "radically unsettles, at least potentially, philosophical, epistemological and ontological ground on which both the natural sciences and the social sciences/humanities have traditionally stood" (Baskin, 2014, p. 3).

Seemingly familiar terms such as *water* also need to be considered afresh as complex socio-ecological and political systems in their own right, and are more usefully understood as "water assemblages" (Figure 8.1). They comprise molecular matter, biophysical components, social relationships, decision-making processes, institutional norms and practices, the pragmatics of plumbing, and many other everyday practices that often go without remark (Gibbs, 2012). Central to this re-imagining is the potential to conceive of water assemblages with both power and agency that can shape or prompt events, actions, and reactions across ecological systems.

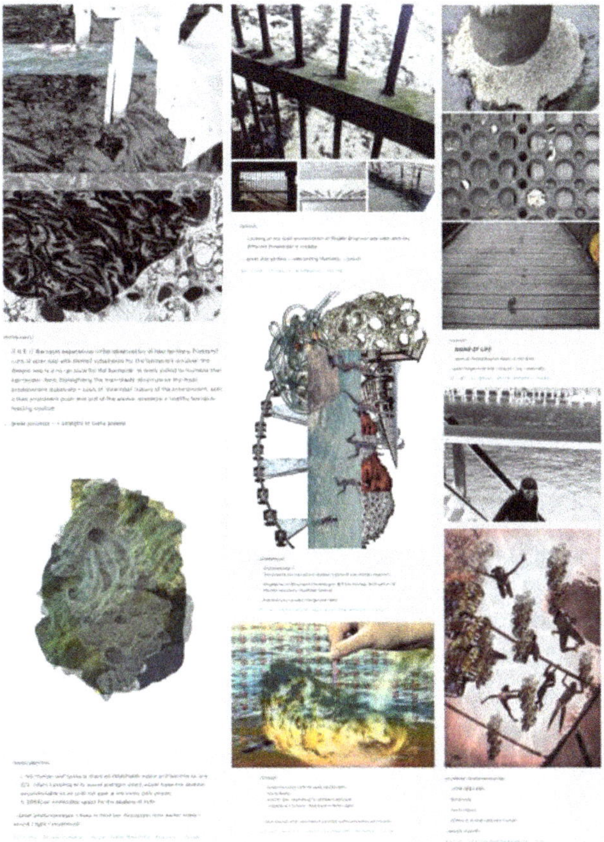

Figure 8.1: Digital and Dynamic Moments of Water Assemblages
Source: Tumblr Screenshots: Student Images and Comments, 2015

Interconnected

Notions of assemblage forced students to rethink their inclination to neatly divide the social from the natural, and also to shield their individual progress from others' eyes. The common impulse to produce neat and bounded categories of the world delineating subjects and objects is rendered absurd in the context of global transformation. As our planet has been so comprehensively impacted by human activity that "even the molecular composition of the atmosphere bears our signature"

(Head, 2016, p. 69), it is clear that we need to reconceive relationships between humans and the non-human. We cannot protect or conserve this *thing* that students refer to as nature, especially by attempting to keep it at a distance from our own actions. Non-humans clearly co-constitute human society, due to our ecological dependence on them and—perhaps more problematically—as a source of protein, clothing, and biogenetic research matter (Panelli, 2010; Philo & Wilbert, 2000). By referring to the more-than-human we seek to reconcile our (human) influence on, and interactions with, the non-human, including the weather, ocean, plants, rocks, and other animals (Head, 2016). The studio looked to acknowledge this hybrid composition as a common world entwined with, and mutually constituted by, the environment and humans (Harrison, 2013; Latour, 2004).

Moreover, the Anthropocene demands that we respond to the challenges of climate change on a planetary scale. In this context, climate is rendered not just as a background condition, but a mode of cultural discourse; as well as the context and content for spatial practice and socially engaged action (Rice, 2011). The interior—when considered as the intimate experience of space—is the site of all negotiations of social interaction. It follows that design for the enclosure of socially-experienced space extends beyond simple architectural pragmatics. The challenge of the studio was therefore to overturn expectations and move beyond disciplinary control.

The studio called for students to radically rethink their position towards interior architecture and, even more importantly, their position as designers and makers in the world. To do this, students were encouraged to develop new communication skills in order to move beyond the usual representations of fixed sites, subjects, and objects that are employed by spatial practitioners. Students were also encouraged to practice the application of new critical and responsive perspectives in the (often literally) disruptive context of the ocean. Finally, the studio provided an arena in which students could question the privileging of perspectives, highlighting the great need for empathy in a designerly skillset.

AN OVERVIEW OF SUBMERSION SUBVERSION

Unbounded

Studio investigations were physically focused on a site at the Middle Brighton Sea Baths, in the south east of Melbourne's Port Phillip Bay. The timber-screened ocean swimming enclosure has been built and rebuilt several times over the past 130 years. The sea baths are some of the last remaining in Australia, recently redeveloped alongside an Art Deco dining pavilion. The enclosed ocean operates as a private recreational centre for the wealthy and older demographic of Melbourne's southeastern bayside suburbs. This liquid leisure facility defines a large interiorised landscape. The strict definition of rigid architectural boundaries is at odds with its fluid and shifting content and sensory experience. Below the surface, many other species besides well-tanned and toned humans can be found: abalone, crabs, barnacles, mussels, sponges, seaweed, and occasional visitors, such as jellyfish, juvenile rays, and penguins.

Individual, small group, and studio-wide projects were presented and discussed in a studio space on campus at MADA (Monash Art Design & Architecture) in Caulfield East. The studio was also *digitally* located on social media platforms via students' ongoing communication of design process, cinematic study, and reflexive critique. Students used the hashtags #submersionsubversion and #madainterior for posts of in-process work to individual Tumblr accounts. These were shared and commented upon by all students and the tutor through the studio's collective account (http://submersionsubversion.tumblr.com). Students were also encouraged to curate what they perceived to be their best works, and to post these images and videos to Instagram as more polished "sneak peeks." Using the same hashtags, this work was picked up by the department's Instagram account (@monashinterior) and reposted to the wider student cohort at MADA, and well beyond. By following each other, and the studio's social media activity, students were able to create a wider *digital studio*—electronically peeking-over-the-shoulders of fellow students, and trialling new ideas in a (mediated) public sphere. This iterative process encouraged students to shift their benchmarking and critique of work beyond the confines of typical student-tutor power relationships. Critical feedback and supportive commentary was sought and provided outside of both the physical and digital studio environments, and new interactions and networks were established between different students, year levels, and graduates. Leveraging this age of destabilisation, the studio pushed beyond the temporal and geographic limits of the campus, reinforcing the pedagogical potential of an extended period of shared process in lieu of the individual drive toward a "hero project image" for the end of semester. A review of students' production and engagement in this digital space is included in the Design Epiphany section below.

Decentred

Visitors were regularly invited into the physical space of the *Submersion Subversion* studio. By way of an example, two-thirds of the way through the semester the studio hosted a public "salon" of work-in-progress, where students were able to discuss their ideas, approaches and experiments with other students, tutors, invited design practitioners, and interested passers-by who happened upon the event. By removing the demands of an assessment framework that often limits capacity to respond and adapt to new engagement, informal discussions that developed from this display meant students could comfortably debate the potential of their approaches before committing to a fixed proposal, and also consider how best to communicate this to a diverse audience. Horizontal networks already created by the social media engagement of students earlier in the semester were expanded and scaled up, ultimately challenging the authority of an anticipated final critique by a design panel jury that typically drives student outcomes in studio. The salon was held several weeks before final studio presentations, and publicised via social media. The invitation to the event asked visitors to observe, engage, and critique the work as they found it, in a rough and pre-finished stage. Students wallpapered the room with their drawings, models, and narratives; and projected cinematic summaries of the design iterations and anticipated futures of their work throughout the space. Projector screens showed looping mash-ups of aquatic documentary scenes and sound recordings of the sea baths made on-site. This mix of performance, process, and possibility created an immersive experience driven by and for students and guests—in keeping with this studio's aims, and in clear contrast to more traditional design studio teaching practices.

It is appropriate that the sea unsettles fixed ideas of space, and that water demands consideration as a paradoxical sensory *thing*. The loose molecular structure and reflective qualities of water allow us an experience that is surface, matter, and depth together at once. Surveillance technologies are disrupted by this subversive materiality, for most scanning methods are unable to capture the depth and obscurity of these spaces (Bélanger, 2014; Elden, 2013; Peters & Steinberg, 2014). We may only experience the rich meaning of water through immersion in its constantly mobile volume. It is also suggested by some authors that this *uncontained* water shapes us, but that knowledge of it can only be gained through repeated (always partial) encounters over time (Bélanger, 2014; Elden, 2013; Peters & Steinberg, 2014). Students were similarly encouraged to regularly test their spatial proposals within water (in the kitchen sink, in the rain, in the sea) and to film, draw or collage dynamic outcomes drawn from this experimentation.

Key moments were visually catalogued, such as:

1. Flotation (above the surface, at the surface, below the surface),
2. submersion (deep beneath the water, by choice, against will),
3. diving (from above, from below, breaching the water surface),
4. swimming (slow, fast, relaxed, in danger),
5. encountering a wave (small, large),
6. approaching the water's edge (hesitant, joyful),
7. the experience of being stranded out at sea, and
8. king tide, storm surge, and heavy rainfall events.

These moments were expanded and refined through critical reflection to become cinematic shorts for wider consumption via social media. Students used filmic methods of non-linear narrative and persuasive storytelling to communicate the deceptive, hidden, and embodied information uncovered as part of their documentation for a digital studio discussion. The use of Tumblr and Instagram to project their design process and conceptual triggers into the public realm enlarged the space and scope of the typically resource-strapped and institutionalised university design studio.

Responsive

For the purposes of assessment, the *Submersion Subversion* studio was presented as six project deliverables, outlined in Table 8.1, with new work iteratively responding to prior actions. Each project was framed by a series of strategies (mapping, physical model-making, observation, cinematic techniques), supporting resources (political texts, site visits, design blogs, films), and design experiences (workshops, material sourcing, large-scale prototyping, salon events, exhibition curation) to reveal alternatives available to those engaging with disruption and discovery.

Table 8.1: Sequence of Studio Actions throughout the Teaching Semester

Project	Critical Operations	Studio Strategies	Student Activities
Weird Science (3 weeks)	Examination of existing ecological conditions, comparative studies of precedent, scientific methods, and experiments documenting contested sites and clients.	Introduction to peers, researching historical records, data collection, mapping site-based experiences, collaborative networks, and a temporary relocation to the ocean.	In small groups students explore the Middle Brighton foreshore and interrogate a variety of ecological interiors (other than the existing captured space of the Sea Baths), and non-human occupants that operate at the threshold of ocean/beach/built form. Speculative photomontages and hand-cast models demonstrate the group findings.
The Protective Cast (3 weeks)	Emphasis on bodily responses to marine environments and temporal conditions of weather/water/ light.	Documentation of non-human shelter and motion, developing narratives through zine production, physical model-making using clay, water, and hand sculpting.	Building on the data collection phase, individual students create a future "protective cast" for an organism (a non-human client) that exists in a defined site to allow it to adjust to rising sea levels and other environmental impacts. Representation via section models, cinematic methods, and narrative techniques of persuasion.
Mid-semester Review (1 week)	The performative nature of interior experiences. Proposing future investigations and responding to critique. Processes of expert engagement and collaboration.	Negotiation with peers, and communication to a wide audience (especially those unfamiliar with non-human design and how it connects with the practice of interior architecture).	Curated presentation of individual and group mappings, data catalogues, cast prototypes, persuasive cinematic studies, detailed section models, and body representations.
The Deep End (2 weeks)	Choreographed and constructed experiences. Physical interventions into space, and the communication of events over time.	Prototyping, time-based documentation, human and non-human observation.	Individually designed spatial education experience proposals within an interiorised water landscape to extend existing bathing program of the Middle Brighton Baths. Swimming and ecological narratives will merge with digital technologies. The designed experience to operate as a shared, even entangled, event between non-human and human clients.

Salon *(1 week)*	Work-in-progress, debate and discussion.	Communication of diverse approaches, individual and group negotiations.	Extended invitation to the public to engage with design processes.
Full Immersion (3 weeks)	Movement of bodies through time, detailed exploration of physical intervention, material specifications, presentation, and communication.	Iterative design processes, new representations of more-than-human relations, refinement of physical proposals.	Resolution of individual proposals with conviction that spatial education experience teaches humans all that non-humans know of the foreshore. Demonstrate non-humans also learn from the shared experience. Creation and coordination of immersive final exhibition and event for end-of-semester presentation.

Reflective remaking of the occupation, representation, and sensation of water environments was critical to studio activities (Figure 8.2). These imagined sites of water as complex ecological interiors consisting of volume, atmosphere, materiality, and depth, as well as a variety of mutually entwined social relations, could be reconfigured through a series of design exercises. Representation of these ecological interiors described a physical space somehow captured within the wider environment, but also showed that the enclosure of such an interior could be ambiguous and ephemeral—the daily tide identified as a possible edge condition, albeit a constantly shifting one. Deliberately ad hoc approaches to experimental practice and exploration encouraged physical immersion to fully comprehend the parameters of the site. Students were invited to move directly into the sea and explore the intertidal zones; to search for non-human clients among the coastal detritus, and to study both the vast scales of the sea and the minutely cascading sensations it provided for their bodies.

Figure 8.2: "Weird Science" as Spatial Practice
Source: Tumblr Screenshots: Student Images and Video Still, with Comments, 2015

Shifting

The studio aimed to be differentiated in conception, but not in its foundation of spatial analysis practice, from the usual starting point of a construction site or built interior project simply waiting to be constructed or refurbished. The complex challenge of responding to a dynamic three-dimensional volume became apparent within weeks of commencing the studio, when students were required to map an ecological interior within the intertidal zone of a local beach as the site for their ongoing investigations during the semester (Figure 8.3). Initial mappings were rendered obsolete at the very next visit (sometimes even just hours after the first) as the combined impact of changing tides, wind patterns, detritus left behind by wave action, and activities of human and non-human inhabitants radically altered the delicate and temporal site previously documented.

Figure 8.3: Map Making and Shifting Conditions
Source: Student Images, 2015

The soft sand, porous rock outcrops, intrusive water behaviour, and other displacements caused by the kicking of footballs, dragging of boogie boards, building of sandcastles, running of dogs, and other everyday activities, all intermingled to imprint heavily upon the landscape—to the despair of students desperate to fix the conditions through standard architectural conventions representing topography. Students soon realised the primacy of temporality in these conditions, and moved to create multiple mappings and video accompaniments that faithfully documented the constantly shifting micro-conditions in this territory. The limitations of representations taught previously in other design studios were uncovered, and students began to develop new modes of communication in order to adapt to this seeming chaos. They researched cinematic precedent, art practice, and choreographic notation techniques and used these discoveries to create hybrid methods of recording, reflecting and re-communicating ecological flux (Figure 8.4).

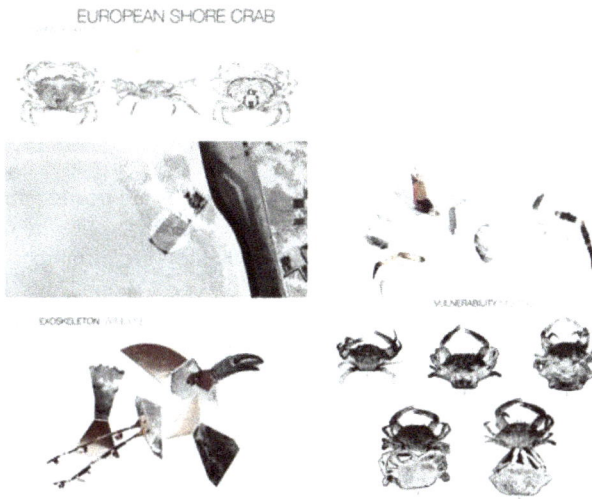

EUROPEAN SHORE CRAB

EXOSKELETON

VULNERABILITY

Figure 8.4: Ecological Interiors in Context
Source: Student Images and Video Stills, 2015

PEDAGOGY

The subsection titles of this chapter have offered qualitative descriptors of the studio concerns: fluid, interconnected, unbounded, decentred, responsive, and shifting. These descriptors are no less evident in the online engagements related to the studio, and in particular, the collective Tumblr account (http://submersionsubversion.tumblr.com).

This online discussion provides an enduring record of the progress of the studio and its developing references and concerns, as well as an example of creative agency and learning in a shared and responsive space. A review of individual student activity offers insight into explorations each was undertaking, and also evidences student's interactions with each other and with the tutor over the course of the semester. As the discussion unfolds for a new reader, students again find examples of projects or images, and suggest their relevance to another's project. Others celebrate the achievements of groups as they prepare a shared site model to support individual schemes. Alongside face-to-face engagements, site visits, and the salon, the studio as a whole develops a trajectory and a set of concerns that offer conceptual landmarks in this fluid space.

Still and moving images, sound, and sketched and textual forms are accompanied by reflections, as well as comments from both studio leader and colleagues. The location of the discussion in the digital realm has offered the opportunity to engage at any time and from any location. Conversations continue, as they can online, in parallel with other aspects of students' lives. Publication of selected images or events via the program's Instagram account offered a further opportunity to extend design work into a public realm, drawing comment from those outside of the studio and of the interior architecture program.

Meanwhile, the shared Tumblr account formed a content-rich timeline that consumed other activities, drawing in images and ideas from digital searches, site visits, design testing, and chance conversations. This record offers evidence of a shared "reflective conversation" (Schön, 1983), in which representations of shared concerns operate alongside those of individual proposals and testing of ideas. They allow the reconceiving of ideas by analogy via Schön's "seeing as," together with his "seeing that" via a construction of design causation. Ideas are posited and revised, and evidence is collated and reallocated to new concerns. At this scale, the representations are still acting to support designerly development, they are "neither 'complete' nor 'objective' … [but] 'operative' in that they are … shaped by [task-relevant] characteristics" (Visser, 2006, p. 122). Visser extends her definition quoting Suchman that such representations make things "visible so that they can be seen, talked about, and potentially, manipulated" (Suchman, 1995, p. 63).

The representations in this digital realm are primarily through referencing and connection to the very wide range of content gathered or linked online, although the records of design tests certainly include sketches and sketch models. The sketching is at a different scale, and forms a multi-handed rhetoric constructed in real time. Individual contributions to the whole create the context as well as offering content for design responses.

Following individual student's posts to the account over the course of the semester offers a different view—the particular within a creative ecosystem. The trajectories of individual students through the studio are evidenced through the volume, the content, and the development of their design ideas, and on this shared Tumblr site are accompanied by students' reflective commentary on the experience and their discoveries. The volume of each post waxes and wanes, with a peak around mid-semester when short posts of single sentences become long strings of images, sketches, and textual consideration.

It is also evident that students' approaches to the project demonstrate different responses to the challenge of balancing more-than-human needs in an ocean environment. Personal concerns are evident within early selected references and align with the proposals each develops. One student commences with posts that focus on ephemerality, celebrating artworks that use water droplets, steam, and reflections. Phenomena that emerge and disperse offer a metaphor that establishes a position on the project and its challenges, and is linked by the student to broader concerns. Speculative photomontage presents translucent images of jellyfish and shadowy shark jaws, with a human form barely in sight. At the conclusion of the project, arrangements of inflatable beads form detached supports for human bodies, sliding across the surface to appear or retreat from the human's world. By contrast, another student commences with images of human bodies submerging in water, and investigates an anemone client's tubular form with tentacles at its opening. Test models are similarly tubular, floating with the aid of inflated containers, and filtering water by the use of frills. Other tests include the wrapping of materials around organic forms including the student's own body, and the final proposal includes a space for human occupation, with waving tentacles at the entrance.

A third student collects images and ideas from a spectacularly broad range of disciplines and content types. Over sixty posts on the shared site demonstrate a productive experimental engagement with scientific research and artistic representation. An early photomontage produced by the student includes the comment: "An exploration of the many human & non-human interactions at sea. This montage focuses on collecting, embracing and immersing ourselves in knowledge of our experiences at sea."

Another montage experiment is inspired by the work of artist Gregory Euclide: "My montage is a scenic representation of space that is collective of all sorts of non-human organisms brought to shore/land and in contact with humans—the human and non-human relationship is explored through this interaction by collection and investigation."

Netting and filtration become key themes explored through materials and precedent research, directly relating to the role of the abalone shell for its fleshy inhabitant, but offering a means to explore the colocation of human and more-than-human life forms at the edge of the oceans. A floating, filtering enclosure at the conclusion of the studio offered sustenance via collection of algae for those who eat it, and support for those who need a rest from swimming.

Each of these examples demonstrates different attempts to resolve the conflict between human and non-human needs that is central to *any* Anthropocene. The design development chronicled on the site demonstrates "exploratory" creativity (Boden, [2004] 1990) in which an existing set of cognitive frameworks is extended via more or less radical transformation (e.g., scale, material), as well as "combinatorial" creativity in which the concepts of one set of frameworks is mapped onto another, or the intersection between these is explored (e.g., via netting). The evidence lies in the reflective comments, and the ongoing design explorations that seek resolution. The first example, above, can be seen as an attempt to translate the ephemeral qualities particular to the ocean (or the other) into a human realm; the second seeks to provide spaces for humans to occupy that mimic the qualities of non-human cohabitants themselves; the third demonstrates an exploration of spatial, systemic, and experiential intersections through material form and scientific representation. Together these approaches form part of a productive, entwined, and responsive system mimicking ocean ecology to focus on and extend the boundaries of the studio experience.

This digital pedagogical space mirrors the physical teaching studio based on the Beaux Arts / Atelier model, in some ways, in that students spent extended periods working alongside each other and contributing to the iterative development of others' schemes. Informal interactions over a drawing board or model are lost, however, when studio teaching becomes a scheduled activity in a "flexible" teaching space, a situation that is all too familiar given current resourcing challenges faced by design departments. The online digital space has been identified as an alternative approach (Zehner et al., 2009) that can take advantage of the (now) familiar practices of social media, as well as an extended space and time for interaction. The *Submersion Subversion* studio and its digital engagements offer a model of this approach.

The role of the tutor deserves special attention in this arrangement. In another mirroring of a traditional studio role, the tutor needed to model the behaviour expected by students online. This included a demonstration of the uses of different digital platforms; for example, as a space to share reflective work in progress within the group (Tumblr), or as a location for finished images presented to the public (Instagram). The collection, sharing and translation of a vast array of resources sourced online was also important to kick-start student activity, as well as to keep new possibilities alive, and to encourage broad exploration by the students themselves. Regular comments on Tumblr are light, positive, and encouraging, characterised by the tutor as "spinning the prayer wheel" to keep the action moving, but also as a means to prompt and test boundaries (including those set or assumed by the students themselves). More broadly, the Tumblr account demonstrates the value placed on the speculative and the development phases of a design proposition, rather than the hero shot at the end. These activities operated alongside more intense interactions in physical studio settings, and on-site visits, but offered ongoing engagement nonetheless.

AGENDA AND EXPERIENCE IN RESPONSE TO THE ANTHROPOCENE

Influenced

The Anthropocene offers a useful lens to describe the nature of accelerated devastation of ecological systems, global warming, rising sea levels, and ocean acidification. The inadequacy of this concept as a pedagogical platform however lies in its unchecked claims and assumptions; that is, a reliance on "planetary managerialism" (Baskin, 2014, p. 6) and "expert" solutions invariably in the form of large-scale technological infrastructure or untested geo-engineering undertakings. Donna Haraway writes that none of the names we use for this age, including "Anthropocene" and "Capitalocene," are the right fit. Instead we "need stories (and theories) that are just big enough to gather up the complexities and keep the edges open and greedy for surprising new and old connections" (2015, p. 160); other such names include "Manthropocene" and "Anthro-obscene" (Ernstson & Swyngedouw, 2015). We should also call for a more radical reconfiguration of design professions so that students become aware of our own "deep-seated anthropomorphism" (Slaughter, 2012, p. 123) that instrumentalises the landscapes, territories, and species assemblages we are entwined with, and instead begin to operate as innovative agents of change outside the conventional modes of spatial practice (Fry, 2009).

The Anthropocene does tend to establish a certain default type—usually Western, white, wealthy, and male—as the *anthropos* (human) centre of this dynamic. By universalising this typical encounter as a species-focused predicament for all humanity, and only humanity, we deny the non-human (simply cast as nature) any agency, and ourselves any variety of response. Placing humans at the centre obscures the intertwined more-than-human experiences of all organisms impacted by these changing circumstances. This framing occludes the diversity of lived experience, the structural inequality of distributed effects, historical responsibility for the causes of climate change, and the cumulative impact of these changes across space and time.

Planetary environmental transformations investigated in this studio were explored through the bodies of intertidal dwellers (such as barnacles, mussels, and abalones), which conveniently also became the project clients for many students. By privileging the small, miniature, and often ignored, the studio sought to introduce students to nuances of empathy and understanding of the other as crucial to designing in the context of rapid environmental change. Sponges, molluscs, crustaceans, echinoderms, and crabs were selected as subjects for the studio, as much for their small-scale and lack of anthropomorphic qualities as for their vulnerability to climate change impacts. Critically for these organisms, the colossal quantity of carbon dioxide (CO_2) absorbed by the ocean in response to our burning of fossil fuels and deforestation changes the chemical composition of marine environments. Indeed, the increased acidity caused by increased CO_2 levels limits the very capacity of marine organisms to maintain or even create their skeletons and shells (Department of the Environment, 2011; International Programme on the State of the Ocean, 2013). The perilous lived experience of water-y bodies was therefore also highlighted. Project briefs integrated storm surges, increasingly regular urban flooding, and the chaos of king tides as parameters over the semester.

Entangled

In its concluding phases, *Submersion Subversion* sought to broaden the perceived agency of student designers as a response to the challenges of discovery and disruption we experience in this Anthropocene. The final project asked students to subvert what they had already learned in the studio, and conduct a scientific investigation of new organisms in their site at the Middle Brighton Sea Baths; that is, the various humans occupying the space. Activities focused on investigating these life forms with the same rigorous experimentation undertaken in response to determining the needs, hopes, and dreams of their earlier non-human clients. Students premised their explorations on the assumption that humans are also strange animals that require observation, objective research, and precise documentation before we can attempt to understand their complex existence. Rather than create an anthropocentric distinction between what or who is valued in design processes, the studio agenda brought all of these bodies—human and non-human—into an expanded more-than-human assemblage of potential discovery for students. By placing all on a similar footing, students were more able to grasp the entangled nature of our Anthropocene, and the necessity for transformed spatial practices in response to its many challenges (Figure 8.5).

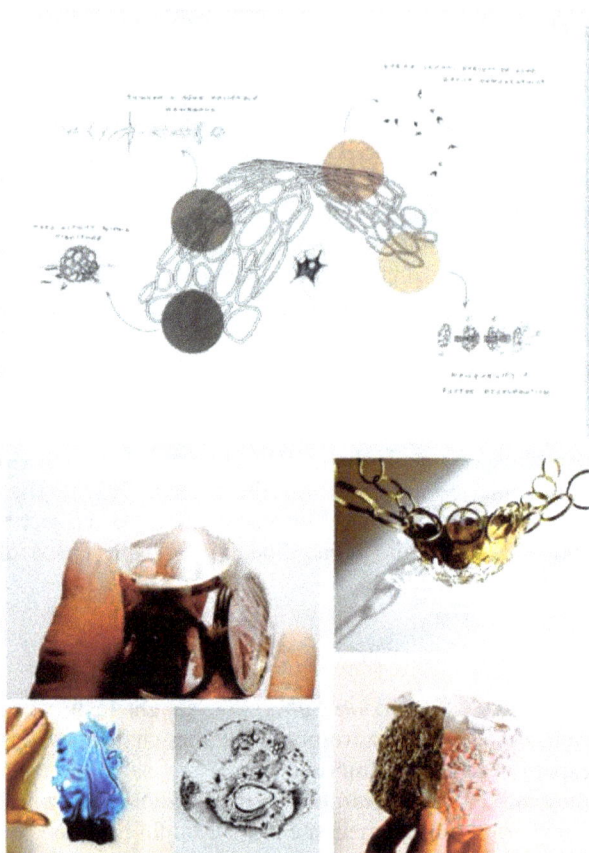

Figure 8.5: Water-y Bodies Understood at Close Range
Source: Student Images and Body Adornment Sketches, 2015

The scope of interior architecture expands significantly once we begin to fully acknowledge the planetary implications of the Anthropocene. This is especially so if we consider spatial practices as fundamentally connected to the intimate exploration of social relations, experience, and sensation. The studio took this position as a starting point for student assumptions, based on the evolving teaching agenda at MADA's Interior Architecture program, and sought to shift this understanding beyond the inside of space. This change aimed to decouple design processes from notions of contained impacts, and encouraged the exploration of interconnected decision-making by students. From the scale of an individual design proposition to the studio-wide coordination of a final immersive multimedia exhibition—via an admittedly steep learning curve in climate change science and environmental politics—students were exposed to the charged potential of spatial and material connectedness. The intersection of evolving ideas of the Anthropocene with a critical development of more-than-human design skills led to a transformed context for the practice of interior architecture by students.

In addition to the projects described above, some of the final projects created by students (Figure 8.6), included:

1. A temporary bio-adhesive bodysuit of barnacle colonies that rejuvenates ocean swimmers' skin before slowly dissolving in the high saline content of the water and providing individual barnacles an opportunity to travel and establish the next site for a new generation of their colonies;

2. a floating sea pavilion that provides therapeutic support for visiting international students (who may have little or no experience of swimming) through an immersive educational introduction to sea sponge functions within intertidal environments, whilst also regenerating seagrass patches in the sea baths that are attractive to sea sponges; and

3. a submerged dazzle-camouflage-style distraction technology that clips on to noise-shy abalones to provide a protective armature and increased security for the vulnerable communities of these organisms who inhabit the sea baths.

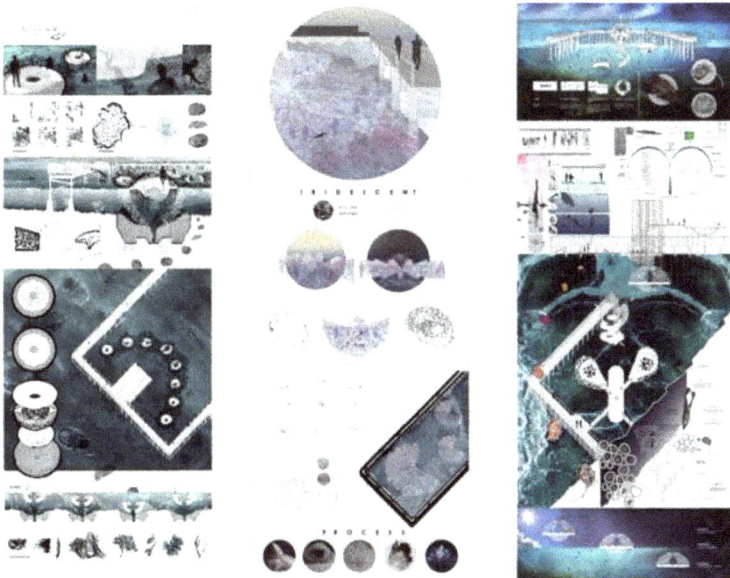

Figure 8.6: Final Presentation Banners of *Full Immersion* Projects, 2015

The final deliverables for each student in studio included, individual items, group models and videos, and the curation of a themed exhibition event to present their end-of-semester work. This was made up of a large hand-sculpted model of the existing landscape constructed by the studio group. It comprised the sea floor and all existing architectural structures on the Middle Brighton Sea Baths site, with a horizontal acrylic surface used to represent water and act as a projection screen for individual cinematic summaries. Each student presented their individual work in several media formats: a zine publication; an oversized banner of collaged oblique drawings, diagrams, and renders; a suite of physical models at various scales; and a cinematic narrative projected onto various surfaces during a final verbal presentation to guest critics. Also, all the students worked together to create an exhibition event for the final presentation of work (Figure 8.7). This included dynamic gallery lighting, data projections, choreographed performances, and soundscapes, as well as colour-matched inner tube seating and ocean-themed snacks for visitors. The final atmosphere was an overwhelming experience of immersion and submersion: a suspension of the typical studio and an otherworldly account of the semester's work.

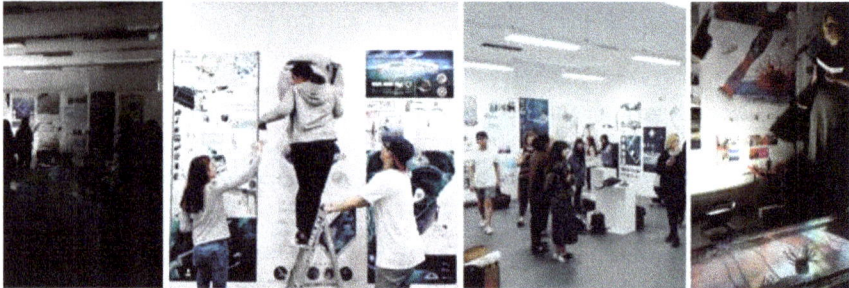

Figure 8.7: Exhibition of *Submersion Subversion* at the
End-of-Semester Presentations, 2015

The ongoing focus on iterative development through intense engagement with their studio peers highlighted entanglement as a fundamental experience of the Anthropocene—and one that can leverage great opportunity from the disruptive nature of our age. The studio consisted of a mix of second- and third-year interior architecture students; all group activities and assessment items required a combination of contributors from each cohort. This guiding parameter encouraged the development of new peer networks and skill transfers between students. An emphasis on small group settings for every discovery activity also shifted student behaviour away from individual and competitive motivations, and towards fostering collaborative networks in the studio. The negotiation of each new disruption to usual studio practices (e.g., trialling new sculpting methods, projecting onto ceiling surfaces in exhibition format, or engaging with new perspectives on interior) was held in the open with all involved in the studio. In these events, the tutor acted in an advisory role rather than as the director or arbiter of action. This shared decision-making and collective engagement was scaffolded via the extension of studio practices into the digital realm by normalising the sharing of in-progress work and inviting commentary from studio peers on Tumblr, and further afield from the public via Instagram.

CONCLUSION

This chapter has considered *Submersion Subversion,* an Interior Architecture design studio at the Monash Art Design & Architecture, Monash University, Australia. The focus of the studio on the sharing of water environments by human and non-human inhabitants has challenged members to move beyond many of the assumptions of a human-centred, land-based (and site boundary-defined) project context. *Submersion Subversion* studied the interior at an ecological scale, considering boundaries between systems, spaces, and occupants as permeable and relative, soluble and negotiated. The form of its delivery, via both physical and online studio modes, has questioned the opportunities of studio interactions, as well as the role of both tutor and student colleagues, in the construction of meaning and intent in creative pedagogy and production. The studio encouraged students to consider the decisions and impact of design within an extending set of connections, and challenged the notion of designerly agency within nested scales that draw on and influence human and more-than-human occupants. The content of the studio has encouraged students to consider new approaches that can extend their current practices. It highlighted the role of empathy, building on an investigation of adaptations developed by non-humans to water environments; first to wonder, second to investigate amplification, and then to ask how human cohabitants might be approached by a designer who supports participation in the Anthropocene.

REFERENCES

Baskin, J. (2014). The ideology of the Anthropocene? *MSSI Research Paper No. 3* (pp. 1–20): Melbourne Sustainable Society Institute, The University of Melbourne. Retrieved from http://sustainable.unimelb.edu.au/sites/default /files/docs/MSSI-ResearchPaper-3_Baskin_2014.pdf

Beck, U. (1996). World risk society as cosmopolitan society? Ecological questions in a framework of manufactured uncertainties. *Theory, Culture & Society, 13*(4), 1–32. http://dx.doi.org/10.1177/0263276496013004001

Bélanger, P. (2014). The other 71 percent. *Harvard Design Magazine, 39,* 3–5. Retrieved from http://www.harvarddesignmagazine.org/issues/39

Boden, M.A. (1990). *The Creative Mind: myths & mechanisms* (2004 ed.). London: George Weidenfeld and Nicolson Ltd.

Brenner, N., & Schmid, C. (2015). Towards a new epistemology of the urban? *City, 19*(2-3), 151–182. doi:10.1080/13604813.2015.1014712

Department of the Environment. (2011). *State of the Environment - Chapter 6: Marine Environment.* Canberra, ACT: Commonwealth of Australia. Retrieved from http://www.environment.gov.au/science/soe/2011

Elden, S. (2013). Secure the volume: Vertical geopolitics and the depth of power. *Political Geography, 34,* 35–51. http://dx.doi.org/10.1016/j.polgeo.2012.12.009

Ernstson, H., & Swyngedouw, E. (2015). Framing the meeting: Rupturing the Anthro-obscene! The political promises of planetary & uneven urban ecologies -

Position paper version 2. Paper presented at the *ANTHRO-OBSCENE Conference: Seminars, lectures & activist forum on political movements, urbanization and ecology*, KTH Environmental Humanities Laboratory, Stockholm, Sweden. Retrieved from http://www.anthro-obscene .situatedecologies.net/framing.html

Fry, T. (2009). *Design futuring: sustainability, ethics and new practice*. Oxford, England: Berg.

Gibbs, L. (2012, August 6). The matter of water [Blog post]. Retrieved from http://www.uowblogs.com/ausccer/2012/08/06/matter-of-water

Haraway, D. (2015). Anthropocene, Capitalocene, Plantationocene, Chthulucene: Making kin. *Environmental Humanities, 6,* 159–65.

Harrison, A. L. (2013). Introduction: Charting posthuman territory. In A. L. Harrison (Ed.), *Architectural theories of the environment: posthuman territory* (pp. 3–36). New York, NY: Routledge.

Head, L. (2016). *Hope and grief in the Anthropocene: Re-conceptualising human–nature relations* (pp. 54–73). London, England: Routledge.

International Programme on the State of the Ocean. (2013). *The state of the ocean report 2013*. Retrieved from http://www.stateoftheocean.org/wp-content /uploads/2015/10/State-of-the-Ocean-2013-report.pdf

Latour, B. (2004). *Politics of nature: how to bring the sciences into democracy* (C. Porter, Trans.). Cambridge, MA: Harvard University Press.

———. (2014). Agency at the time of the Anthropocene. *New Literary History, 45,* 1–18. http://dx.doi.org/10.1353/nlh.2014.0003

Luke, T. W. (2015). The climate change imaginary. *Current Sociology, 63,* 280–296. http://dx.doi.org/10.1177/0011392114556593

Malm, A., & Hornborg, A. (2014). The geology of mankind? A critique of the Anthropocene narrative. *Anthropocene Review, 1,* 62–69. http://dx.doi.org/10.1177/2053019613516291

Mentz, S. (2015). Enter Anthropocene, c.1610. Retrieved from http://arcade.stanford.edu/blogs/enter-anthropocene-c1610

Panelli, R. (2010). More-than-human social geographies: posthuman and other possibilities. *Progress in Human Geography, 34,* 79–87. http://dx.doi.org/10.1177/0309132509105007

Peters, K., & Steinberg, P. E. (2014). Volume and Vision: Toward a Wet Ontology. *Harvard Design Magazine, 39,* 124–129. Retrieved from http://www.harvarddesignmagazine.org/issues/39

Philo, C., & Wilbert, C. (2000). Animal spaces, beastly places. In C. Philo & C. Wilbert (Eds.), *Animal spaces, beastly places* (pp. 1–35). Abingdon: Taylor & Francis.

Rice, C. (2011). The inside of space: Some issues concerning heterogeneity, the interior and the weather. In M. Hensel, C. Hight, & A. Menges (Eds.), *Space Reader: Heterogenous Space in Architecture* (pp. 185–193). London, England: Wiley.

Schön, D. A. (1983). *The Reflective Practitioner: How Professionals Think in Action.* New York, NY: Harper Colophon/Basic Books.

Slaughter, R. A. (2012). Welcome to the anthropocene. *Futures, 44,* 119–26. http://dx.doi.org/10.1016/j.futures.2011.09.004

Suchman, L. (1995). Making work visible. *Communications of the ACM, 38*(9), 56–64. http://dx.doi.org/10.1145/223248.223263

Visser, W. (2006). *The Cognitive artifacts of designing.* Mahwah, NJ: Lawrence Erlbaum Associates.

Zehner, R., Forsyth, G., Musgrave, E., Neale, D., de la Harpe, B., Peterson, F., & Frankham, N. (2009). *Studio Teaching Project Final Report.* Strawberry Hills, NSW, Australia.

Transformative Pedagogies and the Environment

CHAPTER 9

The Anthropocene as a Transformative Pedagogical Platform

Dr. Josh Wodak

ABSTRACT

This essay provides an overview of the centrality of the "Anthropocene" and its relevance for transformative pedagogy in tertiary education. Across all disciplines around the world, there is widespread recognition that we now face environmental changes and crises unprecedented in recorded history. These intractable and compounding challenges not only pose profound ramifications for civilisation in the 21st century, but also for the future of life on Earth. How then can the Anthropocene be a platform from which to develop transformative pedagogy for such environmental challenges?

The chapter is framed through a survey of nascent art and design curriculum on the Anthropocene at universities around the world, to explore the potential for Anthropocene specific pedagogy in relation to art and design education that has atomised related environmental challenges, such as climate change, consumerism, globalization, and food security. To explore what sort of art and design education would be appropriate for the Anthropocene, the chapter draws on the author's research on developing art and design curriculum on the Anthropocene, including a critical reflection of the author's pedagogy in art and design on the Anthropocene.

The first project discussed is the 2014–2016 "Anthropocene Curriculum" project, at Haus der Kulturen der Welt, Berlin, where the author was one of 100 Early Career Researchers from across the natural sciences, physical sciences, social sciences, humanities, art, and design who undertook a nine-day workshop in 2014 on the Anthropocene as a transformative pedagogical platform. The second project discussed is the "Anthropocene Kitchen," the first teaching project on the Anthropocene at UNSW Art & Design, which was also one of the first university courses in Australia to engage with the Anthropocene in the disciplines of art or design.

WELCOME TO THE ANTHROPOCENE

The Anthropocene is a scientific hypothesis based on the assumption that humanity has become a global Earth system factor in sectors such as water circulation, climate, biological productivity, biodiversity, geobiochemical cycles, sedimentation patterns, and overall use of lands and seas. If this hypothesis is correct, and all available data corroborate its correctness, it has a great range of implications … we have managed, inadvertently and unconsciously, to strain these same environmental conditions to their limits. (Leinfelder, 2013, p. 9)

Across all disciplines around the world, there is widespread recognition that we now face environmental changes and crises unprecedented in recorded history (Chakrabarty, 2009; Yusoff, 2009). These intractable and compounding challenges not only pose profound ramifications for civilisation in the 21st century, but also for the future of life on Earth (Oreskes & Conway, 2014). In addition to Leinfelder's above catalogue of anthropogenic influences on the global Earth system, we are in the midst of the Sixth Extinction, being the sixth such mass extinction event since the Cambrian explosion 570 million years ago (Kolbert, 2015). However, in contrast to prior mass extinctions, the causal agent is not asteroids, volcanoes, or other such planetary scale catastrophes. The principal causal agent is human actions, to the extent that scientists argue Earth has been shifted into the Anthropocene—the "Age of Humans"—a new geological era dominated by humans as geological agents (Steffen et al., 2011; Lewis & Maslin, 2015).

The extent to which human actions are pushing the global environment into chaotic realms far removed from the stabilities of the Holocene is tantamount to carrying out an unplanned and unintentional experiment on the biosphere and atmosphere, the results of which risk irreversibly transforming the planet into one that would be unrecognisable by the end of this century (Stilgoe, 2015). Of these environmental challenges, anthropogenic climate change constitutes the most immediate and pressing "superwicked" problem. Attempts to mitigate climate change through international negotiations and policy are widely held not to be addressing the problem in the time and scale required to avert catastrophic levels of climate change, defined as being greater than 2°C warming over pre-industrial levels by the end of this century (Flannery, 2015; Steffen, Broadgate, Deutsch, Gaffney, & Ludwig, 2015). In conjunction with the other "sectors" identified by Leinfelder above, the global biophysical changes that collectively constitute the Anthropocene present a profound transformative platform for all sectors of society, including the focus of this chapter, transformative pedagogy for art and design.

Given the all-encompassing nature of the term "the Anthropocene," the scientific hypothesis has recently become the subject of intense scientific research since it was first formalised by atmospheric chemist Paul Crutzen in 2000 (Crutzen & Stoermer, 2000; Crutzen, 2002). Formally validating the Anthropocene, including defining its official starting date, is the current focus of significant and timely debate such as in the publication of *Transformative Pedagogies and the Environment: Creative Agency through Contemporary Art*. Under the auspices of the Subcommission on Quaternary Stratigraphy, a constituent body of the International Commission on Stratigraphy (ICS), the Anthropocene Working Group was formed in 2009 to formally determine the scientific validity of the proposed geological era. In 2016 they submitted their recommendation to the ICS to formally establish the term, with a provisional starting year of 1950 (Voosen, 2016). The level of scientific scrutiny and inherent conservatism for formal ratification of geological divisions is formidable. A Global Boundary Stratotype Section and Point (GSSP) is a reference point denoting a discernable change in stratigraphic layers, which defines the lower boundary of each geological era, eon, or epoch.

To place the Anthropocene in its immediate geological context, the Holocene era translates to "recent era," referring to the time interval since the last ice age ended 11,700 years ago, which encompasses all human history since the beginning of agriculture around 11,500 years ago. The Holocene featured an abnormally stable and warm climate relative to the 2.5 million year era immediately preceding it, the Pleistocene, when the severity of fluctuations between glacial and inter-glacial periods are argued to have made agriculture physically impossible (Richerson, Boyd, & Bettinger, 2001; Sage, 1995). The starting date for the Holocene was only formally ratified by the ICS and IUGS in 2009 on the basis of its GSSP marked by an abrupt shift in deuterium 1,492.25 metres deep in a Greenland ice core (Walker et al., 2009). That the ICS is receiving a formal proposal only eight years later, in 2016, to define a new geological era, speaks of just how rapidly the spectre of the Anthropocene is being scientifically identified. This proposal may in turn require a radical redefinition of the formal time span of the Holocene.

For instance, the first atomic bomb detonation in 1945 in New Mexico is the most formidable contender for the formal boundary marker between the end of the Holocene and the start of the Anthropocene (Zalasiewicz et al., 2015). The radionuclides from this detonation form a detectable anthropogenic imprint on the global stratigraphic layer that will persist into the geological record, and thus fit the criteria for a GSSP. 1945 is also contemporaneous with the advent of the Great Acceleration, when socio-economic and global Earth system trends all began to significantly increase (Steffen et al., 2015). The extent of the biophysical changes during this time interval have rendered such place-specific 20th-century environmental challenges as population increase, pesticides, soil erosion, industrial effluent and so on as relatively innocuous against the 21st-century environmental challenges that collectively constitute the Anthropocene, where the challenges and the complexity of their causality operate simultaneously at a local and global scale; for example, ocean acidification, the stratospheric ozone layer, and the phosphorus cycle.

In terms of responses to 20th-century environmental challenges, Rachel Carson's landmark publication *Silent Spring* (1962) is considered the origin text for the post-war environmental movement. Her fidelity to evidencing the place-based deleterious effects of pesticides in the USA was unparalleled in its time. However, a 21st-century version would be *Silent Biosphere*, as the environmental challenges of the Anthropocene operate at temporal and spatial scales orders of magnitude larger than the terrestrial ecosystems in a sub-continent documented over decadal time intervals in *Silent Spring*. That is, the Anthropocene encompasses such place- and time-specific environmental challenges, in conjunction with those that will be stratigraphically detectable many millions of years from now. In *The Earth After Us: What Legacy Will Humans Leave in the Rocks?* (2008), Jan Zalasiewicz, Chair of Anthropocene

Working Group, outlines that the technofossils of the "human stratum" that will remain are concrete, plastic, metal, cities, and other human creations.

The rapid increase in scientific research supporting a formal definition of the Anthropocene is occurring against the backdrop of increasing sociocultural engagement with the concept, which is the focus of this chapter. However, while the scope and incomparable importance of the term is readily accepted in scientific domains, in art and design the term has only much more recently become a site of research. In art and design, the "Anthropocene Project" at the House of World Cultures (HKW) in Berlin (2013–2016) is considered the first large scale international project, while *Anthropocene Humanities*, the 2012 annual conference of the Consortium of Humanities Centres and Institutes (CHCI) in Canberra, Australia, is considered the first large scale international project in the humanities. The status of these respective key points (2013 and 2012) are determined in part by the scale and scope of their respective organisations: HKW as one of the world's leading contemporary art organisations, and CHCI as the most formidable and reputable global organisation for the humanities.

Prior engagement with the Anthropocene in the humanities and creative arts has generally been of a more limited scale. For example, the author was one of the conveners of *The Arts of Environmental Anxiety: A Multi-Media Event*, which featured academic presentations and performing arts events on the Anthropocene at the National Museum of Australia, Canberra in 2009. However, it is only in the last couple of years the term has been the subject of sustained investigation, through two large scale high profile exhibitions: *The Great Acceleration: Art in the Anthropocene*, the 2015 Taipei Biennial, the first international art biennial with this focus; and *Welcome to the Anthropocene* exhibition at the Deutsches Museum, 2014–2016, the first large-scale exhibition on the Anthropocene, in which the author exhibited.

STATE OF THE ART: EXISTING UNIVERSITY CURRICULUM ON THE ANTHROPOCENE

In line with how the Anthropocene has rapidly become a field of research in the past five years across art, design, humanities, and social sciences, there is likely to be a significant increase in Anthropocene-specific university curricula in light of developments such as the Anthropocene Working Group's formal submission to the ICS in August 2016 (Voosen, 2016). In the context of this timeline, it is unsurprising that the formal development of university curricula on the Anthropocene in these disciplines is similarly recent. Research by the author indicates that as of 2016 there were less than a dozen Anthropocene-specific courses outside of the sciences, which are generally post-graduate electives in the environmental humanities at Euro-American universities. The pace at which biophysical and sociocultural events are unfolding has repercussions for current undergraduate students going through university at a time when the Anthropocene has become a site of concerted investigation in art and design, but before existing curricula have been reconsidered in light of this paradigm shift and the concept has been integrated into existing curricula.

In Australia, the term is now part of the glossary for Senior Secondary Curriculum in Geography (classified within Humanities and Social Sciences) and is defined as:

> An informal term commonly used to define the most recent period of geologic time. It is used to highlight the extent to which human activities have impacted on the Earth's ecosystems. Evidence of human impact such as the proliferation and spread of managed and constructed elements of environments – together with climate change, habitat loss and species extinctions – are cited by scientists as evidence that human impact has significantly changed the nature of the earth's biodiversity. (Australian Curriculum Geographic Glossary v7.1, 2015)

Since 2014, the author has taught on the Anthropocene to more than 400 students at UNSW Art & Design; however, when asked if they had heard of the term all students responded in the negative, except for those who had taken prior courses by the author. Similarly, during the 2013 development phase of the Anthropocene Project at HKW and the Deutsches Museum the curators' surveys found that 86 percent of the institution's visitors had not heard of the term (Robin et al., 2014, p. 7).

In light of the current level of Anthropocene-specific university curricula, the following draws on the nascent state of existing literature on Anthropocene pedagogy in art and design, in tandem with more established lines of enquiry in science and geography. In so doing, it offers an art and design response to articles about Anthropocene pedagogy, such as "What Sort of Geographical Education for the Anthropocene?" (Pawson, 2015) and "The Anthropocene Mass Extinction: An Emerging Curriculum Theme for Science Educators" (Wagler, 2011). This gap in the literature exists in many disciplines outside of science, which has been the focus of Anthropocene studies to date. Pawson argues that there is considerable scope to develop Anthropocene pedagogy in the humanities and social science as to date "much less attention has been paid to the social implications, such as the dissolution of the division between humanity and nature that broadly held in the west for two millennia, or the suddenness with which previously predictable historical experience has begun to change" (2015, p. 306).

The unifying and all-encompassing nature of the Anthropocene itself raises a pressing relevance for art and design pedagogy on the Anthropocene. Both Pawson and Wagler highlight commonalities between geology, as the seat of Anthropocene research and field in which the term originated, and all non-geology disciplines, in part due to how geology is routinely concerned with interrelated and massive global processes and their inherent "catastrophes." Pawson, working from within geology, remarks how "for many people beyond the discipline of geology … the Anthropocene as social concept is beginning to encapsulate anxiety: anxiety about the human future, about risk, and about limits. It conveys a prophetic sense of concern and unease about people's place in nature, the very thing that the embrace of industrial capitalism was supposed to remove" (2015, p. 307).

In response to such anxiety, the unifying and all-encompassing nature of the Anthropocene is being used to construct greater collaboration across disciplines, with the aim of facilitating better understanding of the myriad implications of the hypothesis. In the past three years, three journals have been launched on the Anthropocene. Two of these, *Anthropocene*, and *Elementa: Science of the Anthropocene*, chiefly concern the scientific, technical, and engineering aspects of the hypothesis. In contrast, the third, *The Anthropocene Review*, was announced in 2014 by its founders as providing the basis for creating collaboration across an even broader range of disciplines. Their opening article was "The Anthropocene Review: Its Significance, Implications and the Rationale for a New Transdisciplinary Journal" (Oldfield et al., 2014). Thus far, this has included articles on museology, historiography, and critical thinking.

In tandem, this chapter discusses the implications of how such pedagogy has emerged from the sciences and progressed into art and design. This pedagogy has been facilitated through the cross-disciplinary innovation of scientists such as Reinhold Leinfelder, whose definition of the Anthropocene began this chapter. Leinfelder is a geologist, reef geobiologist, museologist, and communication scientist at the Freie Universität, Berlin. He has championed the use of the concept of the Anthropocene as a way to develop transformative pedagogy across all disciplines. These initiatives include the two main projects that are the subject of this chapter:

1.   The Anthropocene Project at HKW, co-initiated, developed and facilitated by Leinfelder, in which the author participated for the 2014 HKW "Anthropocene Campus," and

2.   The "Anthropocene Kitchen" research project at Humboldt University, directed by Leinfelder, which included a collaborative project between UNSW Art & Design students and the author.

Before considering these case studies of Anthropocene pedagogy in art and design, it is instructive to first contextualise the existing uptake of the subject in university curricula more broadly, as this uptake determines the potential of the concept to operate as a transformative pedagogical platform.

In his 2012 article "Welcome to the Anthropocene," Richard Slaughter provides a global survey of university engagement with the Anthropocene. Slaughter frames the term according to the fields of future studies and social innovation, which critically examine contemporary trends, whether prevalent or rare, with a speculative forward-looking perspective. In accord with many such surveys of university engagement with the Anthropocene, Slaughter's argument holds true: "as far as I'm aware, not one university anywhere in the world has taken up the challenge set out so clearly by Don Aitkin, former Vice Chancellor of the University of Canberra, more than a decade ago" (Slaughter, 2012, p. 123). It is worth quoting Aitkin's 1997 assessment on university engagement with 21st century environmental challenges as it offers a rare example of a frank disclosure of the discrepancy between university curricula and these challenges:

> It seems to me that humanity may have only two generations left in which to sort out how to modify the impact of the human species on the planet. If it does not learn how to do that, then the world is likely to experience a catastrophe even more severe than that of the Roman Empire. Compared with 1500 years ago, we do know in some detail what is happening and we know at least some of what needs to be done. Moreover, we understand that where we do not know something, we can set about finding it out. The principle institution in humanity's race to save itself, if we set aside enlightened governments, is the modern university. (Aitkin in Slaughter, 2012, p. 123)

The level of university curricula needed to match the timeframe of the challenges Aitkin identified in 1997 continues to cause consternation in literature around Anthropocene pedagogy (Thomas, 2004; Jagodzinski, 2013). Given that literally all biophysical "sectors" in Leinfelder's usage, and all human sectors (such as social, cultural, economic, and psychological) are inextricably enmeshed in the Anthropocene there is immense potential for universities to increase transformative learning and ecological literacy in all curricula, from A (accounting) to Z (zoology). While zoology as a book-end for the alphabet may appear more immediately relevant to the Anthropocene, Kala Saravanamuthu, from the Newcastle Business School at the University of Newcastle, Australia, argues that the Anthropocene is immediately relevant at the opposite end of the alphabet in accounting curricula. In his article "Instilling a Sustainability Ethos in Accounting Education through the Transformative Learning Pedagogy: A Case-Study," Saravanamuthu describes his use of transformative pedagogy to "challenge the unproblematic perpetuation of economic rationalism in accounting's predominately technical curriculum, and sow the seeds of a sustainability ethos" (2015, p. 1). For the intervening letters of the alphabet one could randomly select a course for each letter and find disciplinary-specific relevance to the Anthropocene for each of them.

A decade after Aitkin's sombre assessment of the timeframe to respond to environmental challenges, the Australian Vice-Chancellor's Committee articulated their "Policy on Education for Sustainable Development," which included that its members

> build capacity in the community by educating the next generation of professionals and leaders to become fully aware of sustainability: for students, consider embedding elements of sustainability at appropriate levels in academic programs; for staff, consider implementing Professional Development programs on sustainability themes. (AVCC, 2006, p. 1)

A decade later, in 2016, this capacity remains unfulfilled, with educational theorists such as Ian Thomas from Australia's RMIT School of Global Studies, Social Science and Planning citing the biophysical impossibility of the out-dated notion of "Sustainable Development" as further diminishing the building of such capacity (2009, p. 246).

In his own 2015 survey of the state of Anthropocene pedagogy, Matthew Nisbet, an Associate Professor of Communication at Northeastern University, USA, writes of how "universities and colleges will play a central role by sponsoring interdisciplinary courses, degree programs and related initiatives" in terms of forging a "hopeful path forward in the Anthropocene." In this endeavour transformative learning emerges as a relevant pedagogical methodology, wherein "the goal is not for students, faculty and staff to choose among competing perspectives about the Age of Us and its many problems and opportunities. Instead, the purpose is to acquire skills, experience and connections that help the campus community grapple with the Anthropocene's many tensions and uncertainties" (Nisbet, 2015). For Nisbet, art and design have a distinct contribution to realising this "catalyst role." According to his breakdown of the relationship between the four principal academic disciplines:

> Problems like climate change require that efforts to engage students and campuses be truly multi-disciplinary, bridging the expertise of the four major academic disciplines ... the sciences provide data and models that allow us to understand the world and to make predictions. Philosophy and religion help us recognize what is good, what is right, and what is of value. The social sciences provide theories and data that enable us to understand societal choices and decisions. The creative arts and communication professions tell inspiring stories that shape human actions, promote learning and encourage critical self-reflection. (Nisbit, 2015)

While this model overly simplifies disciplinarity and academia, it is still useful for a broad schema of the role that art and design may play, particularly around encouraging "critical self-reflection," with transformative pedagogy as the principal methodology to do so.

WHAT SORT OF ART AND DESIGN EDUCATION FOR THE ANTHROPOCENE?

Having covered the broader relevance of art and design to engaging with the Anthropocene, the following outlines the requirements for the concept to become a transformative pedagogical platform. The literature on Anthropocene pedagogy for art and design shares many of the same requirements that are extensively cited in existing literature for sustainability and ecological literacy in art and design. Educational theorist Joanna Boehnert provides a survey of the current state of such pedagogy in her 2015 article "Ecological Literacy in Art & Design Education: A Theoretical Introduction." Her conclusions are broadly representative of such survey literature, including Slaughter's survey of university engagement with the Anthropocene, noted above, namely that sustainability and ecological literacy is next to non-existent across university disciplines, being confined to a "token 'green week' fashion" as "an elective that staff and students can decide to ignore" (Boehnert, 2015, p. 1).

While there is considerable potential for the Anthropocene to become a transformative pedagogical platform, the first requirement of this development would be an exponential increase in sustainability and ecology literacy, as any concerted engagement with the Anthropocene is best built upon a working literacy of these fields. In terms more specific to the basis of *transformation*, if students are to be taught *how* to think through a process of transformative learning, they must already have at least an introduction to *what* their topic entails. The subject matter of the Anthropocene requires an understanding accessible to non-scientists: first of the scientific basis of the Anthropocene in geology, biology, physics, and chemistry; and second, a framing of the subject from the field of environmental humanities in history, philosophy, and ethics.

These diverse disciplines can be thought of as individual elements, where the assembly of the elements is determined by the aim of the particular pedagogy. In art and design, this aim is more closely aligned to the field of environmental humanities, in seeking to facilitate the *how* of students' thinking. Nevertheless, in surveying existing curricula of the Anthropocene in the humanities and social sciences, what constitutes a well-assembled curriculum is generally a specific aspect of the Anthropocene, such as its implications for environmental justice or social justice. While art and design curricula on the Anthropocene have a different pedagogical aim to non-art or design disciplines, their assembly ideally utilises elements from material that would otherwise form an entire semester-long course in science, humanities, and social science. Such seemingly onerous requirements for art and design pedagogy reinforce the necessity of students to gain a rudimentary knowledge of sustainability and ecology, requiring great sensitivity and potentially onerous responsibility for the educator. In their polemical article "Learning about Global Issues: Why Most Educators Only Make Things Worse," David Hicks and Andy Bord argue that the required sensitivity and responsibility create a "paradox" that lies "at the heart of this issue." They ask:

> By what right do we expose young people to the extensive traumas of the world? Is this not some sort of betrayal of those students who do have great enthusiasm for life? Many first year students arrive with what might be described as false hope or unrealistic optimism about the world, partly through lack of knowledge but also because they themselves have yet to be tempered by life. In a sense the task is an existential one – to shatter their innocence about the human condition so that a more grounded journey can begin. The real betrayal would be not to awaken them to the human/global condition.... A true sense of empowerment thus comes from both head and heart – but this requires educators who have also worked through these issues for themselves. (Hicks & Bord, 2001, p. 424)

Hicks and Bord have found that this "paradox" exists across all disciplines, and it has been the subject of their research at the School of Education at Bath Spa University College, UK.

Leinfelder addresses a different aspect of the pedagogical responsibilities created by the Anthropocene in his article "Assuming Responsibility for the Anthropocene: Challenges and Opportunities in Education." These are the responsibilities for how educators may facilitate the Anthropocene becoming a transformative pedagogical platform, rather than the sensitivity issues in so doing that concern Hicks and Bord. To explore these responsibilities, Leinfelder outlined the requirements and challenges for meeting such a pedagogical responsibility. One of the key challenges he identifies is how the concept of the Anthropocene rejects the western "intellectual tradition characterized by atomism, mechanism, anthropocentrism, rationalism, individualism" (2013, p. 2). Leinfelder argues that:

> Education about environmental problems, when it occurs at all, usually presents them as discrete and isolated, often prioritizing certain problems over others. Is it more important to address climate change than biodiversity loss? Isn't food and water availability the primordial problem? Hence another educational challenge is to make the interconnectivity of processes and anthropogenic influence understandable. (2013, p. 11)

To counter this "educational challenge" Leinfelder provides a critical reflection on his membership of the German Advisory Council on Global Change (WBGU), a large-scale project where academics advised the German government on how to comprehensively respond to 21st-century environmental challenges. In conjunction with scientific reports and policy advice (WBGU, 2011; WBGU, 2013), this WBGU project resulted in *The Great Transformation: Climate – Can We Beat the Heat?* (Hamann, Zea-Schmidt, & Leinfelder, 2014). This was a comic book about the Anthropocene by artists and designers, commissioned by the WGBU to visualise and translate their 2011 report *World in Transition – A Social Contract for Sustainability* for entirely new audiences outside of academia, policy, and governance, through the medium of the graphic novel. The transformative nature of the subject matter and the pedagogy is expressed on the rear of the book cover:

> A major transformation is needed to stop climate change; in other words, we have to learn to live and to produce what we need in sustainable ways. Any transformation of society must begin in people's minds; only then can it be achieved technically with any chance of economic success. Scientists, politicians and citizens will have to work together to achieve this. In this comic, nine top scientists, the members of WBGU as comic-book heroes, show us that we can beat the heat – and how to do it! (Hamann, Zea-Schmidt, & Leinfelder, 2014)

The book was produced and edited by Leinfelder in collaboration with Alexandra Hamann and Claudia Zea-Schmidt. Leinfelder and Hamann collaborated on a subsequent graphic novel about the Anthropocene through Leinfelder's Anthropocene Kitchen project, discussed below.

Across all these domains—science reports, policy, and art-based research—Leinfelder foregrounds the centrality of transformation: in society, in education, and in the biophysical world-at-large. Under the heading "The Role of Education in a Social Contract for a Great Transformation" he argues that "A 'Great Transformation' will require that individual states and the global community facilitate transformative processes through top-down regulations, whereas NGOs, innovative thinkers, visionary companies, and societal movements will play a bottom-up role as pioneers of change" (Leinfelder, 2013, p. 13). Furthermore, he argues that realising such a transformative "societal movement" is based on education, which

> must be embedded in new forms of transformative and transdisciplinary education in order to allow the participation, discourse, reflection, and societal structures that are necessary for a transformation towards an Anthropocene that allows fair use and development chances for future generations. Such a knowledge-based transformation movement will therefore have to begin with new forms of education. (2013, p. 13)

These "new forms" are based around harnessing the different qualities of "transformative education" versus "transformation education." Leinfelder defines the former as stemming from actual "'transformative' processes" with "research and education directed towards finding concrete solutions to specific problems." The corresponding mode of education—transformative—accordingly concerns "causal relations for transformation processes, on learning from history, as well as on the interaction between society, the Earth system, and technological development, and above all on human preconditions for change" (2013, p. 14). In contrast, the subject of "transformation education" is derived from actual "'transformative' processes" concerning "research and education which focus on the larger contexts: how we have gotten where we are and what conditions are necessary for realizing the Great Transformation."

Transformative education is *about* the global transformations occurring under the advent of the Anthropocene and is analogous to Boehnert's arguments for sustainability and ecology literacy as prerequisites for Anthropocene pedagogy. Transformation education is the desired pedagogical platform of the Anthropocene: for education *itself* about such transformations to be transformative. The pedagogy would then possess the quality of teaching *how* to think, ideally drawing on *what* students have already been taught, if sustainability and ecology literacy are regarded as prerequisite education. For this to occur Leinfelder argues "transformative education … must cease to be treated as unidirectional knowledge transfer and instead be embedded in a culture of reflection and discussion" (2013, pp. 13–14).

The etymological similarity between "transformative" and "transformation" requires clear delineation, especially as both terms are required in order for the Anthropocene to become a coherent pedagogical platform. In their article *Click, Clack, Move: Facilitation of the Arts as Transformative Pedagogy* educational theorists Elinor Vettraino, Warren Linds, and Linda Goulet define these terms to demonstrate their similar meanings and the slippage that can occur between them:

> Transformative pedagogy is the ethos, process, and approach to learning/education that entails creating spaces, where critical questioning of the world is possible.... Through the reframing of views of the world, personal and social transformation becomes possible. Transformative

> learning is the product of transformative experiences and pedagogical approaches and also potentially a process in its own right. Central to our understanding of transformational learning is the emphasis on actualization of the person and society through liberation and freedom. (2013, p. 4)

While the authors define these terms in relation to their art-based pedagogy, their usage is not directed toward sustainability or ecology literacy per se. To illustrate the purchase of ecological literacy for the authors' "critical questioning of the world", two of the key terms used in their above quote, *liberation* and *freedom*, are seen in a distinctly different light when viewed through the framework of the Anthropocene. In "The Climate of History: Four Theses," Dipesh Chakrabarty lays bare his "critical questioning" of such terms in one of the most widely lauded articles about the Anthropocene: "In no discussion of freedom in the period since the Enlightenment was there ever any awareness of the geological agency that human beings were acquiring at the same time as and through processes closely linked to their acquisition of freedom...The mansion of modern freedoms stands on an ever-expanding base of fossil-fuel use." (2009, p. 208)

Boehnert's definition of "transformative" and "transformation" aligns with that of Vettraino, Linds, and Goulet while also incorporating Chakrabarty's revelatory reappraisal of such basic presumptions as "freedom" and "liberty." In so doing, Boehnert also outlines why transformative pedagogy is problematic for the subject of the Anthropocene. This arises from how "transformative learning involves becoming aware of one's assumptions in order to address issues from a critical perspective and take action on the basis of new knowledge" so that the pedagogy "engages an ecological view of education that is relational, holistic, participatory and practical." Despite the admirable merits of such pedagogy, Boehnert argues in her article "Transformative Learning for Sustainable Education" that it stands in opposition to the general tenet of university education:

> While transformative learning is a process with the potential to transcend the notorious value/action gap that divides our awareness of environmental threats from our capacity to take appropriate action, it remains a severe challenge due to the fact that individuals are often intensely threatened by the prospect of re-examining accepted norms of beliefs and behaviour. Transformational learning is complete when an individual is able to act according to beliefs he or she has validated through critical reflection. (2011, p. 4)

In addition, she further explains that the barriers to developing such literacy are exacerbated by the transformative nature of the particular knowledge required, as such learning "is not simply a collection of facts to be added onto what we already know, but rather it is a kind of learning that requires an interrogation of many basic premises" and therefore "remains marginal in education and in practice" (2015, p. 1). Her findings accord with those of Hicks and Bord, who similarly found that the *what* of such learning can be confronting and overwhelming for the great majority of students who were previously unaware of the extent of 21st century environmental challenges. With the Anthropocene now being incorporated into primary and high school curricula in Canada, the USA, and Australia, the emerging literature on this pedagogy has revealed that these responsibilities only increase as the subject is introduced to younger and younger students (Lloro-Bidart, 2015; Mychajliw, Kemp, & Hadly, 2015; Thorne, 2015).

Having outlined the requirements for the Anthropocene to become a transformative pedagogical platform, this chapter will turn to explore them through Anthropocene pedagogy the author has collaboratively enacted.

ANTHROPOCENE PROJECT, HAUS DER KULTUREN DER WELT, BERLIN

The humanities and the natural sciences, as today's established forms of knowledge, have reached a limit in their capacities to approach the challenges of the Anthropocene. The entanglement of industrial metabolism, climate change, rapid urbanization, soil erosion, and species extinction poses problems too complex for any one field to address in total: the transformation and re-organization of the complex interconnections between humanity and Earth require different approaches to what it means to be in the world, to be connected to materials and dynamic processes. Like a speck of Saharan dust that is carried by trade winds to nourish the Amazon basin, granulate plastics accumulate in far away ocean gyres. Our anthropic traces are inseparable from earthly matters. We must approach the Earth with a renewed sense of wonder: how do we re-sensitize ourselves to the world we live in? How do we connect what we do with what we know? (Klingan, Sepahvand, Rosol, & Müller, 2014, p. 1)

The foremost attempt to create "Anthropocene curriculum" and pedagogy has been under the auspices of the Anthropocene Project at HKW, a multi-faceted, multi-year collaboration between the German organisations HKW and Max Planck Society; Deutsches Museum, Munich; Rachel Carson Center for Environment and Society, Ludwig Maximilian University, Munich; and Institute for Advanced Sustainability Studies, Potsdam. The above quotation is the opening paragraph from the organisations' principal communiqué about their Anthropocene Project. The excerpt demonstrates a common mainstay of Anthropocene research and pedagogy: a concrete and somewhat startling fact that dust from Earth's largest desert travels 5000 km across the Atlantic to fertilise Earth's largest tropical rain forest is used to demonstrate the inextricably interrelated functioning of global Earth systems. And from this, a movement toward a more "metaphorical" insight: the notion that "our anthropic traces are inseparable from earthly matters" which in turns raises two key terms in art and humanistic inquiry: *sense of wonder* and sensitivity to the *world we live in*. The excerpt ends with a question that recalls Boehnert's "value/action" gap discussed above (2011, p. 4), connecting action (the *how* of behaviour) with the *what* of knowledge. The organisations probe the further dimensions of this question with a series of subsequent questions:

> How can teaching and research face the challenges of rapid global change in a responsible way? What forms of knowledge production and transmission are appropriate responses? What does it mean to question the borders between institutionalized disciplines, or even to renegotiate them entirely? What new fields of knowledge emerge when an atmospheric chemist, a historian of technology, and an architect develop a joint curriculum? (Klingan, Sepahvand, Rosol, & Müller 2014, p. 13)

These questions constitute the framing statement for Anthropocene Campus and Anthropocene Curriculum, the two sub-projects within the Anthropocene Project that addressed pedagogy and curriculum development, respectively.

HKW focuses on contemporary art and "world" cultures (generally denoting non Euro-American) in the areas of literature, humanities, visual arts, film, music, and performing arts. In their collaboration with the above German universities, research centres, and cultural organisations, HKW broadened their disciplinary framework to stage the first Anthropocene Campus in 2014, where the author was one of 100 Early Career Researchers from across the natural sciences, physical sciences, social sciences, humanities, art, and design who undertook a nine-day workshop on developing the Anthropocene as a pedagogical platform at HKW. The 27 facilitators were also drawn from across these disciplines, including scientists from the Anthropocene Working Group, with whom HKW has a close association having hosted some of their formal committee meetings within the Anthropocene Project.

In the lead up to the workshop, HKW informed participants that the "immediate" aim of this "Campus" was "to collaboratively compose a transdisciplinary curriculum for higher education, presenting a workable and pedagogically feasible design for shared knowledge-building under the Anthropocene auspices" (Klingan, Rosol, Brinzanik, & Laubichler, 2014, p. 2). Participants were required to nominate three seminars, each of which was a two day workshop run by three facilitators, each from a different discipline and/or organisation; for instance, an anthropologist, a geologist, and an artist; or a chemist, an architect, and a historian. Each seminar had its own prerequisite reading to be completed beforehand, with online communication and collaboration encouraged between participants, and between participants and facilitators, via the website www.anthropocene-curriculum.org. Broadly, this may be seen as ensuring the foundation of sustainability and ecology literacy discussed above, whereby participants knew of the *what* before going through the experimental pedagogies of formulating novel *hows* in the seminars. Such prerequisite knowledge was also insisted upon due to how the Campus deliberately took participants and facilitators out of their disciplinary comfort zones, to explore the potential for collaboration across seemingly disparate terrain. For instance, artists were prescribed readings about the geology of the Anthropocene, chemists about the cultural history of the Anthropocene, architects about the anthropology of the Anthropocene, and so on.

The nine days were unchartered waters for the organisers, participants, and facilitators—testing, probing, extending, experimenting across how such transdisciplinary pedagogy could be realised. In the Campus outline, HKW informed participants of their expectations in this regard:

> In the end, the experimental cooperations across the disciplinary divides that are exemplified in this project seek to address the educational skills needed to tackle the critical environmental and humanitarian challenges that the Anthropocene poses. It is thus an attempt at knowledge and educational practice to turn "earthbound," that is to adapt to the manifold ways in which earth and humans have become enmeshed. (Klingan, Rosol, et al., 2014, p. 2)

The author collaborated with fellow participants across the breadth of the disciplines represented, although grounded in the context of exploring what sort of art and design education would be appropriate for the Anthropocene. The results of the Campus are still being formulated through the open access *Anthropocene CourseBook* and *Anthropocene CourseSite* website. Both feature contributions from all the participants and facilitators, and are being edited by the HKW Campus organisers, for print+digital publication in 2017, subsequent to an extension of the 2014 Anthropocene Campus as a follow up nine-day Campus, staged in April 2016.

At the time of publication, the influence of the Campus on new university curricula is still in a formative stage, as the Campus experiments in pedagogy and disciplinarity are still in production. One such example is the author's post-Campus "Slow Media" artwork with the historian Anna Åberg, the geologist Jens Kirstein, and the comics scholar Hugo Almeida (Åberg, Almeida, Wodak, & Kirstein, 2016). This collaboration arose from our Campus participation in the Slow Media seminar facilitated by Leinfelder with environmental historians Libby Robin and Helmuth Trischler. Nevertheless, the following critical reflection illustrates how participation in the Campus informed the author's design, teaching, and coordination of the first teaching project on the Anthropocene at UNSW Art & Design.

ANTHROPOCENE KITCHEN

> The requirements for authenticity and the standards for documenting phenomena and issues in knowledge-based non-fiction comics are comparable with academic publications in terms of their strictness. Given these different qualities, non-fiction comics have an incredibly broad potential for creative knowledge transfer and to promote power motivation or motivation for action. Moreover, they can be conceptualized as a participative, dialogic and structuring process with which to generate scholarly approaches and to identify new research needs. (Leinfelder, Kirstein, Schleunitz, & Hamann, 2015)

For the Slow Media seminar the author co-conceived and created a comic with the above-mentioned historian, geologist, and comics scholar (Åberg, Kirstein, and Almeida, respectively). The comic visualised interrelationships between micro- and macro-processes that constitute the Anthropocene, such as that of Sahara dust fertilising the Amazon rainforest. The medium used, comics, thus lent itself well to a subsequent collaboration with Leinfelder as part of a graphic novel produced for the "Anthropocene Kitchen: A Laboratory Connecting Home and World," a current international research project directed by Leinfelder and led by Humboldt University as part of their *Image Knowledge Gestaltung: An Interdisciplinary Laboratory Cluster of Excellence*. The graphic novel, "Eating Anthropocene: Curd Rice, Bienenstich and a Pinch of Phosphorus - Around the World in Ten Dishes" (Leinfelder, Kirstein, Schleunitz, & Hamann, 2016), formed part of this "interdisciplinary laboratory," concerning how different disciplines across the humanities, natural and technological sciences, medicine, design, and architecture could collaborate "to investigate the fundamental *Gestaltung* processes of the sciences" (*Image Knowledge Gestaltung*, 2016). *Gestaltung* is a polysemic term that does not have a direct translation in English, although the terms "designing," "forming," and "framing" are the closest in intention in this context.

The Anthropocene Kitchen is a collaboration between Leinfelder, Kirstein, Marc Schleunitz, (biologist and political scientist), and Alexandra Hamann (Media Designer). The project uses the kitchen as a lens through which to examine material and cross-cultural exchange around food and culinary resources. A kitchen is where globalised food production, processing, and transportation meet the domestic sphere of food consumption via the resource intensity exemplified by refrigerating, freezing, and heating. On this premise the project has sought to reveal how "our food behaviour is reflected in how we handle resources and, since most of us are no longer aware of the connection between production and processing due to the growing availability of food products from all over the world, it has consequences that extend far beyond our own immediate surroundings" (Leinfelder et al., 2016).

Through participatory ethnographic research the project involved ten protagonists from around the world, to investigate their diverse perspectives on food and kitchens. Each of the ten chapters in the subsequent book explores the subject matter through a protagonist and artist from each of the following countries: Brazil, China, Germany, Japan, India, Morocco, Norway, Australia/Kiribati, Uganda, and the United States. The quotation that begins this section is from Humboldt University's communiqué for a symposium they staged in Berlin in October 2015, where all ten artists spent one week collaboratively developing their respective chapters. The communiqué foregrounded the rigorous academic methodology, developed through Leinfelder and Hamann's prior non-fiction comic projects *The Great Transformation: Climate – Can We Beat the Heat?* (Hamann, Zea-Schmidt, & Leinfelder, 2014) and *Anthropocene – 30 Milestones on the Way to a New Era: A Comic Anthology* (Hamann, Leinfelder, Trischler, & Wagenbreth, 2014).

To formulate the context and content for the chapter on the "Australia-Pacific region," the author collaborated with this Humboldt University team. Given the focus on the protagonists' perspectives, of what the Humboldt editors term *expert citizens*, the author invited Katerina Teaiwa from Banaba, a six-square kilometre Pacific Island of the Republic of Kiribati, to collaborate on the project and to be the protagonist for the students' comic book chapters. Associate Professor Teaiwa, Head of the

Department of Gender, Media and Cultural Studies at the Australian National University, is an anthropologist whose work concerns the history of phosphate mining in the central Pacific. In particular, her fieldwork and publications concern phosphate resource extraction through the mining of 22 million tons of Banaban rock by a British-Australian-New Zealand mining company. This mining resulted in the indigenous inhabitants being dislocated, because Banaba was rendered uninhabitable, as the topsoil of the island was converted into superphosphate fertiliser that was instrumental for the development of Australian and New Zealand agriculture in the 20th century (Teaiwa, 2015).

A related dimension of Teaiwa's research is her project "Indigenous Peoples and the Global Remix" concerning the meaning of indigeneity in the context of the 21st century globalising world. Through this project Teaiwa has *remixed* her text, photographic and filmic fieldwork in Banaba into films and installations that have been shown in galleries and museums, including a permanent exhibition about Banaban phosphate mining at the Museum of New Zealand Te Papa Tongarewa. Teaiwa and Wodak thus approached the Anthropocene Kitchen as a new form of remixing her research for art and design students in a course at UNSW Australia Art & Design (Teaiwa & Wodak, 2017). This process, with art and design students remixing Teaiwa's research aimed to challenge conventional, linear, and textual modes of knowledge production, and move knowledge beyond the academy by inspiring public engagement with Pacific histories, including exploitative colonial relations that deeply implicate Australia.

Drawing on the aims of the Humboldt colleagues under the auspices of their Anthropocene Kitchen, and Teaiwa's aims for her "Indigenous Peoples and the Global Remix" research (2015), the author adapted a project to realise it through undergraduate art and design pedagogy. The project was developed into the major assignment for the second year "Graphics Media: Visual Communication" course, taken by 170 students between March and June 2015 at UNSW Art & Design. The majority of the students were undertaking a Bachelor of Design (Honours), with the remainder doing a Bachelor of Media Arts (Honours) or a Bachelor of Fine Arts (Honours). This course, convened by Dr Ian McArthur, was delivered in seven studio classes, each with 24 students. The author taught one of these classes and did not have face-to-face contact with the other six classes.

Consequently, the author delivered all project resources online, such as an introductory lecture on the Anthropocene, client background, client brief, protagonist background, and assignment requirements. These resources comprised written documents, journal articles, websites, and videos. As it was not possible for students to meet Teaiwa in person, media designer Hamann interviewed her to establish the synopsis of her chapter, and the author collated questions from the students to relay to Teaiwa via email. Face-to-face meetings were held between the author and the six teachers of the other classes, where the project and its background were explained. This was essential as the term "Anthropocene" was unfamiliar to the other teachers. The term was also unfamiliar to most students, other than those who had taken prior courses by the author where the term had been introduced.

Moodle, an online learning management system, was used for students of other classes to communicate directly with the author about the subject matter of the project and the coordination of the assignment. The project was delivered as a real-world brief and commission, with Humboldt University as both the client and commissioning body that would ultimately select one student from the course to write the chapter for the publication. As such, the brief was for each student to write and illustrate how food may be used to probe the Anthropocene in the specific context of a kitchen. It was a way to visualize this subject matter, and, importantly, create a narrative device through which to communicate these complex relationships. Students were required to devise a title page, chapter title, and three pages of the chapter for their assignment. The commissioned student would then write a full-length chapter of 18 pages. They were not expected to communicate a complete beginning-middle-end narrative, but rather to encapsulate the essence of how they would do this as a full chapter.

The subject matter of the assignment and its production constituted the second half of the semester. Within the limitations of this timeframe, the focus of the transformative pedagogy was on developing the *what* of students' understanding of the relationship between the Anthropocene, the Anthropocene Kitchen research project, and Teaiwa's research on how Australian industrial agriculture has been developed through phosphate mined from neighbouring Pacific Islands. To develop students' understanding of the *what*, a flipped classroom method was used in the author's class, where students were provided with textual, photographic, and video resources to be researched online before attending classes. The *how* of their thinking was then developing through in-class workshops, consultation, critiques, and feedback, where each student's critical reflection was encouraged as a catalyst to their creative interpretation, and original visualisation, of these relationships.

For this formative research stage students worked in groups of four, with roles and responsibilities negotiated within each group as to how they would collectively formulate a response to the brief, and determine which of the following five transformations would form the basis of their comic book chapter:

1. Dietary transformations
2. Transformation of the homeland
3. Transformation of the landscape
4. Transformation of beliefs and values
5. Transformation of commodity and resource flows: spreading phosphate on the island all over the world

Students selected their transformation-specific subject in dialogue with their group members, before shifting to the second phase of the project, when each worked independently to draft their storyboard. The shift from group work to solo studio work was integral in terms of developing the transformative pedagogy of students' engagement with the Anthropocene. Not only were they working through a visual narrative explicating the Anthropocene, but also a mode of knowledge production that employed Nisbet's above mentioned role of "the creative arts and communication professions" in contributing to the Anthropocene by telling "inspiring stories that shape human actions, promote learning and encourage critical self-reflection" (Nisbet, 2015). In the fourth week of the project students pinned their draft storyboards to the walls of the classroom, where each gave a verbal presentation in front of their storyboard, followed by a critique. Such feedback was also pivotal for encouraging critical self-reflection as it provided for formal peer review as to what was, and was not, being conveyed in each storyboard. Each teacher across the seven classes also provided weekly individual consultation as to the development of students' comic book chapters.

Following completion of the course, each teacher nominated three students from each class for possible selection to write a full chapter. From the nominated students, McArthur and the author short-listed ten, whose work was submitted to the Humboldt University team for their consideration. Then, in July 2015 the author met with the team in Berlin to make the final selection. UNSW student Samuel Jaramillo was commissioned by Humboldt University to write the full comic book chapter, a project that included attending the week-long symposium in Berlin in October 2015 (Figures 9.1 and 9.2). While the project was successful in terms of introducing a new audience to the subject of the Anthropocene, and of facilitating students' creative engagement with the subject, the timeframe for the project did not permit sustained or in-depth engagement, nor the realisation of the full potential of the Anthropocene as a transformative pedagogical platform. Nevertheless, a critical reflection has been provided in order to frame future literature in Anthropocene pedagogy, with the staging of the Anthropocene Kitchen project in Australia representing one of the first university courses in Australia to engage with the Anthropocene in the disciplines of art or design.

Figure 9.1

Source: From "Kiribati and Fiji," by S. Jaramillo [co-edited by K. Teaiwa & J. Wodak], in R. Leinfelder, A. Hamann, J. Kirstein and M. Schleunitz (Eds.), Eating Anthropocene: Curd Rice, Bienenstich and a Pinch of Phosphorus - Around the World in Ten Dishes *(p. 7), 2016, Berlin/Heidelberg, Germany: Springer-Verlag. Copyright 2016 by Cluster of Excellence Image Knowledge Gestaltung of Humboldt-Universität zu Berlin. Reprinted with permission.*

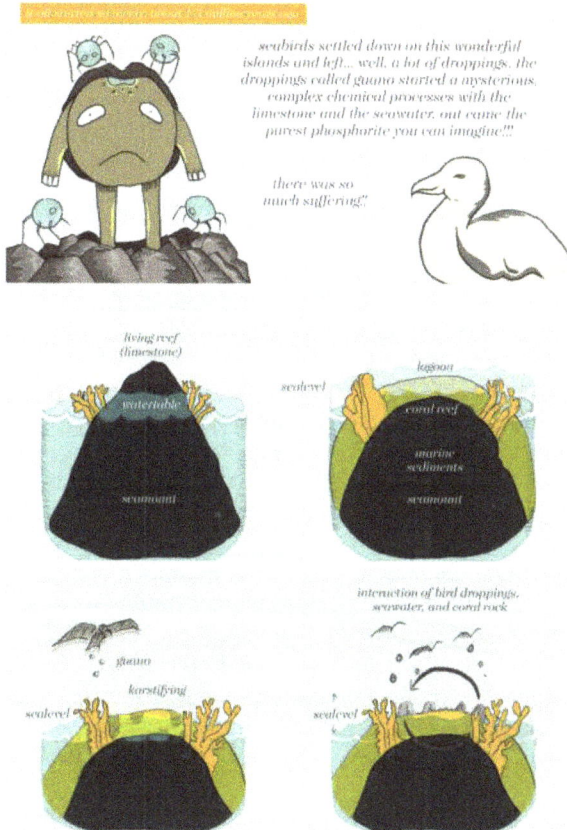

Figure 9.2

Source: From "Kiribati and Fiji," by S. Jaramillo [co-edited by K. Teaiwa & J. Wodak], in R. Leinfelder, A. Hamann, J. Kirstein and M. Schleunitz (Eds.), Eating Anthropocene: Curd Rice, Bienenstich and a Pinch of Phosphorus - Around the World in Ten Dishes *(p. 9), 2016, Berlin/Heidelberg, Germany: Springer-Verlag. Copyright 2016 by Cluster of Excellence Image Knowledge Gestaltung of Humboldt-Universität zu Berlin. Reprinted with permission.*

CONCLUSION

Irrespective of whether the term "Anthropocene" is formally ratified by the International Commission of Stratigraphy in 2016 (Voosen, 2016), it is only likely to grow in the near future as a potential catalyst for wider societal engagement with 21st-century environmental challenges; in that context the same challenges it denotes will grow in complexity, as the timeframe to respond with any efficacy decreases in inverse proportion. This is not a metaphor: there are decadal lags between increases in biophysical drivers like carbon dioxide concentration and their full impact on global climate. As Will Steffen, one of the members of the Anthropocene Working Group reasons:

> As the Earth System changes in response to human activities, it operates at a time scale that is mismatched with human decision-making or with the workings of the economic system. The long-term momentum built into the Earth System means that by the time humans realize that a business-as-usual approach may not work, the world will be committed to further decades or even centuries of environmental change. (Steffen, Crutzen, & McNeill, 2007)

What remains to be seen is whether university curriculum will embrace the potential of the Anthropocene as a pedagogical platform, in which case the transformative basis of its pedagogy may come into being. The closing section of this chapter highlights what such an embrace would entail, and what the immediate hindrances are.

With Anthropocene pedagogy in a nascent stage, particularly in the disciplines of art and design, it cannot yet form the basis of recommendations for practical applications to teaching. The much more longstanding pedagogy of art and design that deals with environment and sustainability can be drawn upon instead. In the interest of formulating *practical* teaching applications, these fields may be more readily utilised for transformative pedagogy, although their framework is long outdated and of limited contemporary relevance. Returning to the analogy between Carson's *Silent Spring* of 1962 and the contemporary equivalent of the *Silent Biosphere* occurring through mass species extinction, pedagogy around sustainability and environment hails from a former era, and a pedagogical mindset that is myopic when applied to the biophysical conditions of the Anthropocene.

Nevertheless, with regard to practical applications, the increase of such longstanding pedagogy would accord with the arguments by Slaughter, Thomas, and Boehnert that the ability for the Anthropocene to become a transformative pedagogical platform is conditional on an exponential increase in ecology and sustainability literacy in every academic discipline. So long as this base literacy remains marginal and elective, rather than central and core, students engaging with the Anthropocene face a long process of coming to understand the *what* of the subject matter, with the transformative potential of the *how* of their thinking remaining an unknown entity.

To embrace the fuller potential for universities to increase transformative learning, Leinfelder, Slaughter, and Thomas argue for a re-orientation of the function, role, and operation of universities, in accordance with the scale of the biophysical and human changes currently underway. To realise "their potentially catalytic role in creating and sustaining social foresight," Slaughter argues that universities "need to invest much more seriously and comprehensively than hitherto in preparing the individuals and creating the enabling structures to support them" (2012, pp. 124–25).

In effect, this does constitute a practical application to teaching, although the practicality of this application faces further hindrances, such as a fulsome embrace of transdisciplinarity so that art and design students can engage with the scientific basis of the Anthropocene, and the framing of the concept in the field of environmental humanities. Experiments such as HKW's Anthropocene Project, Anthropocene Curriculum and Anthropocene Campus have demonstrated that such transdisciplinarity is possible, and indeed enthusiastically embraced by the project organisers, facilitators, and participants. It remains to be seen whether the two decades since Don Aitkin's pronouncement on the timeline available for Leinfelder's "Great Transformation," or the decade since the Australian Vice-Chancellor's Committee "Policy on Education for Sustainable Development," will now be met with a seismic shift in pedagogy in light of the Anthropocene.

REFERENCES

Australian Vice-Chancellors' Committee (AVCC). (2006). *AVCC Policy on education for sustainable development.* Retrieved from http://sustainability.unsw .edu.au/sites/all/files/resource_file/14-Policy-on-Education-for-Sustainable -Development-Aug2006.pdf

Australian Curriculum Geography Glossary v7.1. (2015). Retrieved from http://www.australiancurriculum.edu.au/seniorsecondary/humanities-and -social-sciences/geography/glossary

Åberg, A., Almeida, H., Wodak, J., & Kirstein, J. (2016). Around the world in eighty days: Time(s) at the scale(s) of the Anthropocene. *Resilience: A Journal of the Environmental Humanities, 5*(1), 42–68.

Boehnert, J. (2011). Transformative learning in sustainable design education. In K. Niedderer, K. Mey, & S. Roworth-Stokes (Eds.), *SkinDeep - experiential knowledge and multi sensory communication: Proceedings of the International Conference 2011 of the Design Research Society Special Interest Group on Experiential Knowledge.* Farnham, UK: University for the Creative Arts. Retrieved from http://experientialknowledge.org.uk /proceedings_11.html

———. (2015). Ecological literacy in design education: A theoretical introduction. *FORMakademisk, 8*(1), 1–11. Retrieved from https://journals.hioa.no /index.php/formakademisk/article/view/1405

Carson, R. (1962). *Silent spring.* New York, NY: Houghton Mifflin Harcourt.

Chakrabarty, D. (2009). The climate of history: Four theses. *Critical Inquiry, 35,* 197–222. http://dx.doi.org/10.1086/596640

Crutzen, P. J. (2002). Geology of mankind. *Nature, 415*(6867), 23. http:dx.doi.org/10.1038/415023a

Crutzen, P. J., & Stoermer, E. F. (2000). The "Anthropocene." *Global Change Newsletter, 41,* 17–18. Retrieved from http://www.igbp.net/download /18.316f1832132347017758000I40I/1376383088452/NL41.pdf

Flannery, T. (2015). *Atmosphere of hope: Searching for solutions to the climate crisis.* New York, NY: Atlantic Monthly Press.

Hamann, A., Leinfelder, R., Trischler, H., & Wagenbreth, H. (Eds.). (2014). *Anthropocene: 30 Milestones on the way to a new era: A comic anthology.* Munich, Germany: Deutsches Museum.

Hamann, A., Zea-Schmidt, C., & Leinfelder, R. (Eds.). (2014). *The great transformation. Climate - Can we beat the heat?* Berlin, Germany: German Advisory Council on Global Change (WBGU).

Hicks, D., & Bord, A. (2001). Learning about global issues: Why most educators only make things worse. *Environmental Education Research, 7,* 413–25. http://dx.doi.org/10.1080/13504620120081287

Image Knowledge Gestaltung: An Interdisciplinary Laboratory. (2016). *Image Knowledge Gestaltung: An Interdisciplinary Laboratory.* Retrieved from https://www.interdisciplinary-laboratory.hu-berlin.de/en

Jagodzinski, J. (2013). Art and its education in the Anthropocene: The need for an avant-garde without authority. *Journal of Curriculum and Pedagogy, 10,* 31–34. http://dx.doi.org/10.1080/15505170.2013.790000

Jaramillo, S. (2016). Kiribati and Fiji [Co-edited by K. Teaiwa & J. Wodak]. In R. Leinfelder, A. Hamann, J. Kirstein, & M. Schleunitz (Eds.), *Eating Anthropocene: Curd rice, bienenstich and a pinch of phosphorus - Around the world in ten dishes* (pp. 114–31). Berlin, Germany: Springer-Verlag.

Klingan, K., Sepahvand, A., Rosol, C., Müller, J. (2014). *The Anthropocene project: A report.* Berlin, Germany: HKW. Retrieved from http://www.hkw.de/en /programm/projekte/2014/anthropozaenprojekt_ein_bericht/anthropozaenpro jekt_ein_bericht.php

Klingan, K., Rosol, C., Brinzanik, R., & Laubichler, M. (2014). *Anthropocene curriculum: Project outline.* Berlin, Germany: HKW.

Kolbert, E. (2015). *The sixth extinction: An unnatural history.* New York, NY: Picador.

Leinfelder, R. (2013). Assuming responsibility for the Anthropocene: Challenges and opportunities in education. In H. Trischler (Ed.), *Anthropocene: Exploring the future of the age of humans, RCC Perspectives, 3,* 9–28.

Leinfelder, R., Kirstein, J., Schleunitz, M., & Hamann, A. (2015). *Science meets comics – A symbiosis of image, knowledge and gestaltung.* Unpublished conferenced outline.

———. (2016). *The Anthropocene kitchen.* Berlin, Germany: Humboldt University.

Lewis, S., & Maslin, M. (2015). Defining the Anthropocene. *Nature, 519*(7542), 171–80.

Lloro-Bidart, T. (2015). A political ecology of education in/for the Anthropocene. *Environment and Society: Advances in Research, 6,* 128–48. doi:10.3167/ares.2015.060108

Mychajliw, A., Kemp, M., & Hadly, E. (2015). Using the Anthropocene as a teaching, communication and community engagement opportunity. *The Anthropocene Review, 2,* 267–78. http://dx.doi.org/10.1177/2053019615601444

Nisbet, M. (2015). Universities in the Anthropocene: Engaging students and communities. Retrieved from http://theconversation.com/universities-in-the -anthropocene-engaging-students-and-communities-36472

Oldfield, F., Barnosky, A., Dearing, J., Fischer-Kowalski, M., McNeill, J., Steffen, W., & Zalasiewicz, J. (2014). The Anthropocene review: Its significance, implications and the rationale for a new transdisciplinary journal. *The Anthropocene Review, 1,* 3–7. http://dx.doi.org/10.1177/2053019613500445

Oreskes, N., & Conway, E. (2014). *The collapse of western civilization: A view from the future.* New York, NY: Columbia University Press.

Pawson, E. (2015). What sort of geographical education for the Anthropocene? *Geographical Research, 53,* 306–312. http://dx.doi.org/10.1111/1745-5871.12122

Richerson, P., Boyd, R., & Bettinger, R. (2001). Was agriculture impossible during the Pleistocene but mandatory during the Holocene? A climate change hypothesis. *American Antiquity, 66,* 387. http://dx.doi.org/10.2307/2694241

Robin, L., Avango, D., Keogh, L., Mollers, N., Scherer, B., & Trischler, H. (2014). Three galleries of the Anthropocene. *The Anthropocene Review, 1,* 207–24. http://dx.doi.org/10.1177/2053019614550533

Sage, R. F. (1995). Was low atmospheric CO_2 during the Pleistocene a limiting factor for the origin of agriculture? *Global Change Biology, 1,* 93–106. http://dx.doi.org/10.1111/j.1365-2486.1995.tb00009.x

Saravanamuthu, K. (2015). Instilling a sustainability ethos in accounting education through the transformative learning pedagogy: A case-study. *Critical Perspectives on Accounting, 32,* 1–36. http://dx.doi.org/10.1016/j.cpa.2015.05.008

Slaughter, R. (2012). Welcome to the Anthropocene. *Futures, 44,* 119–26. http://dx.doi.org/10.1016/j.futures.2011.09.004

Steffen, W., Crutzen, P., & McNeill, J. (2007). The Anthropocene: Are humans now overwhelming the great forces of nature. *AMBIO: A Journal of the Human Environment, 36,* 614–621. Retrieved from http://www.jstor.org/stable/25547826

Steffen, W., Persson, Å., Deutsch, L., Zalasiewicz, J., Williams, M., Richardson, K., & Crumley, C. (2011). The Anthropocene: From global change to planetary stewardship. *AMBIO: A Journal of the Human Environment, 40,* 739–61. http://dx.doi.org/10.1007/s13280-011-0185-x

Steffen, W., Broadgate, W., Deutsch, L., Gaffney, O., & Ludwig, C. (2015). The Trajectory of the Anthropocene: The great acceleration. *The Anthropocene Review, 2,* 81–98. http://dx.doi.org/10.1177/2053019614564785

Stilgoe, J. (2015). *Experiment Earth: Responsible innovation in geoengineering.* London, England: Routledge.

Teaiwa, K. (2015). *Consuming Ocean Island: Stories of people and phosphate from Banaba.* Bloomington, IN: Indiana University Press.

Teaiwa, K., & Wodak, J. (2017). Re-imaging Banaba: Reflections on a visual and pedagogical process. In P. Carter, M. Hinkson, & A. Ravetz (Eds.), *Images on the Edge: Visual cultures of placemaking in a precarious age.* London, England: Bloomsbury.

Thomas, I. (2004). Sustainability in tertiary curricula: What is stopping it happening? *International Journal of Sustainability in Higher Education, 5,* 33–47. http://dx.doi.org/10.1108/14676370410517387

———. (2009). Critical thinking, transformative learning, sustainable education, and problem-based learning in universities. *Journal of Transformative Education, 7,* 245–64. http://dx.doi.org/10.1177/1541344610385753

Thorne, M. (2015). Learning for stewardship in the Anthropocene: A study with young adolescents in the wet tropics. *Etropic*, *14*(1), 28–36. Retrieved from https://journals.jcu.edu.au/etropic/article/view/3363

Vettraino, E., Linds, W., & Goulet, L. (2013). Click, clack, move: Facilitation of the arts as transformative pedagogy. *Journal of Transformative Education, 11,* 190–208. http://dx.doi.org/10.1177/1541344613499826

Voosen, P. (2016, August). Atomic bombs and oil addiction herald Earth's new epoch: The Anthropocene. *Science: News.* http://dx.doi.org/10.1126/science.aah7220

Wagler, R. (2011). The Anthropocene mass extinction: An emerging curriculum theme for science educators. *The American Biology Teacher, 73,* 78–83. doi:10.1525/abt.2011.73.2.5

Walker, M., Johnsen, S., Rasmussen, S., Popp, T., Steffensen, J., Gibbard, P., … Schwander, J. (2009). Formal definition and dating of the GSSP (Global Stratotype Section and Point) for the base of the Holocene using the Greenland NGRIP ice core, and selected auxiliary records. *Journal of Quaternary Science, 24,* 3–17. http://dx.doi.org/10.1002/jqs.1227

WBGU (German Advisory Council on Global Change). (2011). *World in transition: A social contract for sustainability*. Berlin, Germany: Economia.

———. (2013). *World in transition: Governing the marine heritage*. Berlin, Germany: Economia.

Yusoff, K. (2009). Excess, catastrophe, and climate change. *Environment and Planning D: Society and Space, 27,* 1010–29. http://dx.doi.org/10.1068/d7407

Zalasiewicz, J. (2008). *The Earth after us: What legacy will humans leave in the rocks?* Oxford, England: Oxford University Press.

Zalasiewicz, J., Waters, C., Williams, M., Barnosky, A., Cearreta, A., Crutzen, P., Ellis, E., et al. (2015). When did the Anthropocene begin? A mid-twentieth century boundary level is stratigraphically optimal. *Quaternary International, 383,* 196–203. http://dx.doi.org/10.1016/j.quaint.2014.11.045

Transformative Pedagogies and the Environment

CHAPTER 10

Creative Agency, Pedagogy, and the Environment

Marie Sierra and Kit Wise

The chapters in this book have examined transformative pedagogies in art and design tertiary education that address issues of the environment, and how these can be driven by the capacities and forms of creative agency inherent to art and design disciplines. Acknowledging the inherent interdisciplinary pedagogical scope of social change agendas, which are able to generate novel, relevant, and timely engagement with global issues, the authors offer studio practice and field-based case studies embracing ecological and broader environmental imperatives, and the dimensions of social responsibility and engagement these imperatives impart. These range from personal response to activism, to exercising the public platform of exhibition in preparation for professional immersion, to engagement with the local as an instance of the global, and the urban as an instance of the wild. As Noel Castree and Bruce Braun note, a fundamental question to be asked is "who constructs what kinds of nature(s) to what ends and with what social and ecological effects?" (2001, p. xi).

In mapping these chapters and their case studies a continuum becomes apparent, indicative of opposing pedagogical approaches being granted equal importance. There are those that employ a critical, rational reflection in studio practice at one end of the spectrum, employing methodologies, such as critique and student presentation to jury panels who decide a final mark, inclusion for an exhibition, or selection for a real commission. Then there are the intuitive approaches with their espousal of emotive, individualised reflection, often privately journaled or tested in small groups among trusted peers prior to wider airing. This dual model mirrors much of the developed world's contested relationship with environmental issues, echoing as it does the dichotomies of personal/public, aspirational aims/hard data, and freedom/ responsibility of empowerment. Therefore, when used together, these conflicting approaches form an appropriate methodological platform for transformative learning that engages environmental issues, the tension they hold becoming a driver of art and design outcomes. Because they operate on a continuum, these approaches are scalable—a course can have few critique sessions, or many; the approaches can also be combined—most studio courses require outcomes that are both broadcast (e.g., exhibition, critique), and individual (e.g., journal, sketchbook). In relation to transformative pedagogy and the environment, some of the tensions encountered in art and design teaching can be posited as a series of questions:

- *Why* is transformative pedagogy well suited to art and design teaching, particularly when it turns its attention to intractable issues? why should agency underpin art and design practices? and why is it important that students are empowered with creative agency and come to understand its consequent responsibilities?

- *Who* determines the partnerships, roles and dynamics that are required to address environmental agendas, including those agenda's social ramifications? Who are the stakeholders? And upon whom does the transformative operate?

- *What* outcomes should we prioritise for transformation and what must we disregard? What brief can be defined when addressing a *wicked problem*? What are the drivers for innovation in teaching practices, as well as the challenges they confront? And what is the acceptable level of risk in relation to transformative pedagogy, when experiences and exposures may be confronting?

- *How* may we identify specific goals within broad environmental agendas, including those associated with the Anthropocene? How are the best methodologies developed? And how do we define what is good in this field, build on success, and learn from failure?

Each of the chapters in this book addresses these questions with different emphasis, supplying a range of examples that may seed new manifestations of transformative pedagogical development. As a sequence, they progressively explore, and provide vehicles for a broad scope of environmental concerns.

In "The Interdisciplinary Witness: Interdisciplinary Pedagogy and Speaking the New" Sierra, Wise, and Brewin considered approaches to and outcomes from interdisciplinarity, and how this intersects with environment, creative practice as both responsive and responsible, and transitioning to a profession. It reviewed the alignment and influence of different epistemic communities as they manifest in academic disciplines. Two of the three case studies were associated with water, a substance that imparts confluence and dissolution of boundaries. The role of collaborative education in relation to speaking of new ideas came into consideration, ultimately questioning how empowerment and entanglement are governed through practice.

In "A Placement for Everyone," Cross pursues this examination of agency through collective endeavour, focusing on his experiences as an artist, educator, and activist confronting the politics of fossil fuel divestment by tertiary institutions. Focusing on group activity, meta-issues, and citizenship he relates his involvement in a series of real-world events as they unfolded at the University of Arts London between December 2010 and March 2016, questioning local and global responsibility through art and design, and the role of art and design as an ethical compass.

Similarly, Ings considers the role of individual action through a discussion of three heuristic approaches to engaging with the physical environment through artistic practice in "Private Properties: Heuristic Inquiry, Land and the Artistic Researcher." Subjective and place-based models of landscape were explored, again from an activist perspective, as well as indigenous and embodied perspectives, here focusing on individual rather than collective practice.

Bleach, Fountain, and Vella return to the role of collaborative practices, but embedded in specific locations and communities, in "The Whether Project: Transformative 'Extra Tertiary' Projects in Tasmania." Using the metaphor of "the weather" to describe the various vectors operating in their pedagogic projects, they explore how education operates outside of the academy, exposed to the elements but equally, liberated from normative behaviours. In the wilds of Tasmania, new forms of curriculum, designed in an instance of Frayling's description of research *into*, *for*, and *through* the community are realised (Frayling, 1993/4).

Ferris, Stuart, and Zaraftis explore a specific model of community engaged education, in their account of collaboration between the Eden Local Aboriginal Land Council and the Australian National University's School of Art and Design. "Truly, Madly, Deeply: Sharing Story on Bundian Way" outlines formative research into Ramsden's effective teaching, as applied to engaging with land through cross-cultural practices. As such, it also considers the role of affect as creative agency in environment, developed through both in situ and studio based research.

How networked approaches to pedagogy can create to new forms is also reviewed by Norrie, but in relation to design, in her chapter "Transformative Participation and Collaborative Practice-Led Design Research." Focusing primarily senior year level design students engaging with specific rural urban communities, she employs Dascălu's theory of generating relations. Through the work with RUSL, community has an active discourse in the decision-making processes of design of their spaces, and students work not only with community but also local government, managing expectations and aspiration across all the constituent connections.

Architectural design pedagogy is also the focus of Carter, but here providing a counterpoint to the practice and community-based focus of Norrie and other authors. In "The Humanist Don Quixote and the Windmills of Sustainability: How Innovative Pedagogy Can Help Support Classical Subjects for a Sustainable Future," she gives an impassioned account of the value of arts-driven curricula "providing awareness" through an innovative approach to praxis in the School of Architecture & Design at the University of Lincoln. The success of these initiatives is notable, and positions the students to keenly observe the architecture vernacular in their immediate environment through hand drawing, thus also building this skill and its corollary, observation. This grounds the students' learning where they live, work, and study emphasising the local as relatable and performed. Carter also cautions against the pressure of economic rationalism declaring humanities courses peripheral to the study of architecture, noting the technical and artistic must coexist in this discipline. She posits that sustainability of the discipline within the university drives sustainability beyond it.

In "Submersion Subversion: Re-Thinking the Anthropocene as a Pedagogical Platform for Disruption and Discovery," Edwards and Tregloan return us to the water, this time through an examination of architectural models of design education. Using the Anthropocene as a framework for a "re-thinking and re-making of the political in design," they outline a pedagogic approach that capsizes the human and non-human, an aim being to develop empathy as a key designerly skill. Concurrently, their work reinscribes the standard hierarchies of client and designer, using models of disruption and discovery, as well as social media platforms, to shift their approach to studio production.

Finally, Wodak emphasises the shared subject of these transformative pedagogies—the environment—in his text, "The Anthropocene as a Transformative Pedagogical Platform." His thorough survey of international curricula associated with the Anthropocene considers the pedagogy of the climate change parameter, focusing on the role of art and design within wider interdisciplinary contexts. Stepping back from the focus on Australian and Asia-Pacific models found in most previous chapters, Wodak reminds us of the need for global approaches to curriculum and, indeed, to reconsidering the role of universities in order to realise their "potentially catalytic role in creating and sustaining social foresight" (Slaughter, 2012, pp. 124–25).

In relation to transformative pedagogy, it was noted above that the very practice of art and design, by virtue of its ability, indeed its remit, to hold opposing views in tension, provides a platform to engage with environmental issues, with the additional asset of scalability between the individual and the group. This combination is ideal for transformative learning. Patricia Cranton notes the "emancipatory" quality of transformative learning when it is hybridised with critical theory, leading to an

> emancipatory Scholarship of Teaching and Learning in which the assumptions, beliefs, norms and values of the discipline, the institution, the community and the state are directly and critically questioned. Such an approach has the potential to yield a deep shift in perspective on teaching and learning at both an individual level and a social level. (Cranton, 2011, p. 84)

Cranton also notes the way Brookfield (2005) "set out to illustrate how critical theory can be used as a perspective to understand teaching and learning practice," and his devising of "seven interrelated learning tasks in critical theory." With a nod to Marcuse, she says:

> Marcuse (1964), in *One dimensional man*, argues that people can escape one-dimensional thought and ideological domination through imagination and the arts. One-dimensional thought focuses on improving current social systems rather than breaking away from them or replacing them with new ways of thinking about social issues. Engagement with art and aesthetics allows individuals to be able to see the collectivity of humanity in a new manner. The world of higher education focuses almost exclusively on cognitive learning (with the exception of fine arts and some courses in the humanities). (Cranton, 2011, p. 79)

If that is the case—and many art and design academics would argue it is—then two final questions arise for the domain addressed in this book:

- What are the responsibilities of art and design education within the university sector if art and design imparts a collective view of humanity that could, in turn, produce understandings of global environmental issues?

- What level of responsibility will a university take for the art and design sector doing such work?

Many of the case studies indicate a strong sense of responsibility on behalf of those who designed, ran, engaged external partners and communities, and surveyed the noted projects, courses, and events. As Bleach et al. correctly identified, there is now an "extra tertiary" zone, where the reach of university education extends well beyond the campus into communities, their histories and their futures. The tools of critique and reflective practice, critical theory, visual literacy, and the kinaesthetic knowledge imbued in making and performing are all part of the art and design language suite that can be deployed on the wicked problems of environment. By moving beyond essentialist "nature art," the case studies herein demonstrate collective research that identifies, connects, and progresses toward meeting the challenges of such intractable issues.

The "clients" in this scenario, however, are not only the students, but also the universities themselves, as art and design disciplines do important work on their behalf. In the way that a client has some authority over a hired designer or commissioned artist, an art and design school within a university structure is subordinate to the university that manages its finances and students; several case studies noted the subtext of this power relationship. So, what level of responsibility will a university take for art and design schools and their courses and programs? Studio classes are expensive pedagogical models to support and regularly cause art and design schools to have one of the lowest financial returns to university coffers. All authors in this book work in countries where universities are subsidised by the Federal government, meaning munificence is not familiar. Perhaps this is where Edwards and Tregloan's work with conceiving of the client as "more-than-human" could come into play, and this client could be understood to be one that needs active engagement in its own educative process.

The work that art and design can do in relation to the environment is truly transformative. As Juhani Pallasmaa observed, "The duty of architecture [design] and art is to survey ideals and new modes of perception and experience, and thus open up and widen the boundaries of our lived world" (Pallasmaa, 2009, p. 150). The case studies herein point to ways and means for such environmental engagement to occur.

REFERENCES

Brookfield, S. D. (2005). *The power of critical theory: Liberating adult learning and teaching.* San Francisco, CA: Jossey-Bass.

Castree, N., & Braun, B. (Eds.) (2001). *Social nature: theory, practice and politics.* Malden, MA: Blackwell.

Cranton, P. (2011). A transformative perspective on the Scholarship of Teaching and Learning, *Higher Education Research & Development, 30*(1), 75–86, http://dx.doi.org/10.1080/07294360.2011.536974

Dascălu, D. (2013). Architecture as tool for building social capital. *Acta Technia Napocensis: Civil Engineering & Architecture, 56,* 204–20.

Frayling, C. (1993/4). Research in art and design. *Royal College of Art Research Papers*, *1*(1), 1–5. Retrieved from http://researchonline.rca.ac.uk/384/3 /frayling_research_in_art_and_design_1993.pdf

Marcuse, H. (1964). *One dimensional man.* Boston, MA: Beacon Press.

Pallasmaa, J. (2009). *The thinking hand: Existential and embodied wisdom in architecture.* Chichester, England: John Wiley & Sons.

Slaughter, R. (2012). Welcome to the Anthropocene. *Futures, 44,* 119–26. http://dx.doi.org/10.1016/j.futures.2011.09.004

CONTRIBUTORS' INFORMATION

Editors' Biographies

Marie Sierra

Professor Marie Sierra is Deputy Dean and Head of School at UNSW Art & Design. Previously she was the Head, Tasmanian College of the Arts, University of Tasmania, where she remains an Adjunct Professor. Prior roles include Victorian College of the Arts, University of Melbourne, as Head of Sculpture & Spatial Practice, and Coordinator of Higher Degree Research, both in the School of Art, and Associate Dean Research for the Faculty of the VCA. Marie also worked at RMIT in the Faculty of Art, Design and Communication, where she held Associate Dean/Director positions in Research, and Teaching and Learning while lecturing in Sculpture. Her practice as an artist is focused on nature as a social construct, as was her PhD by thesis from RMIT's School of Architecture & Design, which she completed in 2004.

Marie has held numerous solo exhibitions within Australia, and has participated in over thirty group shows in Australia, the US, and France. She has been awarded five Australia Council Grants, and is a chief investigator on a 2015 Australian Office of Teaching and Learning Grant, *Developing new approaches to ethics and research integrity training through challenges posed by creative practice research*. She was also a chief investigator on two Australia Research Council Linkage Infrastructure, Equipment and Facilities Grants, awarded for the Design Art Australia Online (DAAO) project, a collaborative e-research tool.

Active in visual arts advocacy, Marie has served as Deputy Chair of Gertrude Street Contemporary Art Spaces; board member for Australian Centre for Contemporary Art; Chair of the Public Art Committee, and Deputy Chair for the Cultural Affairs Committee for the City of Melbourne. She is the immediate past Chair of the Australian Council of University Art and Design Schools, and the Treasurer for the peak body Deans and Directors of Creative Arts.

Kit Wise

Kit Wise is Professor of Fine Art and Director of the Tasmanian College of the Arts, University of Tasmania, and an Adjunct Professor of Fine Art at Monash University. After graduating from Oxford University and the Royal College of Art with an MFA in Sculpture, he received the Wingate Rome Scholarship in Fine Art in 1999 to study at the British School at Rome. In 2001 he received a Boise Travel Scholarship, administered by the Slade School of Fine Art, for subsequent research in New York and Australia. Since moving permanently to Australia in 2002, he has received four Australia Council grants, as well as grants and commissions from Arts Victoria, Arts

Tasmania, the Besen Family Foundation, and the Museum of Old and New Art, Tasmania. He completed his PhD at Monash University in 2012.

Kit has held several senior educational leadership and governance roles. In his role as Associate Dean Education in the Faculty of Art Design & Architecture at Monash University (MADA), he led the development of interdisciplinary education. He has authored a number of publications in that field, and in 2014 he received an Australian Office of Learning and Teaching Innovation & Development Grant, *Benchmarking quality assessment tasks to facilitate interdisciplinary learning in the creative arts and humanities*. He has engaged in an advisory capacity on course design and interdisciplinarity with creative arts schools nationally and internationally.

He was a member of the Steering Committee for the Creative Arts Learning and Teaching Network, which in 2012 established the peak body Deans and Directors of Creative Arts (DDCA), of which he is now also a Board Member. He is also Deputy Chair of the Executive Council of Australian Council of University Art and Design Schools. His artwork is represented by Sarah Scout Presents, Melbourne.

Contributing Authors

Lucy Bleach

Lucy Bleach is Lecturer and Coordinator of the Sculpture Studio at the Tasmanian College of the Arts (TCoTA), University of Tasmania. Lucy co-designs and delivers diverse University outreach programs in Tasmania. Her service to the community is attuned to increasing engagement and tertiary attainment across Tasmania whilst simultaneously increasing TCotA's reputational capacity. She has been acknowledged by a 2011 Vice Chancellor's Award for Outstanding Community Engagement, a 2014 VC Citation for Outstanding Contribution to Student Learning, and a 2015 Australian Office of Learning and Teaching Citation for Outstanding Contributions to Student Learning.

She is an active researcher achieving increasingly significant published outputs across esteemed national and international contexts funded through competitive grants, awards, and commissions. Her research focuses on varied human relationships to tenuous, contingent, and at times volatile environments, seeking engagement with communities that authentically experience such relationships. She participated in the 4th Echigo-Tsumari Art Triennial in Japan (2009); developed collaborative work for the Heavy Metal Project, MONA (2014); exhibited in Dark Mofo (2015); and produced solo commissioned works for the TMAG (2011), Devonport Regional Gallery (2011), and Contemporary Art Tasmania (2015).

Ross Brewin

Ross Brewin is an Architect and Senior Lecturer in the Department of Architecture at MADA (Monash University Art Design + Architecture) in Melbourne, which he helped establish and build from its inception in 2008. Ross teaches urban-focused architecture design studios that build on his design-led, research-based practice, which engages in culture- and environment-focused urban and regional revitalisation projects. Ross is a past recipient of an Australian Government Office of Learning and Teaching citation for outstanding contributions to student learning.

Doina Carter

Prior to joining the Lincoln School of Architecture in 2006, Doina Carter worked for over ten years in London for large commercial practices, such as *Foster and Partners* and *EPR* architects, mainly on high-end corporate headquarters and masterplanning. She graduated from the *"Ion Mincu" School of Architecture and Urban Design* in Bucharest, Romania, and became a registered architect in the UK in 1996. While in practice, she also taught in schools of design and architecture at *Middlesex University* and *Sheffield* in the UK. Doina's lectures and studio tutoring are informed and driven by experience in practice; making theory relevant to architectural practice underpins her approach to research and teaching. Research interests revolve around architectural theory, hand-drawing, and image production for documentation and presentation, photorealistic versus non-photorealistic delineation in architecture.

In the last few years Doina has been conducting action research projects, in the humanities module she coordinated, in the spirit of the *student as producer* ethos of Lincoln University, with rewarding results in terms of architectural pedagogy for enhanced student experience, attainment and engagement. Her chapter is an overview of this work, from inception (context, reasoning, and theoretical pedagogical grounding) to examples of students' submissions—the most articulate testaments of their formative and transformative experiences.

David Cross

As an artist, David Cross began collaborating with Matthew Cornford while studying at Saint Martin's School of Art in 1987, and graduated from the Royal College of Art in 1991. Cornford & Cross have held residencies at the London School of Economics, and Vitamin in Guangzhou, China. In London, their work has been exhibited at the Camden Arts Centre, the ICA, the Photographers' Gallery, and the South London Gallery. In Britain, Cornford & Cross have exhibited in "East International," the Northern Gallery for Contemporary Art, the De La Warr Pavilion, and the Wolverhampton Art Gallery. In Europe, they have exhibited in Athens, Bologna, Bruges, Rome, and Stockholm, and in the USA: New York, Philadelphia, and San

Francisco. Perceiving a conflict between his internationalism and his environmentalism, David stopped using jet travel in 2005.

David is a Reader in Art and Design at the University of the Arts London. Informing his research, practice, and teaching is a critical engagement with the relationship between visual culture and the contested ideal of "sustainable" development. Since 2012, he has been attempting to move beyond the separation between his artistic and academic activities, and to engage staff and students in discussion on aligning the university's operations with its values, commencing with institutional divestment from fossil fuel, and switching banks.

Charity Edwards

Charity Edwards is a lecturer and urban researcher in the Department of Architecture at MADA (Monash University Art Design + Architecture) in Melbourne, and a registered architect. She currently collaborates with other spatial practitioners to create interiors, buildings and landscapes.

Charity's research explores uneven and more-than-human impacts of urbanisation and climate change at the scale of the planet. She foregrounds the long-disregarded space of the world ocean in these processes in particular, and uses image-making and video practices to investigate spatial experience within urban theory. Charity is currently undertaking a research project on "Antarctic Geo-Imaginaries" and the increasing urbanisation of the Southern Ocean, asking how and why this so often conflicts with our popular understanding of Antarctica as "like being on another planet." She is also a member of the Water Sensitive Cities international research team (led by Monash University's Sustainable Development Institute) to revitalise informal urban settlements in Fiji and Indonesia.

At MADA, she teaches design studio, theory, and urban processes in both the Interior Architecture and Architecture programs. As part of Melbourne's wider culture of design discourse, she has partnered with visiting international practitioners on urban interventions; and continues to contribute to local, national, and international architecture and design media and events such as the National Gallery of Victoria's *Art Book Fair* public roundtable "Architecture: What Matters?", *Architect Victoria*, *Parlour*, and *IDEA Journal*. Charity has most recently been an active "re-writer" of notable Australian women architects into history as part of the international *Women.Wikipedia.Design* initiative.

Denise Ferris

Denise Ferris is the Head of the School of Art and Design at the Australian National University, where she has taught Photography since 1987. In 2007 she completed a doctorate in Humanities and Social Sciences at the University of Technology, Sydney. Her research *Spoilt Milk: Photography, Recollection and Constructing a Maternal* articulated maternal ambivalence and contradiction through innovative and unique milk prints, made from a mixture of casein and dichromate in UV light. The thesis also examined the social anxieties surrounding a "maternal genealogy," the lineage of mothers in fine art photographing their children, and the issues surrounding consumption of these photographs, made for both private recollection and for viewing in public. Her published chapters have been concerned with maternal philosophy and the visual representation of motherhood.

Denise has exhibited a large range of UV contact processes, including cyanotype, van dyke, brown print, and casein. She is best known for the research, development, and innovation of the milk print, and envisages her photography as a non-documentary ahistorical archive. It is a "street photography" genre she considers her extensive Perisher Valley archive to align with, rather than landscape photography. Denise's photographs are in Australian public collections including the National Gallery of Australia, the National Library of Australia, and Canberra Museum and Gallery, as well as international collections, including the District Six Museum, Cape Town and Nara City, Japan. Her most recent exhibition was the extensive "Encounter and Immersion" with painter Ruth Waller, shown at Taipei's National Taiwan University of the Arts in 2015.

Wendy Fountain

Wendy Fountain is an educational designer and design researcher with two decades' experience in vocational, adult, and higher education. From foundations in design practice and teaching, Wendy has worked on the design of learning environments in Australia, New Zealand, Sweden, and the UK, engaging increasingly with the creative arts in adopting participatory, co-creation pedagogies. Her recent doctoral study proposed "design research for resilience," and embraced participatory design to spatialise targeted practices in the integration of housing and food systems, and make space for the crafts of everyday living. This research has sparked a social-ecological systems view of design for learning, in which the human, digital, material, and immaterial are considered in inter-scalar interplay.

Welby Ings

Welby Ings is a Professor of Design at AUT University and is an international award-winning designer, filmmaker, and artist. He has supervised more than 80 practice-led PhDs and master's theses to completion.

He has published and spoken widely on issues of cultural voice, methodology, subjectivity, and pedagogy. His films have been shortlisted for the Oscars and selected for special screenings at Cannes and Berlin. In 2001 he was awarded the Prime Minister's inaugural Supreme Award for Tertiary Teaching Excellence, and in 2013 the AUT University medal for his contributions to research and education.

Welby has a number of significant recent publications related to self-oriented methodologies and their supervision implications, most recently: "Telling tales:

pedagogical challenges to the supervision of illustrated story design theses" (2016), "The Authored Voice: Emerging approaches to exegesis design in creative practice PhDs" (2015), "Narcissus and the muse: supervisory implications of autobiographical, practice-led PhD design theses" (2014), and "Embodied Drawing. A case study in narrative design" (2014).

These publications interface with a number of international keynote addresses of which his TEDX Talk *Disobedient Thinking* (2013), and his opening address *Productive unknowing: Materiality, imagination and the design of a fictional world* at the 2014 Fifth Art of Research Conference in Helsinki, are indicative:

- https://www.youtube.com/watch?v=aumxbgOdkRU
- https://www.youtube.com/watch?v=UIw1erpD6tU&t=34s

In 2017, his treatise on educational reform, *Disobedient Teaching: Survival and change in Education*, was published by Otago University Press.

Dr. Helen Norrie

Helen Norrie is a design academic working across scales from the curation of ideas through text and exhibitions, to the design of buildings and urban environments. Helen teaches in the School of Architecture & Design at the University of Tasmania, and is an architectural critic and regular contributor to architecture, design, and art journals.

Helen is the theme leader of the UTAS Creative Exchange Institute (CxI) Regional Urban Studies Laboratory (RUSL; pronounced Russell), a collaborative urban design research project that engages directly with local councils and communities to examine urban spatial, temporal, and social issues in small towns and cities. RUSL develops practice-led research through the medium of design. It examines urban issues in new ways, utilizing processes of mapping, auditing, research, and speculation to reveal productive relationships and opportunities. Projects engage constructively in the teaching-research nexus, working collaboratively with local councils to examine issues that are at the periphery of day-to-day practice.

Marie Sierra

Marie is Professor, Deputy Dean, and Head of School at UNSW Art & Design. Previously she was the Head, Tasmanian College of the Arts, University of Tasmania, where she remains an Adjunct Professor. Prior roles include Victorian College of the Arts, University of Melbourne, as Head of Sculpture & Spatial Practice, and Coordinator of Higher Degree Research, both in the School of Art, and Associate Dean Research for the Faculty of the VCA. Marie also worked at RMIT in the Faculty of Art, Design and Communication, where she held Associate Dean/Director positions in Research, and Teaching and Learning, while also lecturing in Sculpture. Her practice as an artist is focused on nature as a social construct, as was her PhD by thesis from RMIT's School of Architecture & Design, which she completed in 2004.

Marie has held numerous solo exhibitions within Australia, and has participated in more than thirty group shows in Australia, the US, and France. She has been awarded five Australia Council Grants, and is a chief investigator on a 2015 Australian Office of Teaching and Learning Grant, *Developing new approaches to ethics and research integrity training through challenges posed by creative practice research*. She was also a chief investigator on two Australia Research Council Linkage Infrastructure, Equipment and Facilities Grants, awarded for the Design Art Australia Online (DAAO) project, a collaborative e-research tool.

Active in visual arts advocacy, Marie has served as Deputy Chair of Gertrude Street Contemporary Art Spaces; board member for Australian Centre for Contemporary Art; Chair of the Public Art Committee, and Deputy Chair for the Cultural Affairs Committee for the City of Melbourne. She is the immediate past Chair of the Australian Council of University Art and Design Schools, and the Treasurer for the peak body Deans and Directors of Creative Arts.

Amanda Stuart

Amanda is a Canberra-based visual artist, writer, curator, and art educator. Her sculptural works produce objects that sit in the environment to invite psychic re-imaginings of old, unhealed wounds between humans and unwanted animals. Embedded in a materiality of the Australian regional landscape and its fauna, her works refer to the social, cultural, ethical, and political difficulties surrounding contested, estranged human–animal relations within contested landscapes. Stuart's practice embraces drawing, installation, object making, and in-situ photographic documentation.

Stuart has a PhD in Visual Arts (Sculpture) and a Bachelor of Science (Land Management), the latter of which quietly informs her art practice and concerns regarding relations with country. She currently lectures in the Environment Studio and Foundation workshops at the ANU School of Art & Design, and co-coordinates the Balawan Elective, with co-founders Amelia Zaraftis and Heike Qualitz.

Kate Tregloan

Kate Tregloan is Associate Dean (Education) at MADA (Monash University Art Design + Architecture) in Melbourne. She has contributed to a number of architecture and interdisciplinary design programs in NSW, Tasmania, and Victoria, and is currently a Senior Lecturer, teaching mainly in the Bachelor of Interior Architecture and Master of Design at MADA.

Kate is a registered architect with professional experience as a designer and maker of buildings, spatial experiences, furniture, jewelry, and other objects. Practice and project interests focus on the relationship between the artefact and its context, fixed and flexible elements, and things that can be understood in multiple ways.

She has a particular research interest in brief development through design processes, and the intersection of qualitative and quantitative judgments that influence both the production and assessment of creative work. Her PhD investigated moments of Design Epiphany and the Opportunities of Wickedness with particular reference to design education and studio delivery.

Current research projects focus on the exploratory activities and cognitive functions that underpin learning, designing, and learning to design. Outcomes aim to develop resources to support creative education, including the contributions of the creative disciplines to interdisciplinary engagements in research and learning. Kate was chief investigator for the Office for Learning and Teaching funded project, Multiple Measures (multiplemeasures.org.au).

John Vella

John is Head of Discipline for Visual Art at the Tasmanian College of the Arts, University of Tasmania.

John has received a number of grants and awards in recognition of his teaching innovations and related community engagement. These include: 2011 ALTC Citation for Australian Learning and Teaching Council for Outstanding Contribution to Student Learning; University of Tasmania Vice-Chancellor's Award for Outstanding Contributions to Teaching and Learning (Citation); and University of Tasmania Vice Chancellor's Award for Outstanding Community Engagement.

John's research Interests include cross-disciplinary research, arts industry–community collaboration, and public art. His works have been included in 11 solo exhibitions and more than 45 group exhibitions since 1994. John has also been awarded five major competitive commissions through Tasmania's Art for Public Building Scheme, and received significant competitive grants from Arts Tasmania and the Australia Council. His work is represented in a number of private and public collections in Australia, including ArtBank, the University of NSW, and the Tasmanian Museum and Art Gallery.

Kit Wise

Kit is Professor of Fine Art and Director of the Tasmanian College of the Arts, University of Tasmania, and an Adjunct Professor of Fine Art at Monash University. After graduating from Oxford University and the Royal College of Art with an MFA in Sculpture, he received the Wingate Rome Scholarship in Fine Art in 1999 to study at the British School at Rome. In 2001 he received a Boise Travel Scholarship, administered by the Slade School of Fine Art, for subsequent research in New York and Australia. Since moving permanently to Australia in 2002, he has received four Australia Council grants, as well as grants and commissions from Arts Victoria, Arts

Tasmania, the Besen Family Foundation, and the Museum of Old and New Art, Tasmania. He completed his PhD at Monash University in 2012.

Kit has previously held several senior educational leadership and governance roles. In his role as Associate Dean (Education) at MADA (Monash University Art Design + Architecture) in Melbourne, he led the development of interdisciplinary education. He has authored a number of publications in that field, and in 2014 he received an Australian Office of Learning and Teaching Innovation & Development Grant, *Benchmarking quality assessment tasks to facilitate interdisciplinary learning in the creative arts and humanities*. He has engaged in an advisory capacity on course design and interdisciplinarity with creative arts schools nationally and internationally.

He was a member of the Steering Committee for the Creative Arts Learning and Teaching Network, which in 2012 established the peak body Deans and Directors of Creative Arts (DDCA), of which he is now also a Board Member. He is also Deputy Chair of the Executive Council of Australian Council of University Art and Design Schools. His artwork is represented by Sarah Scout Presents, Melbourne.

Dr. Josh Wodak

Josh Wodak is a researcher, artist, and design educator at UNSW Art & Design, Australia. His work concerns the social, scientific, and technological responses to mitigate the challenges posed by the Anthropocene, through practice-based research in the creative arts, Environmental Humanities, and Science and Technology Studies. With anthropogenic climate change constituting an unplanned and unintentional experiment with the biosphere and atmosphere, this work critically engages with proposals to intentionally mitigate human impacts on biophysical environments through synthetic biology and geoengineering. The ethics and efficacy of these proposals are investigated in terms of the cultural and ethical entanglements between environmental engineering and conservation biology, in relation to extinction and biodiversity loss in the Anthropocene.

Josh holds a BA (Honours) in Anthropology from the University of Sydney (2002), and a PhD in Interdisciplinary Cross-Cultural Research from the Humanities Research Centre, Australian National University (2011). He has exhibited his media art, sculpture, and interactive installations in art galleries, museums, and festivals across Australia and internationally. Prior to joining UNSW in 2014, Josh held research positions at the Australian National University, the University of Sydney, and Western Sydney University. He is currently a Chief Investigator on the 2016–2018 Australian Research Council Discovery Project *Understanding Australia in the Age of Humans: Localising the Anthropocene*, and a member of the Andrew Mellon Australia-Pacific Observatory in Environmental Humanities at the Sydney Environment Institute.

Amelia Zaraftis

Amelia is an artist and art educator who makes objects, performance, photographic documentation, video, drawing, and installation. Her work is initiated through field research, and frequently references human communication systems to explore ideas of safety and vulnerability in relation to human beings and the environment. Amelia has a broad range of experience working as an educator for local and national institutions. As an undergraduate student Amelia participated in Environment Studio projects and Field Studies, including curating an exhibition of children's art titled You'll Never Get Here by Car" (2006), as part of The Art of Moving project. She worked for four years with ANU Student Equity as Project Officer in the ANU Regional Partnerships Program, developing visual arts enrichment programs for disadvantaged regional primary and secondary schools. Amelia was awarded the EASS M16 Studio Residency Award in 2014, and was an Arts ACT Artist-in-School in 2015. Alongside her teaching role with the Balawan Elective, she sits on the Reconciliation Action Plan Sub-Committee for the ANU College of Arts and Social Sciences, and is currently the Deputy Principal of Burgmann College, which is affiliated with ANU.